JEWS IN THE AMERICAN ACADEMY, 1900–1940

Judaic Traditions in Literature, Music, and Art
Ken Frieden and Harold Bloom, *Series Editors*

JEWS IN THE

AMERICAN ACADEMY

1900–1940

The Dynamics of Intellectual Assimilation

Susanne Klingenstein

Syracuse University Press

Syracuse University Press Edition 1998
98 99 00 01 02 03   6 5 4 3 2 1

Originally published in 1991 by Yale University Press.

Design by James J. Johnson and set in Bembo Roman types by Marathon Typography
Service, Inc.

The paper used in this publication meets the minimum requirements of American
National Standard for Information Sciences—Permanence of Paper for Printed Library
Materials, ANSI Z39.48-1984. ∞™

Library of Congress Cataloging-in-Publication Data
Klingenstein, Susanne, 1959–
Jews in the American academy, 1900–1940 : the dynamics of
intellectual assimilation / Susanne Klingenstein.
p.   cm. — (Judaic traditions in literature, music, and art)
Previously published: New Haven : Yale University Press, c1991.
Includes bibliographical references and index.
ISBN 0-8156-0541-2 (pbk. : alk. paper)
1. Jews—United States—Biography.   2. Jewish college teachers—
United States—Biography.   3. Jews—Cultural assimilation—United
States.   4. United States—Ethnic relations.   I. Title.
II. Series.
E184.37.K55   1998
973'.04924—dc21   98-23703

For Shoshana and Margarete

and

To the memory of Horst Schlötelburg (1931–1982)

The Court wants nothing from you. It receives you when you come, and it dismisses you when you go.

FRANZ KAFKA, *The Trial*

Contents

Illustrations

Preface

This is a book about the integration of Jews into the American academy. More specifically, it is about the gradual acceptance of Jews as professors of English and American literature. The English departments, particularly those at Ivy League schools, thought of themselves as the last bastions of Anglo-Saxon culture. Once their defenses broke down, first with the appointments in 1939 of Lionel Trilling at Columbia University and Harry Levin at Harvard University in 1939, it took another two to three decades for Jewish appointments in this field to become a matter of course, or for the rejection of a Jewish candidate to be freed from the suspicion of residual anti-Semitism.

The present study traces the process of the admission of Jews born around 1880 into the academy. It follows their slow progress via professorships in philology and philosophy to appointments in English literature. It ends with a discussion of Lionel Trilling, who was born in 1905. A sequel will examine the process of normalization, that is, the complete integration of Jews into American English departments achieved by the post-Trilling generation, born between 1912 and 1919, and the gradual rediscovery of Jewish intellectuality by their successors, born between 1924 and 1940.

The process of admission was not a simple, unilateral act of consent, a throwing open of hitherto closed doors by the guardians of Anglo-Saxon culture; rather, it was a complex, bilateral process, a give-and-take between two cultures. Naturally, the majority gave more than it took and almost succeeded in remodeling the minority in its own image. This re-modeling of Jewish intellectuals in the image of America, the restructur-ing of their mode of thought under the impact of either the idea of "America" or its opposite, the gentility of English literature, was only half-enforced. It was half-desired by those Jewish intellectuals who found themselves alienated from their fathers' world. They were puzzled by the Law, to which they had neither emotional nor intellectual access, but from which they also did not feel entirely released. Their alienation, which some Gentiles considered the chief asset of the Jews, was due to a crisis in the world of Judaism.[1] It had been brought on by social emancipation and the Haskalah (Jewish Enlightenment), which confronted a self-absorbed, text-centered Jewry with the world of modern European intellectuality. The crisis came to a head in many centers of European Jewry in the mid- to late nineteenth century. Creations as different as Reform Judaism (in the west) and secular Hebrew culture (in the east) are the results of trans-formations triggered by the Enlightenment.

Jews who emigrated to America came from centers of economic, social, or intellectual crisis. More often than not, their experience of "home," of Judaism and Jewishness, was one of rupture, breakup, discontent—of lim-itation, dullness, and despair. Hence, men of intellectual bent were ready to adopt new views that would change their fathers' culture and make it com-patible with the modern world or that would dissolve that culture alto-gether. Yet these youthful immigrants, among them those who would stage the conquest of the American academy, were still so much part of their fathers' world, had minds so thoroughly formed by Jewish thought, that complete restructuring was not possible. They reinterpreted Gentile cul-ture and the idea of America to fit their own intellectual grammar.

The encounter between Jewish minds and the idea of America (as well as its sometimes sordid reality) can be observed particularly well in the works of immigrant academics who grapple with American philosophy or literature. A careful reading of those works may often find traces of a dual redefinition: Judaism (or Jewishness) is remodeled in the light of what America has to offer, while "America" is reinterpreted to accommo-date a Jewish mode of thought.

The portraits that follow document the academy's changes in attitude toward the Jews. The focus is on Harvard and Columbia, which represent the major social and intellectual trends in the academy at the time. The process of intellectual assimilation is presented here as the increasingly transformative effect that exposure to the idea of America and to English and American literature had on the intellectual grammar of Jewish academics. For them, changes in their understanding of Judaism or Jewishness as well as a variety of emerging working definitions of "America" eased the acceptability of the new culture.

The focus of this study is not on the American finish line, but on the points of departure of the Jewish intellectuals portrayed here. Taking seriously their descent culture, that is, the culture into which they were born, reveals immediately that late-nineteenth-century Jewry is not a monolithic culture. This study presents men (no female academics in the humanities could be found) from a broad variety of Jewish cultural niches. The men portrayed here come from German-tinged bourgeois Russian culture (Leo Wiener), from the Haskalah-touched world of the Lithuanian *yeshivot*, or Talmud academies (Harry Wolfson), from the impoverished world of the traditional shtetl (Morris Cohen), from German Orthodoxy (Horace Kallen), from German Reform Judaism (Felix Adler), and from the post-Romantic Prussian-German bourgeoisie (Ludwig Lewisohn). The last portrait (Lionel Trilling) leads into the next generation but also refers back to the beginning of the study. Trilling's father came from the city of Bialystok, which Leo Wiener had left in his youth.

It is obvious that for men of such different social and cultural backgrounds, "America" had to provide very different things. The ideal consent communities which these men envisioned and sometimes (though infrequently) called "America" were vastly different. These differences at the point of arrival can be explained by the differences at their points of departure. (The utopia of consent is envisioned as an improvement of some sort over the given, over their point of departure, or their conditions of descent.) Hence it did not make sense to construct, as Werner Sollors advised, one composite biography for all the subjects of this study before their entry into the United States. Because the cultural and intellectual atmospheres and pressures experienced in childhood determine to a great extent the "cultural interests and symbolic equipment"[2] of adults, each individual's biography is presented separately, even at the risk of structural repetition.

That structural similarities emerged, yet not simply those arising from the narration of a series of biographies, was one of the surprises of this study. The most important structural feature common to the intellectuals under consideration here is that they all in their responses to America developed a mode of thinking in dichotomies. Their dialectic mode of thought reflects on the one hand their sociological circumstances, their passage from an old into a new world, and on the other hand reactivates intellectual structures acquired in their fathers' world. The world of their mothers—the observant home—was of lesser importance to these intellectuals because America changed their behavior. None of them remained observant. It took much longer for the New World to change the newcomers' minds, their intellectual habits formed in the world of Jewish learning, from which women had been largely excluded.

Thinking in binary oppositions is a general feature of Western culture, but it is particularly indispensable in Jewish thought. In the first chapter of Genesis, the world comes into being by God's creation of a series of opposites which exclude but define each other: heaven/earth, light/darkness, firmament/water, and so forth. The fundamental opposition in Judaism, however, was that between transcendence and immanence. The complete separation of the two realms (identical with the positing of an absolute God, One and Eternal) opposed Judaism to the surrounding pagan cultures that saw the divine suffused in nature. One of Judaism's basic tenets, which one may phrase as "God is not in nature" (although God might make creation an instrument of communication), meant an enormous gain in freedom for man, because one of its consequences was man's sovereignty over nature (signified in Adam's naming of creation) in exchange for the acceptance of God's sovereignty over man (God's naming of Adam).

In Judaism, man is not perceived as subject to nature (except in death). Genesis 1 is an extended metaphor for the dominance of mind over matter. That claim represents progress (man's gain in independence) over the thinking prevalent in pagan cultures which saw man subject to the irrational whims of nature and its gods. In Judaism natural catastrophes like drought are interpreted as God's punishment for man's failure to abide by the terms of their contract.

Although God could choose nature as a channel of communication, JHWH was not part of nature. God's interaction with man was regulated by a contract (the Covenant, or *brit*). This contract is the central idea in Judaism. It declares, as do Genesis 1 and 2 in metaphorical form, the separation of immanence and transcendence and at the same time connects the two realms through the very words of the contract, Torah, of which Genesis is the first part. The contract decrees that God will keep out of immanence (that is, grant man sovereignty expressed metaphorically by the promise of descendants and territory) if man will do certain things. In other words, man will testify to the existence of a God outside the world of phenomena through the performance of certain acts. The sign of man's obedience (the acknowledgment of an invisible God's sovereignty over man) was a particular behavior.

These acts, which at first consisted in the execution of simple ethical commands, became more and more complex, just as the first oral covenant (the simple acknowledgment of a transcendent God in the act of Abraham's separation of himself from his familiar environment) developed into an elaborate document (Torah) which regulated Jewish behavior. Torah prescribed minutely the acts that would testify to God's existence. Jewish life itself—consuming food, measuring time, making love—became a constant reenactment of that first separation between transcendence and immanence, the holy and the profane. *Kashrut, menuhat shabbat, taharat ha-mishpahah*—that is, dietary laws, sabbath repose, and conjugal relations—center upon distinction-making.

Each act of practical distinction-making recalls and reflects the fundamental separation between transcendence (God) and immanence (people), and yet connects the two. Since God was nothing *but* the collective acts of the people, these actions expressed God. Their collectivity was God's manifestation in history. Hence this people could call itself the *goy kadosh*, that is, the people separated from all other peoples (*goyim*). Just as the Jews preserved this separation throughout history, so the separation preserved them. The obligation to recognize and implement distinctions in all areas of life had an enormous effect on the intellect of the Jewish people; it shaped decisively what I call their *intellectual grammar*. The inescapability of the binary grid sharpened their sense for intellectual games based on binary thinking, hence the well-known Jewish penchant for paradox, dialectics, a fortiori reasoning—known in rabbinic exegesis as *kal ve-homer*—and so forth.

One of the vexing problems in Judaism, certainly for its intellectuals, was the relationship between bondage and freedom. Life was so tightly regulated and group cohesion so intense that individual freedom in the realm of action (self-realization) seemed impossible. And yet the life of observance was, supposedly, the life that granted man sovereignty, the life that made man sublimely free.

The paradoxical interdependence of freedom and bondage (the obligation to abide by the terms of the contract, that is, to obey the Law) is recognized and formulated in a famous passage in the Talmud. In Erubin 54a two rabbis discuss Exodus 32:16, a description of the tables of the Law that Moses brings down from Mount Sinai and that he will break in anger two verses later: "And the tables were the work of God, and the writing was the writing of God, graven upon the tables." The rabbis' discussion is brief: "R[abbi] Eleazar further stated: What is the purport of the Scriptural text, *Graven upon the tablets*? If the first tables had not been broken the Torah would never have been forgotten in Israel. R[abbi] Aḥa b[ar] Jacob said: No nation or tongue would have had any power over them [Israel]; for its says, 'Graven,' read not 'graven' [ḥarut] but 'freedom' [ḥerut]."

Both rabbis claim that the breaking of the first tables is a metaphor for freedom. The answer of the first rabbi can only be understood when the answer of the second is known. The relation of Rabbi Eleazar's answer (that the breaking of the tables permitted the forgetting of the Law, and hence released Israel into lawlessness, or freedom) to the question he posed does not become apparent until the answer of Rabbi Aḥa defines the relation of freedom and obedience, or bondage, as one of interdependence. Without Aḥa's answer, Eleazar's answer makes no sense. Question and first answer stand in juxtaposition. Q: Graven? A: Freedom! To the eye that reads only the world of phenomena there seems to be no connection between question and answer. Q: What does phrase x mean? A: The fact that we are told about two sentences after phrase x means y!

But Rabbi Aḥa saw that Eleazar had given an ingenious answer. He perceived that Eleazar's question (graven?) and the content of his answer (freedom) were linked not in the world of phenomena, but on the level of language. Question and answer were both contained in the Hebrew letters *ḥet-resh-taf*, which in their vocalized form spell either *ḥarut* [graven] or *ḥerut* [freedom]. On one level, Rabbi Aḥa's answer confirms Rabbi Eleazar's by providing the linguistic key to it. The text under consideration, the letter sequence *ḥet-resh-taf*, becomes the basis for consent. It unites the two opinions.

But simultaneously, on a second level, Aḥa disagrees with Eleazar. The first answer, though based on a sophisticated linguistic perception, is very simple in content: The breaking of the tables causes (means) forgetting (i.e., release). The emphasis is on *release* or *freedom*. Aḥa dissents by saying: It is true that there is a relationship of interdependence between the Law and freedom. However it is not, as you suppose, Rabbi Eleazar, one of mutual exclusivity (as if the Law needs to break in order to release or allow freedom). The opposite is true. *Ḥarut* and *ḥerut*, the law and freedom, are identical, *ḥet-resh-taf*. The Law is freedom. No nation or tongue would have had any power over Israel had Israel always remained within the Law. As long as it keeps the Law it will be an independent people. Within one's jurisdiction one is free. The Law (Torah, the elaborate version of the Covenant) is the source of sovereignty.

By juxtaposing "nation" and "tongue" Aḥa defines sovereignty also as the keeping of one's language. This makes sense, not only in light of

Greece's and Rome's linguistic imperialism, but it is also the consequence of Aḥa's own reasoning. For him the source of freedom is the text of the Covenant, "graven upon the tables" and transmitted in the Hebrew of the written Law (*torah she-bi-khtav*).

The intellectual structure of that short passage is a dazzling interplay of paradoxes and inversions. Not only does the understanding of answer 1 presuppose knowledge of answer 2; but answer 2, which makes sense of answer 1 through an act of linguistic consent, at the same time contradicts that answer on the level of content. Hence the rabbis' dialogical analysis of Exodus 32:16 in Erubin 54a illustrates in its structure the answer it gives—that of the paradoxical interdependence of bondage and freedom.

The interplay between *ḥarut* and *ḥerut* is the single most important dichotomy in the complex response of Jewish academics—released from their diverse Jewish niches into the freedom of America—to the breaking of the tables. Many who thought at first that Rabbi Eleazar was right and that breaking and freedom were identical, discovered late in life that the truth lay with Rabbi Aḥa. But whichever rabbi they eventually sided with, they were bound to be free.

The organization of this study is not strictly chronological. A desire to keep the narrative focused on certain places for longer periods of time has occasionally won out against the historian's urge to preserve the sequence of events. Chapter 1 begins at Harvard University with the arrival of the first Jewish academic but quickly broadens to sketch some main currents in American Jewish history.

Chapter 2 returns to Harvard, where the adventures of the migrating Leo Wiener came to an end when he became a professor of Slavic languages. Chapter 3, devoted to three philosophy students at Harvard, Harry Wolfson, Horace Kallen, and Morris Cohen, remains at Harvard, where Wolfson made his home; but then in following the career of Kallen it shifts focus from Cambridge to New York. The metropolis and its City College were Cohen's haven. His search for a father figure introduces Felix Adler, who takes the study briefly to Cornell University. Adler had to leave Cornell after a very short appointment. A quarter of a century later he became a professor at Columbia University, which is the focal point for the remainder of the study.

Chapter 4 is in the main given to Ludwig Lewisohn, who was brought as a child from Berlin to South Carolina. He grew up in the South and wanted to become a professor of English literature. Denied a scholarship

at Columbia because he was a Jew, he left the university without his doctorate. The first section of chapter 4 sketches Lewisohn's childhood and
adolescence in the South and follows him to Columbia. The second section investigates whether Lewisohn's complaints about Columbia's anti-
Semitism had any basis in fact, by examining the school's admissions
policy and treatment of Jews. The third section portrays Columbia's first
Jewish professor of literature, Joel Spingarn, and closes with a sketch of
Jacob Zeitlin, who refuted Lewisohn's complaints as excessive. The fourth
section continues the analysis of Lewisohn's life and works. He ended his
days as a professor of comparative literature at Brandeis University.

Chapter 5, which is entirely about Lionel Trilling, brings the study to
a representative of the next generation. Trilling succeeded in realizing
Lewisohn's dream. A short prefatory section introduces critical views on
Trilling; the second section describes the world of his adolescence and the
elements which determined his intellectual grammar. The third section
presents Trilling at Columbia and analyzes his short fiction. The final
section summarizes the intellectual positions found in his essays and argues that Trilling's mode of thought remains determined by his descent
culture, but that his mode of expression was adopted from his consent
culture. Chapter 6 concludes the study with a brief description of events
at Harvard after Trilling's appointment at Columbia. Surprisingly, Cambridge rather than Morningside Heights became the starting point for a
new generation of Jewish academics, the first to achieve full integration
into an Ivy League English department.

Acknowledgments

I wrote this book, which traces the intellectual effects of the transition from one culture to another, while I was moving from German into American Jewish culture. This may explain an occasional lack of distance, my empathy for those who undertake this journey. It may also account for the book's peculiar perspective. It is that of a European accustomed to perceiving the culture of Jewish thought as separate from that of the Christianity-dominated national cultures. It took time to comprehend how much separateness is woven into togetherness, into a texture of distinctive strands, in the United States on the basis of its Enlightened constitutional documents, and to accept that the idea of "America" does work in daily life.

It is a pleasure to thank my advisers and friends. My major debt is to Cynthia Ozick and Sacvan Bercovitch, who have made themselves available for endless hours of discussion. Without their generosity and trust, my transition and writing would have been much more difficult. Their incisive criticism, their insistence on precision, shaped this book. I owe much to an exchange with Werner Sollors. His *Beyond Ethnicity: Consent and Descent in American Culture* (1986) was essential to the crystallizing of my thoughts. That I fundamentally disagree with his views does not diminish my indebtedness. Dr. George M. Saiger provided important information about Ludwig Lewisohn, and to Michael Greenstein's critical reading of chapter 4 I owe many improvements. Strong encouragement has come from Geoffrey Hartman and unconditional support from my

"Doktorvater," Herwig Friedl. The magnanimity of Harry Bochner, Fritz Fleischmann, Elizabeth Gifford, Simon Hirschhorn, and Jeremy Korzenik permitted me to transform our conversations, dinners, and outings into testing grounds for ideas. I also wish to thank Ellen Graham, Richard Miller, and Melissa Weissberg at Yale University Press for their care, expertise, and patience, all of which made the transformation of the manuscript into a book a pleasure rather than a chore.

Funding has come from the German Academic Exchange Service, the German Marshall Fund of the United States, and the University of Heidelberg, where this book was accepted as a doctoral dissertation in February 1990.

List of Abbreviations

AL   Lionel Trilling, "Some Notes for an Autobiographical Lecture," in *The Last Decade: Essays and Reviews 1965–1975*. Ed. Diana Trilling. New York: Harcourt Brace Jovanovich, 1979.

D   Marshall van Deusen, *J. E. Spingarn*. New York: Twayne, 1971.

DJ   Morris R. Cohen, *A Dreamer's Journey*. New York: Arno, 1975.

EP   Norbert Wiener, *Ex-Prodigy: My Childhood and Youth*. New York: Simon and Schuster, 1953.

FL   Lionel Trilling, "Freud and Literature," in *The Liberal Imagination*. London: Secker and Warburg, 1951.

FW   Lionel Trilling, "Freud: Within and Beyond Culture," in *Beyond Culture: Essays on Literature and Learning*. New York: Harcourt Brace Jovanovich, 1978.

I   Ludwig Lewisohn, *Israel*. New York: Boni and Liveright, 1925.

IB   Lionel Trilling, "Isaac Babel," in *Beyond Culture: Essays on Literature and Learning*. New York: Harcourt Brace Jovanovich, 1978.

Im   Lionel Trilling, "Impediments," in *Of This Time, of That Place, and Other Stories*. Selected by Diana Trilling. New York: Harcourt Brace Jovanovich, 1979.

In   Henry Rosenthal, "Inventions." *Menorah Journal* 14 (January 1928): 49–61.

JA   Lionel Trilling, "Why We Read Jane Austen," in *The Last Decade: Essays and Reviews 1965–1975*. Ed. Diana Trilling. New York: Harcourt Brace Jovanovich, 1979.

MC   Ludwig Lewisohn, *Mid-Channel: An American Chronicle*. New York: Blue Ribbon, 1929.

MM Lionel Trilling, "Manners, Morals, and the Novel," in *The Liberal Imagination*. London: Secker and Warburg, 1951.

N1 "From the Notebooks of Lionel Trilling, Part 1." *Partisan Review* 51 (1984): 496-515.

N2 "From the Notebooks of Lionel Trilling, Part 2." *Partisan Review* 54 (1987): 7-17.

NT Lionel Trilling, "A Novel of the Thirties," in *The Last Decade: Essays and Reviews 1965-1975*. Ed. Diana Trilling. New York: Harcourt Brace Jovanovich, 1979.

O Lionel Trilling, "Of This Time, of That Place," in *Of This Time, of That Place, and Other Stories*. Selected by Diana Trilling. New York: Harcourt Brace Jovanovich, 1979.

OS Lionel Trilling, *The Opposing Self: Nine Essays in Criticism*. New York: Viking, 1955.

P Leonora Cohen Rosenfeld, *Portrait of a Philosopher: Morris R. Cohen in Life and Letters*. New York: Harcourt, Brace & World, 1962.

US Ludwig Lewisohn, *Up Stream: An American Chronicle*. New York: Boni and Liveright, 1922.

WH Leo W. Schwarz, *Wolfson of Harvard: Portrait of a Scholar*. Philadelphia: Jewish Publication Society of America, 1978.

JEWS IN THE AMERICAN ACADEMY, 1900–1940

1   Beginnings

The history of Jewish academics in the United States begins at Harvard University. On June 29, 1720, Judah Monis (1683–1764), an Italian-born Jew, presented to the Harvard Corporation a draft of his Hebrew grammar, later published as *Dickdook Leshon Gnebreet: A Grammar of the Hebrew Tongue* (1735), and a plan to revise the teaching of Hebrew at Harvard. This was a good move, because even though the Puritans did not welcome the Jews, they respected and studied the Hebrew language and literature. Harvard's first two presidents, Henry Dunster (1640–1654) and Charles Chauncy (1654–1672), were excellent Hebraists and made the reputed *Ursprache* part of the curriculum. But the study of Hebrew had declined during Chauncy's presidency and very few theses were submitted in Hebrew. A few years later, in 1681, Cotton Mather caused quite a stir when he decided to argue, for his master's degree, that the vowel points in Hebrew were of divine origin. Despite declining student interest, Harvard was positively disposed toward making use of Judah Monis's services in 1720. Two years elapse before we hear from Monis again; during this period he might have received his M.A. from Harvard. Jews were then excluded from Oxford, Cambridge, and most other European universities. Finally, on March 27, 1722, Judah Monis reemerges: in a ceremony held in College Hall in Cambridge he publicly converted and within a month was appointed instructor in the Hebrew language at Harvard. He held this position until he chose to retire in 1760.[1]

During the century and a half following Judah Monis's conversion to

Christianity and appointment—an ominous sequence of events—there were few Jews at Harvard and none on its faculty. This may be in part because the Jewish community of Boston developed slowly, since the economic opportunities in New York and Newport were far more intriguing.

America's first Jewish professor not appointed to teach a Semitic subject was a British mathematician, James Joseph Sylvester (1814–1897). He arrived at the University of Virginia in Charlottesville late in November 1841. But his stay was short. Tension arose from a combination of Anglophobia, anti-Jewish prejudice, and general student unrest. It was increased by Sylvester's antislavery opinions, and perhaps by the fact that he rather enthusiastically taught a difficult and unpopular subject. The tension finally led to a physical assault on Sylvester by a student in 1842. Sylvester defended himself. Believing that he had killed the assailant, he immediately left town and eventually went back to England.

That Sylvester's ouster was the result of an unfortunate combination of circumstances, rather than of anti-Jewish prejudice alone, becomes evident when we look at the social situation of Jews in antebellum America. Although Americans had an abstract notion of Jews, which included the familiar European religious and economic stereotypes, the actual social relations between them and this tiny minority (0.1 percent of the American population) were stable and secure. Around 1840, on the eve of the German immigration, Jews numbered some 15,000 of an estimated total of 15 million Americans. "Throughout the antebellum period," John Higham concludes in a ground-breaking study, "Jews continued to enjoy almost complete social acceptance and freedom. There was no pattern of discrimination in the sense of exclusion from social and economic opportunities which qualified Jews sought."[2]

This was particularly true in the South, where in Jewish communities such as Savannah's (founded in 1735) and Charleston's (founded in 1749) or in slightly younger ones such as Richmond's (founded in 1789) or New Orleans's (founded in 1828), Jews even belonged to the elite circles of society and as a matter of course shared the general cultural tastes and pastimes. To find the very first instances of American Jewish literature or of secular Jewish intellectual life, one would have to turn to the literary women of the old southern and mid-Atlantic communities, to Penina Moïse and Octavia Harvy Moses, or to Richea and Rebecca Gratz.

By 1876, when James Sylvester returned to the United States to accept a position on America's first graduate school faculty at Johns Hopkins University in Baltimore, the formerly relaxed situation had changed. The German immigration, beginning in the 1840s, swelled the Jewish population to a quarter of a million and thus increased its visibility. Although the German Jews developed remarkable economic and religious strategies for adapting to the environment of the new country (ranging from the invention of the mail-order business to the creation of Reform Judaism), and although they were extremely successful materially as a group, they were socially never as much at ease with their non-Jewish financial peers as antebellum Jewry had been. This unease was in part the result of changes in the psychology and behavior patterns of American society.

The Gilded Age (1860s–1880s) emphasized the significance of money. The middle class was economically on the move. A large part of it even became rich. Pomp and splendor reigned, and money became a mark of social distinction. With more and more successful people demanding admission to prestigious (because exclusive) circles, social climbing, the urban version of the American Dream, became, in Higham's laconic formulation, "a genuine social problem."

Frantic competition for mundane success increased social tension and created the need for new and clearer social stratification markers. A time-tested way of lashing out against competition was ethnic labeling. And no label had a more devastating effect in commercially oriented Christian societies than the appellation "Jew." "Practically," Higham explains, "anti-Semitic discriminations offered another means of stabilizing the social ladder, while, psychologically, a society vexed by its own assertiveness gave a general problem an ethnic focus."[3] Of the anti-Jewish stereotypes latent in American society, the economic form emerged as the most important during the Gilded Age. Jews began to symbolize the "pecuniary vices" and, as they "entered more prominently than any other ethnic group into the struggle for status," they also came to stand for "pushiness."[4] It was exactly the label "pushy Jew," first used for the business manners of the German Jews and their social aspirations, that was—in the eyes of onlooking Americans—dramatically confirmed by the incredible pace at which the ensuing wave of immigrants, the Jews from Eastern Europe, rose from rags to riches.

"Pushiness" was particularly undesirable in the genteel atmosphere of the old colleges and Ivy League schools. Here the adjective "pushy" was used well into the 1940s to describe Jews as unfit for admission into the culture represented and preserved by these institutions. In a letter to Yale philosophy professor William Ernest Hocking concerning the appointment of the Jewish philosopher Paul Weiss, who was a student of Morris Cohen, to a full professorship at Yale, Charles W. Hendel, a Princetonian by education and then titular head of the Yale philosophy department, wrote: "It is difficult for men who like Weiss have been brought out of the lowliest social condition to know how to behave in a society of genuine equality where it is not necessary to assert oneself."[5]

Overtly, class rather than race seemed to be the issue at stake here, since it was a feature of the enlightened culture of men such as Hendel to be above the bigotry of racism or even ethnic prejudice. In this genteel form, *verschoben* (displaced) from the level of ethnicity to the level of class, anti-Jewish prejudice persisted in the academy until well into the 1960s. This is not to say that Mr. Hendel's worry was entirely unjustified. Naturally, the psychology and behavior of American Jews of recent Eastern European descent differed from that of their WASP colleagues who set the tone in the academy. But it is important to keep in mind that politely phrased objections such as Mr. Hendel's had their basis in a very real fear of social displacement, which dated back to a time before the arrival of the Eastern European immigrants. A pattern of ethnic discrimination designed to preserve threatened class status was well established among the middle classes by the late 1870s.

Ethnic discrimination to enhance or secure class status first became obvious in the resort business. In 1876, a hotel on the New Jersey shore advertised in the New York *Tribune* that "Jews are not admitted." In 1877, this heretofore subdued tendency came to public attention when Joseph Seligman, one of America's leading bankers, was refused accommodation at the Grand Union Hotel in Saratoga Springs because he was a Jew. In the 1870s Saratoga was steadily losing ground to Newport, Nahant, and Long Branch as the summer capital of the old upper classes and the policy of ethnic discrimination was adopted in the futile hope to stop the social downward trend.[6]

Metropolitan social clubs and eastern private schools, too, began to exclude Jews in the 1880s, while some of the very best preparatory schools —including Andover, Exeter, and Hotchkiss—as well as elite universities practiced no discrimination on the student level. This was hardly necessary, since a college education was not uppermost on the agenda of German American Jewry. In 1869, the total enrollment at Harvard College was 563 students; only three or four were Jews. Of the students matriculating at Princeton between 1871 and 1875, none was Jewish. And when Yale's class of 1873 enrolled in 1869 not one student was affiliated with a "Jewish church." Jews were present at Yale, however, but in such insignificant numbers that they went unnoticed. The discrimination "that would later infest social life at Yale was apparently nonexistent through the 1870s."[7]

Similarly, the prospect of college and university teaching was not at all attractive to German American Jews. Salaries were low and a professorship in America had none of the social prestige it had in Germany. After the material basis for immediate survival had been secured, German American Jews on the whole were most interested in social acceptability, continuing a trend within German Jewry that dated back to the Enlightenment. The two major routes by which they decided to reach that goal were truly American: money and religion. They created large business empires (and became major philanthropists), and established with Reform Judaism a protestant version of Judaism which made the outward appearance of their ancient religion acceptable to their non-Jewish neighbors. By comparison, their interests in general culture and politics were rather limited. As late as 1881 an article in the German Jewish newspaper *Die Deborah* complained about the lack of intellectual interest in the Jewish community: "A sin. American Jewry is making a great mistake which is bound to have evil consequences later on: it *reads* very little and *plays* very much. Young people who enjoyed all the advantages of the public schools, and who enter into practical life between the ages of 16 and 18 years with a good school education, very soon decline intellectually because the society about them is busy playing theater or cards."[8]

All of this changed with the arrival of two and a half million Eastern European Jews escaping the pogroms that broke out after the assassination of Czar Alexander II in 1881 and continued to erupt until well after the October Revolution of 1917.[9] The immigration of the Eastern European Jews, their transformation into a proletariat and subsequent rapid development into a suburban middle class, their intensive political activities and distinct cultural life have been written about extensively. Therefore a few facts and figures will suffice to recreate the scene and recall an important feature of this immigrant group: their thirst for (secular) education.

Between 1880 and 1917, the Jewish population of the United States increased from 280,000 (0.6 percent) to 3,389,000 (3.5 percent). The immigration rate of about 30,000 Jews a year between 1880 and 1899 rose to more than 90,000 Jewish immigrants annually between 1900 and 1914. Unlike the previous wave of German Jewish immigrants, the Jews from Eastern Europe did not spread evenly throughout the country but settled mainly in the northeast, almost half of them in New York City. "In 1880, the Jews made up only 3 percent of the population of New York City. By 1920, they constituted 30 percent of its population, and they have maintained a similar proportion ever since."[10] The heavy concentration in a few large cities was above all a function of economic opportunity. But settling in groups also suited the cultural temperament of Eastern European Jewry. A main difference between the two groups of immigrants, the German and the Eastern European Jews, was the latter group's emphasis on education as an instrument of social success. The importance of education, any education, is perhaps the single unifying trait among this extraordinarily heterogeneous group commonly labeled Eastern European Jewry. And perhaps their traditional reverence for learning, which became a craze for secular education when Eastern European Jews discovered its ready availability in American cities, is the secret of their success as an immigrant group.[11]

Jewish enrollment in American colleges soared after 1880. A survey of 77 institutions carried out by the Immigration Commission in 1908 found that 8.5 percent of the male student body was composed of first- and second-generation Jews at a time when Jews made up only 2 percent of the American population.[12] By 1918–19 the overall figure had increased only slightly. During that year 14,837 students out of a total of 153,084 students enrolled in 106 institutions (or 9.7 percent) were Jewish.[13] But when only the 30 major (mostly eastern) colleges and universities are considered, the average Jewish enrollment reached 20.4 percent.[14] At this point the elite universities began to worry, as did the rest of America, fearing that they would soon be overrun by the immigrant hordes. Jewish students sensed danger and in 1916 the Menorah Society, an intercollegiate Jewish student organization, published a prophylactic statement. The Menorah survey of Jewish student enrollment at 56 major American institutions of higher learning included the high figures for the popular New York schools, but on the whole permitted the soothing conclusion that "2.5 percent of the population are furnishing 2.8 percent of the students in the colleges."[15]

But this report that the Jews did not take more than their fair share of the American cake failed to have the desired effect. America, and its elite in particular, was determined to protect itself. Some hard thinking resulted in a not very original solution: quotas. These were first adopted in New York City, where the competition was fiercest and the establishment felt most threatened. Columbia and New York University became more selective. As Marcia Synnott points out in her important study, *The Half-Opened Door*, "Columbia cut its undergraduate Jewish enrollment in order to regain its former status as an elite institution for native American sons of downtown business and professional men, its clientele prior to moving to Morningside Heights. Even before World War I, Frederick P. Keppel, dean of the college, was asked: 'Isn't Columbia overrun with European Jews, who are most unpleasant persons socially?' "[16]

Among the Jews who applied for admission during that time were those who would later belong to the core of the so-called New York Intellectuals: Meyer Schapiro and Lionel Trilling (Columbia), Meyer Levin (University of Chicago), Sidney Hook (City College of New York; Ph.D. Columbia), William Phillips (CCNY; M.A. New York University). The slightly older Elliot Cohen was a child prodigy and graduated in 1917 (at age 18) from Yale. Harvard was of no importance to this generation, although some of its teachers, men like Horace Kallen or Morris Cohen, had studied there, and the school had enjoyed a reputation of fair hospitality to Jewish faculty and students since the enlightened reign of President Charles Eliot (1869–1909). But for the early New York Intellectuals (the group born around 1905), Harvard was too isolated, too academic, and, perhaps, too provincial. New York City, with its Olympus of Columbia University, was the intellectual and cultural center and would remain so until the 1960s, when the generation born in the 1930s liberated itself into the rest of America.

Nevertheless, the history proper of Jewish academics in the humanities begins at Harvard. Discounting the abortive start in 1720 and the handful of German Jewish students in the nineteenth century, it commences with the arrival of a singular Russian-born individual whom Harvard's court historian, Samuel Eliot Morison, called "one of the most remarkable linguists and teachers of languages we have ever had."[17] Leo Wiener was not the first Jew appointed at Harvard during Eliot's presidency.[18] But he was the first who stood out as a Jew and the first in a number of "characters" whose scholarly brilliance and fantastic work-energy seduced Harvard into overlooking that they were otherwise not quite comme il faut.

2   A Philologist: The Adventures of
Leo Wiener (1862–1939)

Leo Wiener was born in Bialystok in 1862 to a family of *yiches* (distinguished pedigree). Legend had it that the Wieners were descended from Moses Maimonides. But their relation to another talmudic *ilui* (luminary), Akiba Eger, Grand Rabbi of Posen from 1815 to 1837, is far more certain. According to Gershom Scholem, Eger was "probably the greatest Talmudic scholar in Germany at the beginning of the nineteenth century."[1] But the Wiener family was no longer religious. Instead, Leo's father Solomon believed in German *Kultur* and "sought to replace the Yiddish of his environment by literary German."[2] By the time Leo was thirteen he spoke several languages. His son, Norbert, explains that

> The role of German in his life was reinforced by the fact that because of the German bias of my grandfather my father went to a Lutheran school. He learned French as the language of educated society; and in Eastern Europe, especially in Poland, there were still those who adhered to the Renaissance tradition and used Italian as another language of polite conversation. Moreover, my father soon left the Minsk Gymnasium for that of Warsaw, where the classes were also conducted in Russian, although Polish was the language that he spoke with his playmates. (*EP* 12)

After *gymnasium* (high school), where he excelled in Greek, Latin, and mathematics, Leo Wiener went to Warsaw University to study medicine. But he did not take to the subject and soon left for Berlin to enroll in the

Polytechnicum, a professional school for engineers. It was not a change for the better, even though in the drafting room, where he worked between a Serb and a Greek, he was able to add two more languages to his linguistic repertory (*EP* 14).[3] Disgusted with the debauchery of German student life, he joined a vegetarian society and soon detected that "although the purposes of the new régime were of the most pacific kind, there was also a sprinkling of antisemites among them."[4] The group, however, reinforced "a vein of Tolstoyanism which had long been in him, and he decided to forswear drink, tobacco, and the eating of meat for the rest of his life" (*EP* 14–15). The missionary strain in Tolstoyanism finally gave a direction to Leo Wiener's restless adventurous spirit. Bored with his studies and annoyed by German philistinism as he had been annoyed earlier by "Polish inflammability and Russian apathy," he decided to set out and found a vegetarian-socialist colony in British Belize.

He had enough money to sail steerage to New Orleans, where he arrived in 1880 with the essentials of both Spanish and English (learned from grammar books and Scott's *The Pirate*) and the notorious twenty-five cents in his pocket. By then the harebrained Central America plan had disintegrated, and so he looked for a job. He worked first as a laborer in a cotton factory, then on a railroad construction site. Later he took to the road again, fell in with "the remains of an old Fourierist community in Missouri" (*EP* 19) and eventually found himself at the door of a Catholic church in Kansas City lured by the sign "Gaelic lessons given." He joined the class (though not the faith), and soon became the head of the local Gaelic society.[5] The "Russian Irishman" also became notorious at the public library, where he called for books nobody else would read. It was hardly surprising then that when Leo Wiener decided to end his anomalous existence as laborer, peddler, and farmer and return to intellectual work, the Kansas City superintendent of schools, to whom Wiener had applied for a job, did not hesitate to employ this strange individual.

It may reflect the superintendent's strange sense of humor that he first assigned the applicant to a country school in Odessa, Missouri. But Wiener was soon promoted to a position at the Kansas City High School, where he taught Greek, Latin, and mathematics from 1884 to 1892. Although Wiener was now on his way to becoming an academic, he remained a Tolstoyan and a passionate outdoorsman. To the end of his life, "he was more pleased by raising a better crop than his professional farmer-neighbors than he would have been by the greatest philological discovery" (*EP* 19). Apart from farming and nature excursions, a favorite pastime of Wiener's in Kansas City, in which his later colleague at Harvard, Hugo

Münsterberg, also indulged, was "to attend spiritualistic seances and to try to discover the sleight-of-hand techniques of the mediums" (*EP* 20).[6]

In 1892, Wiener was appointed to an assistant professorship in German and Romance Languages at the University of Missouri, which he held until 1895. During that time he married Bertha Kahn, the daughter of a German Jewish immigrant who owned a department store in St. Joseph, Missouri. The ties of the Kahn family reached even further south, and southern gentility and etiquette—not Wiener's forte—were a matter of considerable importance to them. In the ensuing rift between Wiener and his in-laws, partly caused by the traditional friction between German and Russian Jews and probably precipitated by Wiener's brusqueness, Bertha Kahn stood by her husband the *Ostjude*, even though she could not free herself from the Jewish self-hatred prevalent in her family.

When the Department of Modern Languages at the University of Missouri was reorganized, Leo Wiener found himself left out (*EP* 29) and on the move again.[7] He bought a one-way ticket to Boston on the speculation, reminiscent of Judah Monis, that his fantastic linguistic skills might be in demand at a place reputed for its learning. Through the Boston Public Library he came into contact with Francis James Child, who had become Harvard's first professor of English in 1876. Wiener translated Serbian ballads for Child. The scholar was so intrigued by his discovery that he introduced Wiener to A. A. Coolidge, "to whose enlightened interest and friendly backing his appointment as Instructor in Slavic Languages and Literature was in large measure due (1896)."[8] Child died in 1896. But Harvard's other philologist, George Lyman Kittredge, was still there to appreciate Wiener's extraordinary linguistic knowledge. Wiener was promoted to assistant professor in 1901 and to full professor in 1911; in 1930, he became professor emeritus. Fortunately, Wiener's natural academic habitat was the Department of Slavic Languages and Literatures. At that time the employment of a Jew in an English department was still unthinkable.

In the 1880s, when the departments for language and literature were formed, "the Anglo-Saxon mystique reached its high point in America" and was absorbed, of course, by the academy. "The very decision to divide the new language and literature departments along national lines was an implicit assertion of pride in 'the English speaking race'."[9] In 1896, the year of Wiener's appointment at Harvard, a professor of English at Columbia University named Brander Matthews, who was destined to play a villainous role in the life of Ludwig Lewisohn, wrote: "as literature is a reflection and a reproduction of the life of the peoples speaking the lan-

Leo Wiener.
Photograph by Bachrach Studio. Courtesy Harvard University Archives.

guage in which it is written, this literature is likely to be strong and great in proportion as the peoples who speak the language are strong and great. English literature is therefore likely to grow, as it is the record of the life of the English speaking race and as this race is steadily spreading abroad over the globe."[10] In this world Leo Wiener was not at home.

The second half of Leo Wiener's life, which he spent in Cambridge and its vicinity, was not fundamentally different from his life before his arrival at Harvard. His rebelliousness, restlessness, and impatience, aspects of a deep-seated unease, did not disappear but merely found other outlets: in his indefatigable, almost compulsive academic production, in the frequent buying and selling of the family home, and in the education of his prodigy son. It is difficult to say to what extent his "excitability," his perfectionism which could turn into tyranny (EP 52–53), and his complete inability to ingratiate himself with anyone were part of his personal disposition and to what extent they were due to his fundamental cultural Unbehagen (discontent). He was not only thoroughly uprooted, estranged from his Jewish origins, but he was also, as a Tolstoyan peasant at Harvard, singularly displaced—a social outsider, an oddball.

It is hard to imagine that he was a favorite of students. But as in the case of Morris Cohen, a Russian Jew of similarly tyrannical temper, Leo Wiener seems to have been appreciated by some of the stronger students and a few members of the faculty. Morris Cohen, who came to America a generation later, could never get the appointment he most desired, a professorship in Columbia's philosophy department. By then the screw had been turned tight and his Jewishness and even more so his irascibility (dubbed "Jewish manners") made him a most unlikely proponent of the culture Columbia thought in need of protection from the "wretched refuse." Whether Leo Wiener experienced any anti-Semitism at Harvard is not known. It seems unlikely, because the identity he flaunted was that of a Russian. This is not to say that he denied being Jewish. But his relationship to his Jewishness was complicated, and was certainly not made easier by his wife's Jewish self-hatred.

Bertha Kahn would not only look askance at her husband's relatives —who by and by arrived in America (EP 42, 50–51)—and speak with contempt of the "gluttony of the Jews" as she spoke of the "bigotry of the Irish or the laziness of the Negroes" (EP 146), but she would even deny that her own family was Jewish. Her son Norbert learned by accident that he was a Jew when the legend of the Wieners' descent from Maimonides was mentioned in conversation by an old acquaintance of his father. When the child also found out that his mother's maiden name, Kahn, was a variant of Cohen, he was shocked. "As I reasoned it out to myself," he wrote, "I was a Jew, and if the Jews were marked by those characteristics which my mother found so hateful, why I must have those characteristics myself, and share them with all those dear to me. . . . I could not accept myself as a person of any value" (*EP* 148).

The result was an intense "emotional and intellectual dilemma" in an already troubled child. "I alternated between a phase of cowardly self-abasement and a phase of cowardly assertion, in which I was even more anti-Semitic than my mother" (*EP* 148–149). The necessity to solve this dilemma was combined with a strong rebellious impulse against his parents.[11] Hence, he came to consider his deliberate Jewish reidentification as "forced on [him] as an act of integrity" (*EP* 147). But what could support his self-identification as a Jew? Norbert Wiener had no Jewish education; he had never been inside a synagogue or Jewish school. And while he thought it impossible to hide himself "in the great majority as a fugitive from Judaism" (*EP* 154), a return into the fold also made little sense because he had "never been there" (*EP* 153). He found an ethical rather than ethnic solution: "I could only feel at peace with myself if I hated anti-Jewish prejudice without having the first emphasis on the fact that it was directed against the group to which I belonged. . . . But in resisting prejudice against the Oriental, prejudice against the Catholic, prejudice against the immigrant, prejudice against the Negro, I felt that I had a sound basis on which to resist prejudice against the Jew as well" (*EP* 155).

His father's attempts to come to terms with his Jewish origins and early socialization into cultural alienation seem by comparison less relaxed (perhaps even less mature). Leo Wiener's humanitarian solution, a staunchly advocated Tolstoyanism, never lost the flavor of being an escape, or rebellion, rather than a solution. This romantic return-to-the-soil that he practiced as a farmer was counterpoised by a second, highly abstract, solution to the problems arising in a life led in a confusion of cultures. This second solution, which eased Wiener's cultural Unbehagen, was a philological one. It developed from Wiener's phenomenal linguistic memory. Like Harold Bloom two generations later, Wiener succeeded in transforming an extraordinary natural gift into an academic method. Wiener had a command of about thirty languages, a third of which he spoke fluently.[12] His linguistic competence gave him access to a variety of cultures, ranging from the familiar Slavic, Western European, and Jewish, to the more exotic Gypsy, Arabic, Mayan, and Aztec cultures. The ability to compare liberates one from the confines of one's own culture by creating distance; and it develops structural thinking, because perception of common structures is a way to organize a profusion of material.

When Wiener began as an instructor at Harvard, philology was nationalist and formalistic. Linguistic research, which became more and more Wiener's field, was still mainly interested in the purely formal phonetic aspects. This interest was slowly superseded, as Wiener's son puts it, by a "more historical and empirical point of view" (*EP* 122). Therefore Leo Wiener's linguistic versatility and penchant for intuition (a side effect of his impatience), which permitted him to draw on an enormous store of information, was considered avant-garde. "Philology was for him a piece of deductive work, a magnificent crossword puzzle" (*EP* 122), which he played in any culture that would present him with an interesting problem.[13] For Wiener, philology was the opposite of what it was for his nationalist formalist colleagues: it was transnational and based on experience. Philology eventually became Wiener's substitute for a belief or culture in which to be at home (*EP* 73).

Being a transnational philologist was for Wiener's mind what being a farmer was for his body: it eased tension. And it rooted the self—in the soil and in humanity. It would be misleading, however, to suggest that the activity of philological research completely succeeded in curing Wiener's cultural discontent. Academic research and farm work might be an ideal combination for romantic and other utopian minds, but it was not likely to enhance Wiener's acceptability in the eyes of his colleagues at Harvard. His unusual entry into the guild as well as his unorthodox philological methods made for further isolation. He did not belong. Moreover, his romantic idealism and exuberance seemed out of place "amid the frigid and repressed figures of an uninspiring and decadent Boston" (*EP* 74); and for Wiener's love of Russia, its language and literature, Cambridge was a less welcoming place than New York might have been. At the time of the First World War Wiener's preference for Russia brought him into a head-on collision with his German Jewish colleague at Harvard, Hugo Münsterberg.

Both professors, the philologist as well as the philosopher, thought little of their Jewish descent. On neutral territory they preferred to stick their necks out for their "native" countries, Russia and Germany, even though any native son would have chopped off their distinguished heads with a delighted flourish. Yet nothing burns as fiercely as unrequited love, and thus the two Jews presented to their WASP colleagues the pathetic spectacle described by Abraham Roback in the obituary for Leo Wiener. Here they were, in the diaspora, "blasting each other because of their opposing loyalties. Leo Wiener, the 'Russian' (*klompershten*), was sticking up for the Czarist Government, and Hugo Münsterberg, the 'German' (*nit dogedakht*), was rooting (or as one would say it more expressively in Yiddish, 'hot sikh gerissen dem peltz') for his friend the Kaiser. Wiener would call Münsterberg a commensal to the present Herr Hohenzollern, while his colleague would intimate that Wiener belonged to the horde of barbarians in Eastern Europe."[14]

While it is true that Wiener did not think much of Germany, despite his father's reverence for Kultur, he did not like the czar either. His sympathy was with the Russian people. A newspaper report on a lecture Wiener presented at the Unitarian Club in November 1915 quotes him as saying that "Americans made a great mistake in sending their sons to Germany to finish their education, because Germany had nothing intellectually to give them that was worthwhile." In regard to the ongoing war in Europe, Wiener did not mind that the Russians were lacking in military spirit. The newspaper goes on:

> He believes recent German reports that whole divisions of Russians have laid down their arms and surrendered to the Germans rather than fight, because such acts are quite characteristic of Russian soldiers who are so imbued with the Tolstoi idea of nonresistance that they have no heart to fight anybody. That is the reason the whole campaign has collapsed he declared.
>
> "The only interest of the Russian people is in their internal life," he continued. "They care nothing whatever for politics and they are practically all nihilists. Their Government is thoroughly German in its structure and they care nothing for that, or for the Czar. It is because of the corruption and the despotism of their Government that they are always ready for revolution."[15]

Wiener's loving, romantic view of the Russian people stands in sharp contrast to his distanced, occasionally negative attitude toward his own people. However, this reserve does not show in his writings.[16] Wiener's first book was *The History of Yiddish Literature in the Nineteenth Century* (1899), in which he argues that Judeo-German—as he consistently calls Yiddish in his book—should not be regarded as "an anomaly, but a natural development."[17] But his sympathy does not stretch very far. Wiener does not think it "desirable to preserve the Judeo-German, and to give it a place of honor among the sisterhood of languages." Nevertheless he considers the strong bias against Yiddish "a manifestation of general prejudice against everything Jewish, for passions have been at play to such an extent as to blind the scientific vision to the most obvious and common linguistic phenomena."[18] Wiener himself concludes that "Judeo-German is certainly not inferior to many [other] literary languages," for which he then offers ample proof in his account of nineteenth-century European and American Yiddish literature. He recognizes the high literary quality of many Yiddish writers, but he sees no future for the language itself

Caricature (artist unknown) of
Leo Wiener.
Courtesy Harvard University
Archives.

in a free world. "In America it is certainly doomed to extinction. . . .
In the countries of Europe it will last as long as there are any disabilities
for the Jews, as long as they are secluded in Ghettos and driven into
Pales. It would be idle to speculate when these persecutions will cease."[19]

Although Leo Wiener felt socially most comfortable with Russian Jewish
immigrant intellectuals such as Morris Rosenfeld, the Yiddish sweatshop
poet he discovered and whose work he edited in a translation in 1898, Wiener
was an advocate of assimilation on the national as well as on the international
level, or of what he called "that liberal humanism and secular idealism which
characterized the best minds of Europe in the late nineteenth century."[20]
Hence it is no surprise that in his book Wiener reserves exorbitant praise for
Yitzhak Leib Peretz, an ideologue of Yiddishism and the most programmatic of the distinguished Yiddish writers of his time. Peretz's cultural
nationalism, which anticipates central ideas of Horace Kallen's cultural
pluralism, could on account of its insistence on specific suffering easily be
taken for a much larger, all-inclusive humanism. Peretz's writing was an
instance of blowing "into the narrow end of the shofar [to] be heard far."[21]
This, at least, is how Wiener preferred to understand Peretz's stories.

Although they at times deal with situations taken from Jewish life
[Wiener explains] it is their universal import that interests [Peretz],
not their specifically racial characteristics. It is mere inertia and the
desire to serve his people that keep him in the ranks of Judeo-German

writers. He does not belong there by any criterions [*sic*] that we have applied to his confreres, who themselves complain that his symbolism is inaccessible to the masses for whom he pretends to write. While this accusation is certainly just in the case of some of his works . . . there is sufficient real residue of intelligible story for the humblest of his readers. . . . His sympathies are with humanity at large, and the Jews are but one of the units that are to be redeemed from the social slavery under which the wretched of the world groan.[22]

Wiener's political stance and his psychological needs are hardly separable. He was restless, discontent, and he lacked patience with those surrounding him. His own interpretation of his difficulties in dealing with Jewish organizations and with the Jewish Publication Society of America in particular reflects his confusion of psychology and politics. He claimed "that the friction was the result of an arrogant insistence on the part of the Jewish organizations that a Jew was a Jew before he was a man, and that he owed inalienable allegiance to his own group before humanity itself" (*EP* 146). Just as Wiener was opposed to the separate existence of Jews within another nation, he was opposed to their forming a separate state. In his exchange with Israel Zangwill, whom he considered "one of the most eloquent British Zionists," he pointed to the difficulties arising "from the superimposition of a Jewish colony upon a Moslem background" and insisted "that the future of the Jews in the newer countries lay in their identifying their interest with those of the country, not in opening the wound of a separate new nationalism" (*EP* 56).

Leo Wiener tried hard to overcome his descent in the "freedom" of America. He did not recognize that in some parts of Boston and in academic philology "America" was merely an idea, not a reality, and that he, a farming, language-crazed, mid-nineteenth-century German liberal and Tolstoyan Jew, stuck out like a sore thumb from the genteelly composed WASP community at Harvard. It is hard to say how much he was aware of his failure to bridge the gap between them and himself. It is obvious that he reacted to the psychological pressures that his displacement created. He tried to root himself firmly in the ground, in America's welcoming soil, and simultaneously in the realm he shared with all mankind: language. The soil was hospitable enough, but it could not hold him. He frequently sold his farm and moved. In his academic endeavor—the value-free, experience-based, comparative (transnational) study of languages—he excelled. His was an idiosyncratic solution to the problems of deracination and cultural incoherence in his life: the achievement of *heymishkayt* in the realm of language.[23]

3   Three Professors of Philosophy

Despite Norbert Wiener's claim that "Harvard has always hated the eccentric and individual" (*EP* 197), there were quite a few "characters" on Harvard's faculty as well as in its student body during the first two decades of the twentieth century. Among them also were three rather unusual Jewish students of philosophy. All three came from orthodox backgrounds and were born in Europe. Although none of them became a professor of English (in their time this was still impossible for Jews), their metamorphoses from *yeshive bocherim* (Talmud students) into secular academics, and the very different solutions they found to the psychological problems arising from these transformations, had a profound influence on the following generation of Jewish intellectuals (American-born and literature-oriented) as well as on the academy itself. These three Jewish students of philosophy are part of the indispensable transition generation whose thinking to a considerable degree smoothed the passage of the Jewish mind from shtetl culture into the world of artistic (Gentile) literature. Why this transition was made via the study of philosophy (or, in other words, why the study of philosophy and not of literature should appeal to immigrants from Orthodox backgrounds) is explained through analogy by the youngest of the three, Harry Austryn Wolfson:

> That philosophy should have been the vehicle through which the first linguistically emancipated Jews should break into the world's literature was only natural, for outside the Bible philosophy was the only

field of knowledge which the Jews shared in common with the rest of Europe. It is characteristic of all these early Jewish pioneers in European letters [such as Moses Mendelssohn and Salomon Maimon] that even in their new state they continued to draw upon their early knowledge and training and to show the unmistakable influence of their early traditions and interests.[1]

Small wonder then that the early Jewish pioneers in American letters should all have been affiliated with Harvard. Its philosophy department was reputed to be the best in the country, and only after the death of William James, in 1910, did its golden age slowly come to an end. Horace Kallen, a favorite of James's, was "probably the first Jew to have completed both his undergraduate and his graduate work in [Harvard's] Faculty of Arts and Sciences" (B.A. 1903, Ph.D. 1908).[2] He was followed by Harry Wolfson (B.A. 1911, Ph.D. 1915), whereas Morris Cohen spent only two years at Harvard (1904–1906). For a short period, when Harvard saw "probably the most distinguished assemblage of students in its history," the three were exposed to the same teachers and the same social pressures.[3] They responded in completely different ways, reflective of their different personalities, to the challenges and opportunities Harvard and the Gentile world presented: by developing another variant of American philosophy, by withdrawing into traditional scholarship, and by becoming bitter. With the life stories of Kallen and Cohen the focus of this study will shift from Cambridge to New York and remain there for the account of the next generation of Jewish academics. Therefore this chapter will begin with the story of the youngest student, who stayed at Harvard all his life.

A MESSENGER TO THE GENTILES:
HARRY AUSTRYN WOLFSON (1887–1974)

When Wolfson entered Harvard College as a freshman in 1908, the year Kallen received his Ph.D. and was beginning to lecture in philosophy, he had already completed a traditional Jewish course of studies. His personality and the structure of his thinking would always show the imprint of the Lithuanian yeshivot he had attended. He was "painfully shy" (WH 27). One of the few people who seem to have succeeded in winning Wolfson's trust and friendship was Horace Kallen. He took this strangest of Harvardians under his wings, "corrected Wolfson's English grammar, and removed the Yiddishisms from his essays. He appreciated the poems which Wolfson wrote in Hebrew, poems filled with a nationalistic fervor, and translated several of them into English."[4] He introduced Wolfson to Harvard's Menorah Society and shared with him the excitement of the "Hebrew renascence which was blossoming both in Boston and New York in the two decades prior to World War I" (*WH* 27). Both were Zionists. For Kallen, Zionism offered a way to reconcile the Jewish condition of harut [bondage] with the herut [freedom][5] Jews experienced in America and thus became "the secular Hebraic ideal through which he could remain *in* the Jewish community,"[6] whereas for Wolfson, Zionism meant the pre-Messianic, hence partial realization of the *divrei torah* (words of the Torah), that is, the secularization of a religious concept, and thus a way *out* of the community of *talmud torah* (study of Torah) and into Western rationalism.

Harry Wolfson was born Zvi Hirsch (Hershel) ben Mendel Wolfson in Ostrin, a town of two thousand inhabitants, half Jewish, half Christian, with a "sprinkling of Muslim Tartar families" (*WH* 6), 32 miles from Grodno and 120 miles from Vilna, the Jerusalem of Lithuania. To his parents' delight their first son (the second of seven children) turned out to have *a goldener kop*, a sharp mind, and thus would, of course, become a *gelernter*, a Talmud scholar. The *starosta* (lay elder), dropping in from the church opposite the Wolfson house, relished Hershel's storytelling faculties in the local Russian dialect. On the occasion of a big fire that everybody in the village ran to see, the starosta told the police, who were about to pull the eight-year-old Wolfson into the water bucket line: "This boy should be excused. He is a *dachovna*, a spiritual person," and he was excused (*WH* 8). A year later Hershel seemed to have exhausted the educational resources of Ostrin and was sent to a yeshivah in Grodno. He stayed with his maternal grandparents. Rav Shmuel Savitsky, a prominent citizen in the Grodno community and a leading Zionist, gave his young grandson full access to his collection of Hebrew books. A year later Hershel moved on to the yeshivah in Slonim, and in 1898 he enrolled in a yeshivah in Bialystok (Leo Wiener's birthplace). He returned to Ostrin at age thirteen, probably for his bar mitzvah, but he did not stay for long. It was soon decided that Hershel should attend one of the best yeshivot in Europe. Armed with a recommendation from the Ostrin rabbi and accompanied by his uncle, Hershel presented himself to the rector of the "old shul" of Slobodka Yeshivah, also named Knesset Bet Yitzhak after its founder Rabbi Yitzhak Elhanan, the Kovno gaon. Kovno, of which Slobodka was a suburb situated across the river, was then the third largest city in Lithuania and a center of Hebraic culture (*WH* 12). At first, Rabbi

Moses Mordecai Epstein, the dean of the yeshivah, refused to admit Wolfson because he was too young, but finally he gave in. Wolfson did not let him down. He excelled, here too, in the *daf yomi*—the memorization and explication of the daily page of Talmud—as well as in the penetration of the intricacies of other commentaries and codices (*WH* 13).

In Knesset Bet Yitzhak Wolfson spent the three most important years of his adolescence, from ages thirteen to sixteen, studying under the guidance of Rabbi Epstein. During that time, in the years between 1900 and 1903, Wolfson's personality was decisively shaped and the foundation for his later exegetical method, the talmudic hypothetico-deductive method of textual interpretation, securely established.[7]

One has to be somewhat familiar with the rigor of a classical yeshivah education and the intellectual demands of rabbinic texts in order to understand from this bare outline of changing Lithuanian yeshivot why this education, and the particular style of living and thinking that it forged, should be as inescapable as it proved to be, even for someone as creative and independent as Harry Wolfson. In 1912, when he won Harvard's Sheldon Traveling Fellowship, Wolfson decided that he would not become a Hebrew poet and novelist, creating original work outside and against the world of the yeshivot (something he had always wanted to do), but would instead become a scholar, re-creating the arguments of former sages. Thus, the chance to escape the grip of his early education was forfeited. Wolfson's later life-style and scholarship would show to an astonishing degree the imprint of his Lithuanian experiences.

Of course, it must remain largely a matter of speculation which of Wolfson's views, traits, and deeds were in fact aspects of a personality formed in the world of nineteenth-century yeshivot. But it seems safe to assume that among them were Wolfson's reticence about personal matters, set off by his eagerness to flaunt his wit; his indifference towards women;[8] his "divine ritual of study" from the opening until closing time of Harvard's Widener Library; his avoidance of any direct personal reference in his writings (*WH* 5); his difficulty in crediting originality (even in himself), as well as his view that "all the basic positions [in philosophy] had really been worked out, and [that] what philosophers now did was to reiterate them and to write articles in which they argued about one another among themselves"; and furthermore, his emphasis on preserving the continuity of the struggle for understanding, his traditional stance in scholarship, his "resolute self-sufficiency and indifference to novel intellectual movements," and, not least of all, his reluctance to speak out on public issues, even such important ones as President Lowell's attempt to establish a Jewish quota at Harvard in 1922, or Harvard's virtual refusal to welcome to its staff refugee scholars from Nazi Germany. One can understand Wolfson's reluctance to voice adversarial views at Harvard as the continuation of the traditional respect of the talmudist for the institution that shelters his learning. Harvard had clearly succeeded Slobodka Yeshivah in Wolfson's reverence, and it seems to have been impossible for Wolfson to turn against the school. It is far more difficult to comprehend why, in Hillel Goldberg's words, "in one of the most prominent institutions of the world, one of its most prominent Jews sat silent before, during, and after the Holocaust." It was, after all, the world of the yeshivot that went up in flames. Goldberg blames Wolfson's silence on the cowardice of the assimilationist. But that explanation may be too simple. Wolfson was socially paralyzed outside the world of the yeshivot. The younger Jewish sociologists who came to Harvard in the late sixties found such aspects of Wolfson's personality unappealing and alienating. "They took no initiative to meet Wolfson, and he, for his part, felt no urge to meet them."[9]

In Lithuania, the center of the rationalist tradition in talmudic studies and the stronghold of the *mitnadgim* ("opponents" of the *hasidim*, the mystic pietists), the Haskalah (Jewish Enlightenment) had made broad inroads into Jewish culture and had infiltrated the yeshivot. The students there still continued to study tract after tract of the Talmud and commentary upon commentary in the dialogical way that had changed little since the Middle Ages, but in their spare time they read modern Hebrew literature.[10] The yeshivah population, as Robert Alter points out, "was the intellectual elite of central and eastern European premodern Jewry. The Hebrew writers produced by the *yeshivot* were an elite within an elite." But even if most yeshivah students would not become Hebrew writers "as a new Hebrew culture began to shimmer before such unusual students as a radical alternative of Jewish identity to that of the Orthodox system, they would, even in the *yeshivah* milieu, do a good deal of reaching, often surreptitiously, beyond the curriculum—to the parts of the Bible not officially studied, to the medieval philosophers and poets, to those newfangled Hebrew grammars, and, worst of all, to the godless journals, the poetry and fiction, of the new Hebrew literature."[11] At Slobodka Yeshivah students organized sub rosa a Zionist society of which the youngest student, Wolfson, became a leader. Wolfson also edited a small Hebrew journal to which he contributed articles and poems (*WH* 13).

After two years Hershel ben Mendel left Kovno for Vilna, where he stayed for six months "reading classical and modern Hebrew literature in the Strashun Library—one of the best Hebrew collections in Europe"

(*WH* 14). In 1903, the family, emigrating little by little, sent Wolfson and his sister Mamie to America. Despite the family's grinding poverty, it would not have occurred to anyone to put Wolfson to work. Instead he continued his talmudic studies at the Rabbi Isaac Elchanan Theological Seminary on New York's Lower East Side from 1903 to 1905. In those years, his future friend Kallen was serving as instructor of English at Princeton. With the progress of the revolution in Russia, living conditions for Jews deteriorated and passage money for the rest of the Ostrin family was needed. Wolfson found a teaching position at the Montefiore Hebrew School in Scranton, Pennsylvania. During his three-year stay there he learned to speak English (which he had taught himself to read in New York), broadened the knowledge of American life that he had begun to accumulate from some of the seminary's students in New York, particularly from those who were simultaneously studying at the City College, and he put himself through high school. By chance, his superior performance came to the attention of a recent Harvard alumnus, Myer Kabatchnik (class of 1906) who persuaded him that even a poor boy could make it at Harvard if he was smart. Wolfson took the Harvard entrance examinations in June 1908 and won a scholarship of $250, which after the deduction of tuition left him with $100 for the academic year.

He arrived at Harvard in 1908 as a full-fledged *mitnaged*, a Jewish rationalist, equally familiar with Talmud as with modern Hebrew literature. What was he to make of Harvard? And what was Harvard to make of him—of whom even his former American rosh yeshivah had despaired?[12]

Wolfson had the good fortune to meet Horace Kallen, who two years earlier had been among the founders of the Menorah Society and had designed its motto "for the study of Hebraic learning and ideals" (*WH* 27), and also to have George Foot Moore, Josiah Royce, and George Santayana as his teachers. Moore's and Santayana's recommendations were instrumental in earning Wolfson a grant of $1000 to study for a year abroad (the coveted Sheldon Traveling Fellowship). After allocating a part of his funds to his family, Wolfson took off to spend the next two years (his grant was extended for a year) in pursuit of every manuscript on and by Crescas in "the libraries of Paris, Munich, Vienna, Parma, the Vatican, the British Museum, Jews' College, Oxford and Cambridge" with side trips to Berlin, Venice, and Bologna.[13] Wolfson was back in Boston in June 1914 with an abundance of material which by the fall of 1917 had been transformed into a thousand-page manuscript tentatively titled "Crescas' Critique of Aristotle." The thirty months between the summer

Harry Wolfson, May 1905.
Photograph by L. Boressoff. Courtesy Harvard University Archives.

of 1914 and the fall of 1917 were the crucial stretch of time that determined Wolfson's academic future. During this period he transformed his mass of notes into a manuscript which "single-handedly raised Crescas to the status of the second most important medieval Jewish philosopher."[14] But more important, in the process of writing his thesis Wolfson transformed the idiosyncratic hermeneutics of mitnagdic talmudic exegesis into an academic method of scholarly explication de texte acceptable in the post-Enlightenment Gentile West.

Wolfson's decision to write his first professional work on Crescas might have been a spontaneous one and might even have contained, as Lewis Feuer suggests, a "rebellious note" as Crescas tried to undo "the universe built out of the marriage of faith and science by Maimonides and thus [to topple] his master, Aristotle, freeing in this process faith from its concession to reason" (*WH* 53–54)—but the actual writing of the Crescas book was a deliberate attempt at bringing Jewish thought and hermeneutics into an academy dominated by Gentile philosophy. It was a subtly defiant attempt to become a Harvard scholar without giving up the Lithuanian past. The major problem in Wolfson's adjustment to academic scholarship was philological. Nothing seemed to be more at odds than the rabbinic hermeneutics, to which Wolfson had been exposed during the first fifteen years of his education, and the research positivism (or what Gerald Graff called "hard investigation") then still in vogue in the American academy.[15]

A study of Crescas appeared ideally suited to tackling this problem, because the expository part of Crescas's work looked like a talmudic or midrashic text, whereas its critical part adhered to "what may be called the Talmudic method of the text study."[16] Wolfson began his analysis by describing the talmudic attitude toward texts[17] and then presented the "Talmudic hypothetico deductive method of text interpretation" which followed from this attitude. To those familiar with the rules of rabbinic exegesis, it is apparent that under the guise of explaining Crescas's hermeneutics Wolfson proposed in his study an ingenious fusion of rabbinic and Harvardian textual concerns. In analyzing Crescas, Wolfson described not only Crescas's but also his own method of textual analysis.[18]

Wolfson's real achievement in *Crescas*, his combination of two basically irreconcilable methods of textual analysis, of the ahistorical rabbinic hermeneutics and the history-conscious approach then current in the academy, was of limited interest to his colleagues at Harvard. They hardly recognized that one aspect of Wolfson's scholarship was indeed a major asset: his familiarity with talmudic thinking and the rabbinic way of transforming thought into a written text enabled him to see that Crescas's as well as Spinoza's texts, on which he worked next, used a talmudic shorthand. Wolfson saw that for a Gentile readership Crescas's shorthand would have to be translated into a generally understandable longhand:

[The] Talmudic method of reasoning is intelligible enough when it is fully expressed, when its underlying assumptions are clearly stated and every step in the argument distinctly marked out. But in the literature in which this method is followed, owing to the intimacy of the circle to which it was addressed, the arguments are often given in an abbreviated form in which the essential assumptions are entirely omitted or only alluded to, the intermediary steps suppressed or only hinted at, and what we get is merely a resultant conclusion. This abbreviated form of argumentation is characteristic of the recorded minutes of the school-room discussions which make up the text of the Talmud. It was continued in the rabbinic novellae upon the Talmud, reaching its highest point of development in the French school of the Tosafists which began to flourish in the twelfth century. Shortly after, it was introduced into the philosophic literature in the form of novellae upon standard texts, resembling the Talmudic novellae in their external literary form even to the extent of using the same conventional phrases by which questions and answers are introduced. Crescas' work belongs to that type of novellae literature, conforming to the Talmudic novellae literature in all its main characteristics, its attitude toward texts, its method of text interpretation, its abbreviated form of argumentation. (*Crescas*, 28)

Wolfson spelled out Crescas's abbreviations not only by exploring his arguments, the brevity of which "often bordered on obscurity," but also by making good on his promise to give the historical background of Crescas's ideas.[19] Wolfson discussed everything that had been said by every Arab and Jewish philosopher on the themes he delineated in Crescas's texts. "The result was a condensation of the pith and problems of medieval philosophy" (*WH* 54). In the work following the Crescas study, the two volumes on *The Philosophy of Spinoza* (1934), Wolfson's method was essentially the same. Spinoza's *Ethics* was also written in a kind of shorthand:

That the *Ethics* in its literary form is a peculiar piece of writing is quite apparent. But its peculiarity does not consist in the obvious fact that it is divided into propositions and demonstrations instead of chapters and sections. It consists in the fact, which becomes obvious only after a careful study of the work, that the manner in which it makes use of language is rather peculiar. It uses language not as a means of expression but as a system of mnemonic symbols. Words do not stand for simple ideas but for complicated trains of thought. Arguments are not fully unfolded but are merely hinted at by suggestion. Statements are not significant for what they actually affirm but for the denials which they imply.[20]

Wolfson employed the same method in retracing the steps of Spinoza's reasoning that he used to spell out Crescas's arguments. First he equipped himself "with a similar fund of knowledge or philosophical mass of apperception" as the philosopher under consideration.[21] Practically, this meant reading all the books and manuscripts the philosopher mentions or that he may have read. With this store of knowledge Wolfson set out to transcribe the philosophic shorthand into explanatory longhand. For his work on Spinoza, this method required Wolfson to update his reading from the late fourteenth century (where he had stopped for his Crescas study) to the late seventeenth century in the three major literatures—Latin, Hebrew, and Arabic.

As in his study of Crescas, Wolfson finds Greek philosophy to be the common denominator.

> To Spinoza these three literatures, Hebrew, Latin, and Arabic, represented a common tradition. Whatever differences he noticed between them, they concerned only problems of a purely theological and dogmatic nature; the philosophic basis of all such problems, and especially the discussion of problems of a purely philosophic nature, he could not fail to see, were all of a common origin. They were all based upon Greek philosophy, at the centre of which stood Aristotle. The same Greek terminology lay behind the Arabic, Hebrew, and Latin terminology, and the same scientific and philosophic conceptions formed the intellectual background of all those who philosophized in Arabic, Hebrew, or Latin. The three philosophic literatures were in fact one philosophy expressed in different languages, translatable almost literally into one another.[22]

Wolfson's next magnum opus was an investigation into the source of this mutual translatability, which he located in the philosophy of Philo of Alexandria. "Philo is the founder of [a] new school of philosophy, and from him it directly passes on to the Gospel of St. John and the Church Fathers, from whom it passes on to Muslim and hence also to medieval Jewish philosophy. Philo is the direct or indirect source of this type of philosophy which continues uninterruptedly in its main assertions for well-nigh seventeen centuries when at last it is openly challenged by Spinoza."[23]

But the study of Spinoza not only led back to the antique foundations of medieval philosophy; it also took Wolfson back to the beginnings of Jewish involvement in Greek philosophy. Philo's attempt to reconcile Scripture and philosophy did not stand isolated but was in fact part of the culture of Alexandrian Jewish intellectuals since the translation of the Five

Books of Moses into Greek (around 260 B.C.E.). "The Alexandrian Jewish population produced out of its midst a school of philosophers who consciously and deliberately and systematically set about remaking Greek philosophy according to the pattern of a belief and tradition of an entirely different origin."[24]

Philo's work was the most successful attempt at reconciliation. In Wolfson's interpretation of Philo as an original thinker, his Jewishness is strongly emphasized. Philo knew the conceptions of the Greek philosophers and he used their vocabulary. He was, however, not their follower but their critic. In Wolfson's view, Philo's relation to the normative Judaism of Palestine, from which other scholars thought Hellenistic Jewry completely separated, was crucial. Wolfson undertook to prove "how the Alexandrian Jews and Philo justified Greek philosophy" and at the same time tried to remain traditional Jews, an attempt which seemed to create, not least of all, philosophical problems. Philo's working method, "to examine every philosophic view and determine whether or not each view was reconcilable with Scripture" (WH 149), was painstaking. It resembled, however, Wolfson's own procedure in his works on Crescas and Spinoza. With his knowledge of rabbinic and Greek literature,[25] all Wolfson had to do was to follow Philo's line of thought and to show how, concept by concept, Philo achieved "the harmonization of apparent contradictions,"[26] that is "to scripturalize Greek philosophy and to philosophize Scripture" (WH 149).

That Philo used an idiosyncratic abbreviation system and quoted creatively (rather than in a scholarly manner), a feature which had induced former academics to call him an eclectically quoting preacher (WH 143), presented no problem to Wolfson.[27] What might, in fact, have created a problem for him was of a quite different, namely psychological, nature. It arose from the strong resemblance of Alexandrian to post–World War II American Jewry, and from the similarity, mutatis mutandis, of Philo's and Wolfson's endeavors. Since Wolfson hardly ever made any personal remarks in his scholarly works, the closest he came to noting the striking resemblance between the two diaspora Jewries occurs in a passage toward the end of his chapter on "Hellenistic Judaism and Philo":

> These uprooted Jewish intellectuals, whether they found it advantageous to themselves to join any of the numerous heathen religious *thiasoi* or not, certainly had no reason to remain within the religious Jewish community. External political and social and economic conditions of the time did not force de-Judaized Jews to cast in their lot,

despite themselves, with the Jewish community. Still less did external conditions force them to assume communal or religious leadership. It was comparatively easy at that time for a Jew to escape Judaism. Those at that time who cut themselves off from the body Jewish cut themselves off completely, leaving no dangling shreds of festering dead tissue. They wrote neither books against Jews nor books about Jews. . . . Perhaps some of these apostates, either for devious reasons of some practical advantages or for the simple reason that it was easier for them to lose their relish for the God of their fathers than for the cooking of their mothers, had remained within the Jewish part of the city, though without being part of its religious life; and, with all their indifference toward Judaism, they could not completely refrain from taunting their fellow Jews, especially the philosophers among them, for maintaining that Scripture was of divine origin and that its stories were something superior to the mythological fables of the Greeks. [28]

Wolfson had certainly not cut himself off from the "body Jewish," but neither had he remained an observant Jew. [29] His solution was not that of Philo's apostate nephew Tiberius Julius Alexander, but neither was it quite like Philo's cautious messianism, despite Wolfson's sympathy for Zionism. [30] Wolfson's solution to his diaspora situation, presenting him with Philo's "vexatious problem" of many cultural alternatives, was subtle and a direct result of the Haskalah influences in his Lithuanian youth. The outline of his solution can be found as early as 1921, in his essay, "Escaping Judaism," published in the *Menorah Journal*. By that time he had already decided against becoming a Hebrew poet and novelist[31] and had thrown in his lot with Harvard.[32] In his essay he claims that "[w]hat is really necessary for our happiness is an abiding sense of loyalty to one supreme interest, and a willingness to resign ourselves to that loyalty."[33] Wolfson's "supreme interest" was scholarship. To the public eye he became the "cloistered scholar obsessed with the past" (*WH* 109). But his scholarship contained a strong missionary element. His message to the Gentiles, however, was more subtly conveyed than the one to the Jews.

To the Gentile academic community Wolfson's work made clear that the contributions to philosophy by Jewish thinkers needed to be taken seriously. He brought Crescas, Philo, Saadia, and lesser known philosophers to the general attention. Furthermore, Wolfson insisted that the Jewish background of commonly accepted and generally discussed philosophers (such as Spinoza) would have to be considered more seriously. In his elegantly written work on Philo, Wolfson pointed with mild irony

Harry Wolfson, April 1937.
Photograph by Photo Reflex Studio, William Filene's Sons, Boston. Courtesy Harvard University Archives.

to the fact that the philosophic edifices of the Church Fathers and later medieval thinkers rested on foundations laid by a Jew who reconciled pagan thought and Mosaic Scripture. The second part of Wolfson's message to the Gentile academy was even more important: his scholarship established an interfaith community of thought in which the common problems of philosophy overrode theological or dogmatic differences.[34]

Wolfson's message to the Jews was less gently conveyed, as if speaking to family could be done more harshly. Wolfson's publications in the *Menorah Journal* certainly do not mince words, despite their elegant rhetoric:

> The most unfortunate fact about our Jewish religious problem of today is that our awakening to the world of modern thought, toward the end of the eighteenth century, took place at a time when Judaism was at its lowest intellectual ebb, and that the intellectual awakening was accompanied by great political and social upheavals in our life. The great tragedy of our religious history is that the type of enlightened, rationalized, philosophizing Judaism, which had been growing and flourishing for about three centuries, since the days of Saadia, began to decline upon the death of Maimonides and ultimately disappeared. Forces beyond our control put an end to the continued development of rationalized Judaism. Philosophy was gradually hedged in and restricted until it was finally eliminated altogether from Jewish religion. Judaism was flung back into a primitive state of untested tradition, and remained for centuries out of touch with all the currents of the time, so that when it emerged from its secluded ghetto and once more faced the world, as it did in Germany toward the end of the eighteenth century, it was a Judaism infinitely inferior to that of the twelfth century—and amid a world which had passed through centuries of intellectual progress since the Renaissance and the Reformation. . . . Not only were the new horizons of thought that were revealed to [the Jews] out of harmony with their accustomed religious thinking but the newly-discovered life with its manifold opportunities was found to be incompatible with the old life according to tradition or it was found to be closed to them on account of their religious allegiance.[35]

Wolfson saw two ways of reconciling Judaism and modern life: German Reform Judaism, which had developed *die Wissenschaft des Judentums* [the science of Judaism], and the Haskalah, which was of predominantly "literary character." "This was a movement which had its origin among the best classes of Jews who for generations have been the repository of Jewish learning and ideals. The movement culminated in the modern Hebrew renaissance. What is now sometimes called cultural Zionism, the insistence upon Hebrew culture, Hebrew ideals, the inner light of Judaism, are simply the new synthesis of old Judaism and modern culture as worked out by the Hebraized Jews in Russia."[36]

Wolfson's own deepest concern was to revive the "enlightened, rationalized, philosophizing Judaism," a Judaism which was in full communication with the world but still remained true to itself. This Judaism Wolfson finds brilliantly displayed in the works of Crescas, Philo, Saadia,

Maimonides, and Spinoza. Wolfson's intellectual re-creation of their philosophical worlds was at first graciously acknowledged and later honestly respected by Harvard's academic community, who treated him accordingly—with respect, but as "their Jew." For the American Jews he was a *gaon*, a preeminent scholar. But in Israel, his work was hardly recognized.[37] The reasons are not entirely clear, but one would suspect that in its early days Israel was more in need of philosophers of self-assertion than of reconciliation. On the other hand, the mitnaged Wolfson shared the Israeli disdain for that part of Jewish culture associated with the Yiddish language. In Wolfson's classically mitnagdic mind Yiddish language, culture, and politics were linked with social upheaval, revolution, ignorance, and superstition (such as is prevalent in the pious folk-culture of the ḥasidim). In Wolfson's view Yiddish was the language of the Jewish mob. "Although it is true that Yiddish and Hebrew . . . were cognate literatures [at the end of the nineteenth century], and although many of the important writers actually produced work in both languages, only Yiddish evinced a general association with the values and aspirations of the urban proletariat."[38] Hebrew, by contrast, was associated not only with Jewish political autonomy but also (and this was more important to Wolfson) with great achievements in rational Jewish philosophy. For Wolfson, as for many other mitnagdim, Hebrew was the language of physical and intellectual independence, whereas Yiddish was in every respect the language of the ghetto. Wolfson's passage about the "Yidds" in "Escaping Judaism" is, unfortunately, not "biting satire" as Leo Schwarz would have it (*WH* 153), but desperately serious.

> [T]he catastrophic blow fell upon East European Judaism when the great mass of ignorant, superstitious Jews—apprenticed tailors, shoemakers and blacksmiths—benighted, and discontented, were suddenly awakened, within recent times, to a realization of their own rights and of the world around them. Their awakening took place under the auspices of the general revolutionary propaganda which swept like a tornado over all Russia during the last days of Czardom. All kinds of heresies, religious, economic, political, and social, were showered upon their innocent and undiscriminating minds from all directions. These were preached to them by word of mouth and by word of pen, in their own Yiddish language, and in a manner appealing to their intellectual capacity and to their native prejudices. Their religion fell with a snap, along with every other form of thought that was old and established. Broken loose from all bonds of tradition, these Yiddishized masses are gradually becoming a new, distinct people, the Yiddish people. They

are now everywhere contending for supremacy with the Jews, in Poland, in Lithuania, in America, and elsewhere, a contest the full
significance of which is unfortunately not as yet fully understood. In
Soviet Russia they have already gained a decisive victory. There Yiddish satraps are ruthlessly exterminating the old Jewish life, endeavor-
ing to set up on its ruins the new godless Yiddish people.[39]

Speaking about Wolfson's deep aversion to Yiddish, his friend Ben-
Zion Gold, Harvard's Conservative rabbi, at first called it an "instance of
Jewish self-hatred." But later he corrected himself and said: "The word
does not really explain anything. It has become trite and is an accusation
rather than an explanation. Wolfson's aversion to Yiddish [his mother
tongue] was more complex than that. It was a paradoxical fact of his
existence, a paradox which was not solved."[40] Harry Austryn Wolfson,
Harvard's great scholar of Jewish philosophy, who was called *Hershele
Ostrinje* at Slobodka Yeshivah—collected with particular care books by
rabbis from Ostrin, not because they were valuable or erudite but because
they were Ostrinian. In "Escaping Judaism," Wolfson wrote: "I believe
that it is useless to look for solutions for all our difficulties. There are
certain problems in life for which no solution is possible."[41]

Leo Wiener sought to transcend the particularity of his descent by
entering the realm of language, where nationalist prejudice would yield
to "scientific vision" and where insight into the "common linguistic phenomena" would establish equality in the "sisterhood of languages" (and
thus among their speakers).[42] Harry Wolfson, bent on escaping less his
Jewishness than the segregationist doctrines of normative Judaism, sought
to do so by creating in his works a community of philosophers, the members of which might have adhered to different theological doctrines but
who employed "one language" in their philosophical or metaphysical
quests. Wiener and Wolfson attempted to replace descent with consent, to
transcend their particularity by becoming members in a (self-made) universal community in which the particularities of the individuals—the
differences separating the members—were considered apparent and the
unifying element, the One (language or metaphysics) real. It is thus not
entirely correct to describe Wiener's and Wolfson's ideal (and idealistic)
communities as "interlinguistic" or "interfaith," respectively, because
their understanding of the prefix *inter* is more adequately expressed by the
prefix *trans*. They created ideal communities of consent in which the particularities of the members' descent were, if not cancelled out, then of no

33

real importance. The ideal was the *real*, while the "real" differences were only apparent. Horace Kallen thought that precisely the opposite was true.

THE AMERICAN IDEAS OF
HORACE MEYER KALLEN (1882–1974)

On the surface, Horace Kallen's solution to being Jewish in modern America seems similar to the solutions developed by Leo Wiener and Harry Wolfson insofar as Kallen, too, created an ideal community, America, out of a multiplicity of elements, which in his case were not languages or philosophers but social groups, nationalities. But for the student of William James, not the One but the many were real. The One, he claimed, was essentially a construct, existing only by the consent of the many to form a unity in an "associative pattern."[43] The One was the *act of consent*. Thus *America* had no inherent reality but was a word signifying the idea and act of social consent first posited in the Declaration of Independence. " 'American' is a common term for a union of . . . differences."[44] The different nationalities (or ethnic experiences) present in America, however, were real. The conceptual equivalent to the ideal communities conceived by Wiener and Wolfson would have been Zangwill's: America seen as a melting pot. But Kallen's "America" is a society of cultural pluralism — an inter-national society where *inter* signifies "the parity of the different and their free and friendly communication with one another as both co-operators and competitors: it postulates that every individual, every society, thus realizes its own being more freely and abundantly than it can by segregation and isolation and struggle to go it alone."[45]

Kallen's favorite metaphor to describe the "American idea" or cultural pluralism was that of a symphony orchestra. It appears in his first publication on the subject in 1915. He concludes his essay "Democracy Versus the Melting Pot: A Study of American Nationality" with a description of American society as "multiplicity in a unity, an orchestration of mankind":

> As in an orchestra, every type of instrument has its specific timbre and tonality, founded in its substance and form; as every type has its appropriate theme and melody in the whole symphony, so in society each ethnic group is the natural instrument, its spirit and culture are its theme and melody, and the harmony and dissonances and discords of them all make the symphony of civilization, with this difference: a musical symphony is written before it is played; in the symphony of

civilization the playing is the writing, so that there is nothing so fixed and inevitable about its progressions as in music. . . .[46]

Since Kallen's emphasis was not so much on the constructed One ("America," the symphony) but rather on the real Many (the ethnic groups, instruments) it was by no means contradictory that he was as staunch an advocate of Zionism (the attempt at self-realization of his own ethnic group) as of the American idea. In fact, Kallen's advocacy of a "Jewish Commonwealth in Palestine"[47] was the logical consequence of his theory of cultural pluralism, in which diversity was a prerequisite for democracy, and of his understanding of the American idea based on a reading of the term "equal" in the Declaration of Independence not as "same" but "*as different*," or, more precisely, as "*the* inalienable right" to be different.[48] Expanded to the scale of world politics, Kallen's "American idea" included the realization of a Jewish state.

The elegance of Kallen's solution to the problem of being Jewish in America is so intriguing that one is reluctant to notice its paradoxical nature and the shortcomings that have been pointed out by a number of critics.[49] Nevertheless, Kallen's cultural pluralism was, as John Higham points out, "objectively speaking, . . . an extraordinary ethnic achievement: an exercise of mind that abolished any claims of white Protestants to constitute a rightful majority and defined us all as minorities and all minorities as equal."[50] Furthermore, Kallen's theory played a major role in modernizing American Jewish thought, because, as William Toll explains, "Kallen offered a flexible concept of ethnicity for intellectuals who did not feel that traditions must be provincial or that socialism could cure society's ill."[51]

For the young Kallen, as for many other children of observant immigrants, "the Jewish Idea, as it had come to me, was the antithesis of the American Idea."[52] Horace Meyer Kallen was born in 1882 in Berenstadt (Silesia) to a yeshivah-trained father from Latvia who served there as "under rabbi." As a Russian subject Kallen's father was expelled by Bismarck's Prussian government as an alien Jew.[53] He made his way to the United States and returned to Germany in 1887 to move his family to Boston, where he had found a position as rabbi of the German-speaking Orthodox congregation Hevra ha-Moriah.[54] Kallen's Jewish education had begun in Europe in the traditional way that he still remembered eighty-five years later: "I have an image of a maternal aunt standing over me as a three-year-old, and dropping a coin on the book when I read a letter correctly." Rabbi Kallen wanted his son to follow in his footsteps and therefore educated him at home. However, the traditional *ḥeder* (Jewish elementary school) education did not strike the American officials as adequate. When a truant officer threatened the rabbi, his son, then eight years old, was finally permitted to attend elementary school. But instruction at school differed from instruction at home only in degree, not in kind. "My beginning is in the discipline and rigid order of an Orthodox Jewish household, the head of which was a *k'lai kodesh* [religious functionary] supplemented by a somewhat looser control in *ḥeder* and a still looser discipline, but a discipline in the elementary and grammar schools I attended."

To Kallen Jewish education was nothing but "a discipline. It was ritualistic; it was *Shulḥan Arukh.*" He resented his father's coercion, "rebelled and at times ran away from home."[55] But he soon learned that the American freedom he had heard about from his teachers was not to be found right outside his father's home. "In Boston, on the streets and in the schoolyards, the Christian kids taught me what they had learned the Jew should receive in payment for the salvation from eternal death which the death of their crucified Savior brought them. I could endure, and on occasion even overcome, because I knew that I belonged to God's Chosen People and that my pangs and pains were linked in some salubrious way to the divine election."[56]

But except for such occasional moral support he found life according to *halakhah* (Jewish Law) oppressive. His intellectual rebellion as an adolescent was more successful than his spontaneous Huck Finn-like lighting out from home as a boy. In the year of his graduation from high school he chanced upon a German edition of Spinoza's *Tractatus Theologico-Politicus.* "It set me free. . . . His image, his thought, and his story became the point of no return in the ongoing alienation from my father and the ancestral religion. I identified with Spinoza."[57]

Although Spinoza helped Kallen to cut himself loose from his father and his religion, this move did not facilitate his transition into America, because "Americanization" in those days meant "dissipating differences, all directed to self-alienation by the different" either by way of "unquestioning conformity to the requirements of those who claimed to be the nation's elite and used their power to enforce their claims," or by way of emulating the claimants ("keeping up with the Joneses"), or by "willy-nilly melting the Joneses together with oneself into an undefinable new super-identity in Israel Zangwill's 'melting pot'." Kallen, like Moses Mendelssohn in 1783, was not ready to give up his difference if self-alienation was the price, even though his obvious difference from the Joneses of

Boston, his Jewish identity, caused "dumb anxiety": "Non-Jews were troubling my days and nights because, through no fault of my own, I happened to be different from them. My difference diminished me, shackled me, deprived me of my liberty and subjected me to injustice. I must needs rid myself of it and make myself the same as my apparent betters. I must needs change from Jew to—what?"[58] What, after all, *was* an "American"?

By the time Kallen entered Harvard College, in 1900, he was thoroughly alienated from his father's Judaism. He had only the vaguest sense of what his own Jewishness could possibly consist of, and subscribed to Spinoza's belief "that difference, seen clearly and distinctly, made no real difference, that in substance all the families of mankind are one."[59] He had liberated himself from the "confines" into which he had been born, but he could not quite cope with freedom's lack of definition. He was to find that herut made sense only when read before the background of its origin, harut; that "liberty" and "constraint" were not absolute opposites but mutually defining terms.

The man who first gave him a clue how to reconcile harut and herut, how to be a Jew in America, and who is commonly and a little absurdly credited with having brought about Kallen's "rejudaization," was a Harvard professor of literary history. Barrett Wendell, a descendant of an old New England family, introduced American literature into the Harvard curriculum in 1877 and became a pioneer of American studies. "His version of American literary history emphasized the influence of the Hebrew Bible on the Puritan mind, and traced the role of the Hebraic tradition in the development of American character."[60] A central theme was the Hebraic origin of the Puritans' social ideals. Kallen came to recognize beneath "the coercive ritualism [and] all the impositions of *halakhah*" the "prophetic injunctions for social justice and [the] Jobian courage to face nature's irrationalities."[61] And he learned from Wendell that the democratic, horizontal, or consent structure of American society, creating freedom (as opposed to the oppressive aristocratic, hierarchical, or descent structure of most non-American societies) had its origin in the Puritan understanding of the societal organization of Old Israel. "From Barrett Wendell I came to understand the role of the Old Testament in the organization of the Congregational churches as against the Episcopal or ecclesiastical, as liberation. It justified the formation of a free religious society and the movement from congregationalism to the notions of equal liberty of all religious societies."[62]

What Kallen came to perceive was that the tension between harut and

The young Horace Kallen.
Courtesy American Jewish Archives.

ḥerut was not his singular experience alone, his individual problem as a
Jew in America, but that on a larger scale the "tension between an ancient
authoritarian monism of culture and the free cultural pluralism intrinsic
to the American Idea has been the vital spring of the nation's history."[63]
Kallen constructed the problem America (that is, its seventeenth- and
eighteenth-century thinkers and statesmen) had to solve in such a way
that it resembled his own. How was the vertical (hierarchical, authoritarian) structure of a "closed" monistic society to be reconciled with spatial
openness? How would the old (episcopalian) form of societal organiza-

tion have to be transformed in order to accommodate America's horizontal vastness? And what did it mean to a Jew in America that the Puritans had apparently found the model for the solution to this problem in Hebraism? Obviously, *harut* and *herut*, belonging to a "graven" and to a "free" society, being Jewish and being American, thinking "vertically" (hierarchically, or in terms of time) and thinking "horizontally" (democratically, or in terms of space) were not mutually exclusive alternatives, but somehow reconcilable. But how? What was the Puritans' trick? And how could their technique of "Americanization" be applied to twentieth-century problems?

Kallen had no choice but to throw in his lot with America and its culture while he was working out a solution. After his graduation from Harvard in 1903, he went to Princeton as an instructor of English literature and remained there until 1905. His contract was not renewed. It was intimated that he would not have been appointed in the first place had the administration known that Kallen was Jewish. He returned to Harvard as a graduate student and continued his studies in the English Department but eventually returned to philosophy. He wrote his dissertation under the direction of William James on the nature of truth and received his Ph.D. degree in 1908, the year Wolfson arrived there as a freshman.[64] Kallen continued at Harvard for the next three years as a lecturer and assistant to James, Santayana, and Royce. In 1911, he became an instructor of philosophy and psychology at the University of Wisconsin, then known as America's most liberal university. However, even the University of Wisconsin did not remain unaffected by the loyalty craze of the First World War, and Kallen eventually resigned in 1918 over an issue involving questions of academic freedom.[65] In 1919 he received an invitation to join the founding faculty of the New School for Social Research in New York; he gladly accepted. He retired from the New School in 1970. The location, politics, and philosophy of the New School ideally suited Kallen's own frame of mind and cultural theory as they had developed during the for him intellectually decisive decade immediately following his return to Harvard in 1905. During his fifty years at the New School, he modified but did not fundamentally change the philosophical solution to his cultural problems that he had worked out between 1905 and 1915. This solution consisted, logically enough, in the simultaneous development of mutually compatible interpretations of Jewishness and Americanness based on an idiosyncratic reading of the term *equal* and the term *Jew*.

When Kallen returned from Princeton to Harvard in 1905, it was clear to him that although he might reject Judaism, Americans—particularly "those who claimed to be the nation's elite"—would not let him forget that he was a Jew. This insight, in combination with the teachings of James, Wendell, and Royce, who even more than James "appreciated the ethnic diversity of the American people and granted each group its distinctive values so long as each respected the emotional bonds of others,"[66] led Kallen to reclaim his Jewishness, though not his father's Judaism.

He had already taken a first step in that direction, during his studies with Barrett Wendell as an undergraduate. Wendell, Kallen claimed, had emphasized the importance of the "Old Testament" (Hebrew Bible) for the Puritans and of the Hebraic tradition for the development of the American character.[67] The latter, however, is not at all apparent in Wendell's *A Literary History of America* and moreover Wendell's views of Jews as "his social inferiors,"[68] which miraculously excepted Kallen, were well known. But the twenty-year-old Kallen did not see that Wendell made a distinction between ancient Hebrews and present-day Jews. To Kallen, Jews were Jews and he was surprised to find them appreciated by non-Jews. Wendell's views were a challenge. "I was an alienated intellectual being suddenly challenged in his alienation. . . . And the challenge turned not on anything in the Hebraic tradition at all [but] . . . on what Americanism came to mean to me . . . in terms of the philosophical pluralism with which [William] James was identified and . . . in terms of the interpretation of the American tradition by Barrett Wendell . . . . The Zionist meanings came to me rather in terms of the American Idea than in terms of what I had learned of *Torah* at home or in *cheder*."[69]

Kallen began to comprehend that the "American idea" and the "Jewish idea" were not necessarily exclusive. In fact, some of the main ingredients of the "American idea"—dissent, democracy, freedom—had first come to Kallen via the quintessential Jewish story of dissent and freedom.

> In our household the suffering and slavery of Israel were commonplaces of conversation; from Passover to Passover, freedom was an ideal ceremonially reverenced, religiously aspired to. The textbook story of the Declaration of Independence came upon me, nurtured upon the deliverance from Egypt and the bondage in exile, like the clangor of trumpets, like a sudden light. What a resounding battle cry of freedom! And then, what an invincible march of Democracy to triumph over every enemy —over the English king, over the American Indian, over the uncivilized Mexican, over the champions of slavery betraying American freedom, over everything, to the very day of the history lesson![70]

But if the "Jewish idea" as it was presented to him by his "domineering" father[71] and his *melamed* (teacher) in *ḥeder* had seemed to him "the antithesis of the American idea" then there was obviously something wrong somewhere. Kallen decided that the mistake was his father's and began to reinterpret the "Jewish idea" in light of the "American idea" which had been formed by his teachers at Harvard—Wendell, Royce, and James. Kallen called the reinterpretation he developed around 1902 "Zionism."[72] It was a consent version of his father's descent-based Judaism. The elder's "Jewish idea" and the younger's "Zionist idea" would remain exclusive until a few years later, when Kallen developed his concept of cultural pluralism, which allowed him to base the "Zionist idea" on descent and operate with the term *nationality*. But despite this reconsideration, Kallen's reinvention of his Jewish identity effectively replaced the Judaism of his father(s).[73] "Zionism became a replacement and reevaluation of Judaism which enabled me to respect it."[74] Thus Wendell had in fact de-Judaized Kallen and "Zionized" him.

When Kallen returned to Harvard as a graduate student in 1905, he began thinking along these lines.[75] He unpacked the concept *Jew* by distinguishing between Judaic religion and Jewish culture and thought it possible to participate in the latter without embracing the former. He saw Judaism's only chance for survival in its modernization. "[T]he Jewish way of life is no longer a religious way of life. Judaism is no longer identical with Jewishness and Jewishness is no longer identical with Judaism. Jewishness—I prefer to say, Hebraism—is a focus of modernity. It is the Jewish way of life become necessarily secular, humanist, scientific, conditioned on the industrial economy, without having ceased to be livingly Jewish. Judaism will have to be reintegrated with this secular, cultural form of community which is Jewishness if Judaism is to survive."[76]

As a secular culture, Jewishness or Hebraism, a term sanctioned by the famous chapter 4 in Matthew Arnold's *Culture and Anarchy*, could be talked about "in the same terms, in the same refined accents, that the secular high priests of the polite English world used to discuss their culture and history."[77] Once Kallen had distinguished between his father's antiquated Judaism and modern (cultural or ethnic) Jewishness, he was ready to stick his neck out for the latter. To make Jewish culture respectable "among educated Americans" was one aim of the Menorah Society,[78] which Kallen assisted Henry Hurwitz in founding at Harvard in 1906. But its more important (though related) aim was not so much concerned with Americans but with the Jews themselves. "The idea was," to use Mark Krupnick's succinct formulation, "to promote Jewish ideals and learning among Jewish college students so as to offset the negative effects of American anti-Semitism. By demonstrating the interest and dignity of the Jewish past, the Menorah movement encouraged its members to accept and identify themselves as Jews."[79]

The Menorah movement helped create and define a secular Jewish identity for college-educated American Jews. Its dream was to end the diaspora by establishing in America an autonomous cultural center.[80] This goal would become even more pronounced with the founding of the *Menorah Journal* in 1915. By then there were already thirty-four Menorah Societies all over the United States and their number was increasing rapidly. But the *Menorah Journal* was destined to become much more than an organ for an intercollegiate Jewish society, at least during the first sixteen years of its existence. Although it was available by subscription only, it soon developed into one of the most important intellectual magazines in the country. Its contributors were historians, philosophers, sociologists, and writers of the first rank (among them Salo Baron, Cecil Roth, Harry Wolfson, Horace Kallen, Morris Cohen, Ludwig Lewisohn, and Maurice Samuel). An important element in the journal's success was the contributors' relaxed sense of themselves as Jews, which they projected in their articles. This sense of identity seemed most secure in those authors who dealt with Jewish history. Without popularization or its opposite, academic meticulousness, they managed to convey their own sense of the relevance of their subject.[81]

One of the most remarkable features of the magazine during its first sixteen years was the energy and enthusiasm, what Robert Alter called "the quality of excitement," with which the contributors set out to (re-) create in its pages a Jewish secular culture that could match in dignity and interest the culture of America, if not of Europe. There was not only a deep need "to normalize the American Jew's sense of himself" or, as Alter put it, "to validate Jewish cultural phenomena by assimilating them to Western analogues,"[82] but also a firm belief that it could be done and was worth doing.

The first sixteen volumes of the *Menorah Journal* saw two distinct generations of contributors. Members of the first, that is of Kallen's generation, were frequently European born, while members of the second generation—recruited by Elliot Cohen, when he became managing editor in 1925—consisted of young, mainly first-generation American Jews (born around 1905), many of them graduates of Columbia College. This second group, centered around Elliot Cohen, formed the nucleus of the so-called New York Intellectuals: Anita Brenner, Clifton Fadiman, Albert Halper, Meyer Levin, Felix Morrow, Henry Rosenthal, Tess Slesinger, and Lionel Trilling. Most of them left the magazine together with Elliot Cohen when he was fired for political radicalism in 1931. To both generations, although the forms of their "Jewish problem" differed slightly, the magazine was equally important. (The journal's function for the younger group will be discussed in the section on Lionel Trilling). For the older group it provided a forum, respected by the Gentile world, for the expression of their particularity as being different from other hyphenated Americans and for the exploration of the origins of that difference. The group's anti-assimilationist bent was counterbalanced by its equally strong commitment to cosmopolitanism, a seemingly contradictory combination but inherent to the theory of cultural pluralism as promoted by the journal's contributors, Horace Kallen and Randolph Bourne. As Alan Wald puts it, "the journal's program of developing Jewish humanism led directly to the formation of a Jewish intellectual vanguard that aimed to create a Jewish cultural renaissance within the framework of cultural pluralism."[83]

The development of the theory of cultural pluralism was preceded by Kallen's efforts to come to terms with his own heritage. His first attempt at articulating and defining his Jewishness was made three years after the founding of the Menorah Society. His 1909 essay, "Hebraism and Current Tendencies in Philosophy," in which he first describes the principle of Hebraism, is a startling piece of work because it shows so clearly Kallen's need to reconcile the two items in the title. His rhetorical technique for doing so is strikingly simple. He begins by summarizing Matthew Arnold's view of Hebraism and Hellenism by quoting from *Culture and Anarchy* (one of the key works for Jews entering Gentile culture): "The uppermost idea with Hellenism is to see things as they really are; the uppermost idea with Hebraism is conduct and obedience."[84] Kallen contests Arnold's statement. "In truth, Hellenism is not concerned with 'seeing things as they really are,' but with seeing things as they *ought to be*; Hebraism is not concerned with conduct and obedience, it is concerned with making the best of a bad job. The aim of Hellenism is *perfection*; the aim of Hebraism is *righteousness*. Mr. Arnold identifies the two; but they are not and never can be identical."[85]

He then explores the difference between Hebraism and Hellenism from his point of view, taking the book of Job and Plato's *Republic* as examples. Kallen concludes:

> The Greeks saw their world as a composition — a hierarchy of ideas, or forms, each having an especial place in the whole; to them no thing could be explained save by the larger unity to which it belonged. The Jews saw their world as flux, in which events occurred freely according

to no predetermined plan. Sin got its punishment, virtue its rewards. But no man was immutably sinful, no divine fiat eternal and unalterable. There is room for atonement, for a readjustment and a new life; there is a chance "to be born again." . . . In a word, for the Greeks, change is unreal and evil; for the Hebrews the essence of reality is change. The Greek view of reality is static and structural; the Hebrew view is dynamic and functional.[86]

Kallen transforms Arnold's moral characterization of Hebraism and Hellenism into a morally neutral one vaguely reflective of the categories of space (Greek) and time (Hebrew).[87] He claims that the essence of metaphysical insight "was for the Greek, structure, harmony, order immutable, eternal; for the Hebrew, flux, mutation, imminence, disorder."[88] The opposition between stasis and flux, between vertical (hierarchical) structuring and horizontal (democratic) openness resembled an opposition Kallen had experienced as a child: it was that between his orthodox home (dominated by the *siddur*, or prayer book, literally "order," and the *Shulḥan Arukh*, arranging the minutiae of daily life) and the "free" world of America outside. The opposition resembled further a dichotomy Kallen had developed under Wendell's influence, namely the contrast between the old European "episcopalian" (authoritarian) structure of society and its American "congregationalist" modification (via the Hebraic model) paving the way for equality and liberty of all religious societies.

Thus, Kallen's new opposition of Hebraism and Hellenism was a reinterpretation of Matthew Arnold's dichotomy in light of the oppositions observed at home and developed under the influence of Wendell. Its newness and significance consisted in Kallen's understanding of Hebraism, which he associated with America's freedom and flux, while Hellenism came to signify Europe's graven structures. The association of Hellenism with stasis, authority, hierarchy, and bondage, and of Hebraism with flux, equality, democracy, and freedom, was a complete reversal of the current Gentile view; it sounds revolutionary but it was, in fact, not original. This view had already become a stock argument in the teaching of German Jews affiliated with the Hochschule für die Wissenschaft des Judentums (Academy for the Science of Judaism).[89] What was new in Kallen's use of the argument was the unambiguous identification of Hebraism with America and of Hellenism with Europe.

Hence, Kallen disagreed with Arnold's view of the "apparent overemphasis of Hebraism" in European culture. Kallen claimed that "Hebraism has never dominated European life to the degree in which Hellenism has dominated it, that the 'supremacy' of Hebraism is, if one reads the signs of the times aright, yet to come."[90] The material from which Kallen read "the signs of the times" was supplied by an ingenious combination of men: a scientist, a Jew, and an American (members of groups predisposed to cosmopolitanism)—namely Charles Darwin, Henri Bergson (with whom Kallen studied as a Sheldon Fellow in Paris in 1907), and William James. In the second half of his eight-page 1909 essay, "Hebraism and Current Tendencies in Philosophy," Kallen performed an almost talmudic exegetical feat.

Having spent the first half describing Hebraism as the principle of flux and Job as its representative man illustrating "the invincible loyalty of life to itself, in the face of overwhelming odds," Kallen then abstracts the essence from the teachings of the three men. He finds that the theory of each is governed by the principle of flux. Darwin, dealing the "death-blow to scientific Hellenism" in his book on survival against overwhelming odds, *The Origin of Species*, abandons in this work "the notion of the eternity of forms and of the structural order of the universe. [To give species an origin] is to espouse the flux, to allow for the reality of individuals as against classes, to allow for genuine freedom and chance in the world, to insist on the concrete instance rather than on the general law . . . ." For James, who introduces "the postulates of 'spontaneous variation' and the 'survival of the fit' into the inner nature of the universe, . . . [a]n idea is true if it leads prosperously, if it has genuine survival-value, if it endures, by working, in the flux—if it is fit." And for Bergson, who like James "finds knowledge, ideas, concepts to be entirely practical" (their existence being justified by their use), "reality is a *moving act*. Ideas are cinematographic portraits of it." But it is only "in *doing* [that] you get at the *élan vital* of things and really know them and possess them as they are."[91] The element basic to the theories of the three men (or as Kallen might put it, the essence of their metaphysical insight) is the preponderance of the principle of flux, Bergson's élan vital, or simply, "life itself."

With this, Kallen has arrived at a key term in Judaism, *ḥay* (life). For the preservation of life in a critical situation specific laws of the Torah not only may be but must be temporarily suspended. The supremacy of life is the one crack in the "fence around the Law"[92] through which the particularist may escape into the universal. Having abstracted the principle of life from the teachings of Darwin, James, and Bergson, Kallen was now able to reconcile, through the crack in the fence, the essence of being Jewish (survival as Jews against all odds) with the world of modern philosophy to which he wanted to belong.

45

But how could he reconcile being a Jew and an American? He had formulated his understanding of Jewishness theoretically, as Hebraism (principle of flux, or élan vital), and he saw that, practically, this meant that being Jewish had to be based on experience, which comprised the remembrance of a unique past as well as the living particularist present. Consequently, Kallen was vehemently opposed to the solution that German Jews had developed and that Wolfson had considered an intellectual possibility—namely, Reform Judaism. As Kallen put it, "sects and dogmas pass, ethnic groups and cultures endure. The blindness and insensibility of 'reform' lies in the failure or refusal to recognize this fact and in the consequent attempt to thin the richness of Jewish existence to the verbal tenuousness of a few unproved dogmas and to substitute for concrete Jewish living the anatomical horror of their 'Jewish science.' "[93]

Kallen abhorred Reform Judaism because it abstracted "ideas like the Unity of God and the Brotherhood of Man from their distinctive roots in Jewish history."[94] And he was fascinated by cultural movements that activated Jewish roots (such as the revival of Hebrew culture during his time at Harvard) or by cultures that were as immediately experiential, folk- and experience-based, as Yiddish culture seemed to be. Wolfson, in turn, despised Yiddish culture for precisely these features.

In order to integrate an understanding of Jewishness so thoroughly based on the preservation of the distinctive ethnic experience with being an American, Kallen had to unpack and reassemble the concept *American*. Here William James's philosophical pluralism and Josiah Royce's "conception of culture as a harmonious federation of different provincialisms" played an important role.[95] Kallen began his unpacking in 1915, not only in response to his own developing understanding of himself as a Jew by descent and American by consent, but also in response to the increasing uneasiness of large numbers of people born in America about the cultural effects of mass immigration. By the time of World War I, this uneasiness had developed into a deep concern "and was specifically linked with the dangers posed to national unity by the divided loyalties of 'hyphenated Americans'."[96]

Kallen begins his famous 1915 essay, "Democracy Versus the Melting Pot," with a reading of America's constitutional document, the Declaration of Independence, in which he focuses on the term *equal*. In the light of recent American history (i.e., mass immigration), he interprets *equal* to mean not "same" but having "the right to be different." Kallen believes that each nation (or ethnic group) in America should preserve its cultural distinctness and thus exercise the right to self-realization. But each nation should also cooperate politically and economically with all other nations in "a possible great and truly democratic commonwealth."

> Its form is that of the Federal republic; its substance a democracy of nationalities, cooperating voluntarily and autonomously in the enterprise of self-realization through the perfection of men according to their kind. The common language of the commonwealth, the language of its great political tradition, is English, but each nationality expresses its emotional and voluntary life in its own language, in its own inevitable aesthetic and intellectual forms. The common life of the commonwealth is politico-economic, and serves as the foundation and background for the realization of the distinctive individuality of each *natio* that composes it. Thus "American civilization" may come to mean the perfection of the cooperative harmonies of "European civilization," the waste, the squalor, and the distress of Europe being eliminated—a multiplicity in a unity, an orchestration of mankind.[97]

Americanization, the creation of *unum e pluribus*, did not mean the production of a new, American, race, "but an intelligence."[98] Americanization was the achievement of an act of consent in "a democracy of nationalities having for its aim the equal growth and the free development of all."[99] The American idea (*e pluribus unum*) was, as a pluralistic idea, "ever a design, never an achievement."[100] As such it was an ongoing process of compromise, of transforming dissent into consent to make possible political and economic action for the common welfare without infringing on the dissenter's right to differ. This was the democratic process par excellence and for Kallen it was identical with the American idea. A prerequisite for the democratic process was the diversity of the participating elements. Democracy was essentially an acknowledgment of the reality of the many.[101] The many, which constituted America, were individuals and groups defined by descent. Thus to be an American meant not to shed but to retain one's ethnic culture; only true diversity could set the democratic process in motion. Americanization did not mean assimilation, but denoted "the processes by which the diverse learn to know, to understand and to live with one another as good neighbors in liberty."[102]

Kallen's thinking is a bit schematic here and has provoked some criticism. Among the issues raised, the critique of Kallen's insistence on descent in the definition of groups and his "static notion of eternal groups"[103] is the most serious. If Werner Sollors had not called attention to possibly racist remarks in Kallen's letters to Barrett Wendell,[104] one might have argued that Kallen's "static notion of eternal groups" was a consequence of his insistence on the reality of the many. If ethnic groups are real, they

47

Horace Kallen.
Courtesy American Jewish Archives.

should not change; they should be stable. Kallen's understanding of democracy is built on the existence of the many. Considered within the nationalist thinking of his own time, which was about to give rise to fascism, Kallen's insistence on the reality of the many wins him a point. Taking his stand against the nationalist ideologies of the time, which ranked nations or races hierarchically with the Anglo-Saxons, Germans, or Japanese coming out on top, Kallen insisted on the radical equality of all groups. And while fascism began to eliminate the many in favor of the One, Kallen insisted on the eternal reality, and that includes the de facto existence, of the many. Kallen's theory was opposed to all ideologies that provided "the figure of a victorious One, reconciling, subordinating, harmonizing the centrifugal Many."[105] In the face of a victorious One it is sometimes important to insist that you *are* and to remain what you are.

Philip Gleason argued that Kallen "left the entire political dimension [of cultural pluralism] woefully underdeveloped from the theoretical standpoint" and that his "failure to take up these obvious theoretical problems seems particularly puzzling in a man who was a professional philosopher and a disciple of the great pragmatist, William James."[106] Kallen, for whom *America* signified nothing fixed but an ongoing process of achieving consent, might have responded to this criticism with the words of William James: "It is not necessary to attack the universal problems directly, and as such, in their abstract form. We work at their solution in every way — by living and by solving minor concrete questions, as they are involved in everything. The method of nature is patience and that easy-fitting faith, not tense but smiling, and with a dash of skepticism in it, which is not in despair at postponing a solution."[107]

The development of the concept of cultural pluralism reenforced Kallen's Zionism, because it implied that in order to be a functioning member of a culturally pluralist community one had to belong to one of the smaller groups constituting by consent the larger community. In short, in order to be an American one had to be ethnic. The theory of cultural pluralism made it possible for Kallen to reformulate the Declaration of Independence as "all nationalities are created equal and endowed with certain inalienable rights; among their rights are life, liberty and the pursuit of happiness."[108] The rights of the individual were taken care of (under specific circumstances) by the particular group to which the individual belonged.[109] Hence Kallen could claim that "the nationalist philosophy of Zionism is an extension of the assumptions of liberalism from the individual to the group." Further support for the advocacy of Zionism came from European history: "The nationalism which is only another name for [the rights of freedom of thought and of association] was a development of, not a reaction against, the spirit of the French Revolution. It was that spirit which all over the continent of Europe fought both the imperialism of Napoleon and the oppression of the dynasts. Democracy and nationalism made up a single engine of liberalism; they were together against the oppressor."[110]

Thus, to be a Zionist was not only to be a true American but to be a true liberal. With these arguments Kallen helped Judge Louis Dembitz Brandeis during 1913–1914 "reconcile his belief that dual loyalties were unpatriotic with his newly found emotional attachment to the Zionist cause."[111] The recruitment of Brandeis was an important step in the history of American Zionism, because his social prestige made the movement respectable in the eyes of American Jews. During his affiliation with the Zionist movement, it not only grew enormously in membership and fundraising power, but it developed also into an efficient, goal-oriented organization which succeeded in "muting organizational dispute and factionalism and [turning all its] energies toward the upbuilding of a Jewish homeland in Palestine which would be a model of economic democracy and social justice."[112] Gradually, however, the tension increased between the Americanized leadership, who liked to compare the Palestinian *halutzim* (settlers) to the Pilgrim fathers, and the Eastern European immigrants, who expected from the Zionist movement the same comforts they found in their groups of *lantslayt* (compatriots); by 1921 it had reached such a pitch that Brandeis, Kallen, and others decided to resign.

Kallen had created an idiosyncratic version of Zionism. It was derived neither from Hebraic culture (as was Wolfson's) nor from Yiddish culture, but conceived in the image of Jefferson as a vision of a free society with "liberty and justice for all."[113] Zionism for Kallen was a theoretical rather than a practical concern. Since other forms of Jewish experience were unavailable to him, Kallen thought Zionism, defined as "a 'Jewish separation' that shall be national, positive, dynamic and adequate,"[114] to be the means to put the Jews on a par with all other members (i.e. ethnic groups) constituting American society. By being most particular, one was most American. Kallen solved his dilemma of being Jewish in America by redefining both terms, *American* and *Jew*, so that the realization of the one became identical with the realization of the other.

AN ADAMANT RATIONALIST:
MORRIS RAPHAEL COHEN (1880–1947)

Zionism versus Enlightenment: Kallen versus Cohen

The advocacy of Zionism was denounced as "tribalism" by Kallen's colleague at the City College of New York, Morris Cohen. Cohen acknowledged that "Zionism has rendered the supreme service of increasing men's self-respect, and has helped men to realize that they must be ready to give of their own past experience as well as to accept." But he nonetheless considered "the leaders of Zionism in America [who are] convinced of the compatibility of Zionism and Americanism [to be] profoundly mistaken." Cohen failed to see that for Kallen the compatibility of Zionism and Americanism rested on his idiosyncratic understanding of the two terms as based on his interpretation of the terms *Jew* and *American*, and that consequently Kallen's advocacy of Zionism was not a matter of foreign affairs. It suggested, in fact, a solution to national problems that Cohen himself considered pressing, namely "the problems of the harmonious adjustment of the Jews to American life."[115]

Cohen did not recognize that for Western European Jews, particularly those of German background, living in a harmoniously adjusted way had so far necessitated self-denial and been a mere "blind aping of the Gentile ways."[116] And he had therefore overlooked the fact that Kallen's ingenious reconciliation of two heretofore mutually exclusive affiliations made possible for the first time not only "harmonious" but, more important, dignified "adjustment of the Jews to American life" because it was now based on their acceptance of themselves *as Jews*. What made America unique in the history of the Jewish diaspora was that it was possible to be a Jew *and* an American. America had gone beyond Y. L. Gordon's motto, "be a man abroad, a Jew at home," which demanded concealment of being Jewish from the eyes of the public and relegated it to the sphere of the private and religious. In America one could be a Jew openly and culturally fully "realized" without risking to be thought an alien, someone not belonging to the nation. Only late in life did Cohen begin to take advantage of this singularity of the American *galut* (diaspora). But although he would soften somewhat toward Jewish particularism during the 1930s, which "sharpened and refocused" his vision of America, Cohen rejected "until the day of his death . . . political Zionism as a form of tribalism."[117]

In 1919, when he launched his attack on Zionism in the pages of *The New Republic*, Cohen, like so many other intellectuals liberated from the social and religious confines of the shtetl, regarded America as Enlightenment incarnate and Judaism or a Jewish state as its medieval antithesis. "A national Jewish Palestine must necessarily mean a state founded on a peculiar race, a tribal religion and a mystic belief in a peculiar soil, whereas liberal America stands for separation of church and state, the free mixing of races, and the fact that men can change their habitation and language and still advance the process of civilization."

He was convinced that "no great civilization was ever achieved except by a mixed people freely borrowing from others in religion, language, law and manners." And he pointed out in the same article that such borrowing and mixing had been the case among Jews even at the time "when they produced the bulk of biblical literature, and they certainly increased their contribution to civilization when they left Palestine and mixed with other peoples, as the names Philo, Spinoza, Heine, Karl Marx, Dr. [Paul] Ehrlich, [Mark] Ant[o]kolski, Bergson and [Simon] Flexner will readily indicate."[118] At this point Cohen is farthest from Kallen, who held that a contribution to civilization was most valuable when it was most particular, most itself, and that the degree to which idiosyncrasies were respected was the indicator of a society's degree of enlightenment.

Ironically enough, Cohen based the "policy of assimilation which would make the salvation of Jews and non-Jews depend on the progress of the slow movement known as enlightenment" on the same source which supplied Kallen with arguments for the advocacy of Zionism. As Cohen wrote, "The policy of assimilation was clearly expressed by Spinoza, who pointed out that Jews like other groups are held together by the bond of common suffering; and that as the nations became enlightened and removed their restrictions against the Jews, the latter would adopt the habits of western civilization and the problem would thus be eliminated."[119]

Unfortunately, "restrictions against Jews ha[d] nowhere been completely removed," not even in America as Cohen himself experienced ("witness for example the social restrictions against Jews amongst the supposedly enlightened citizens who form our university clubs"). This, in turn, made "the intellectual Jews peculiarly susceptible to the mystic and romantic nationalism which began in Germany as a reaction against the liberalism of the French Revolution, against the old faith in the power of cosmopolitan reason and enlightenment which overthrew medievalism." For Cohen, Zionism was a romantic nationalism comparable in kind to the racist chauvinisms of Houston Stewart Chamberlain and Mikhail Nikiforovich Katkoff and as such "radically false and profoundly inimical to liberal or humanistic civilization." And he feared that a Jewish national idealism might have similar evil consequences. "Incidentally, the idealistic Zionists are quite willing to ignore the rights of the vast majority of the non-Jewish population of Palestine, quite like the Teutonic idealists with their superior kultur."[120]

To embrace an irrational movement in order to offset the effects of irrationalities resulting from an inadequately realized "rational liberalism" struck Cohen as futile, if not absurd. Instead, "the stress of events [such as "the intensification of the small nationality idea in Europe" and the resultant threat that "the rest of the world will be Balkanized"] calls out loudly the need for a refreshing faith in individual freedom and enlightenment."[121]

Cohen's faith in the Enlightenment as a means of "salvation," in its power to solve the "Jewish problem" through its "policy of assimilation," was absolute. This faith was shared by many Eastern European Jews, who experienced the transition from shtetl culture to America as intellectual liberation. The rejection of Jewish particularism (as unenlightened) was strongest in those who had been most exclusively confined to it in Europe. It was comparatively easy for Jews such as Wolfson and Kallen to accept the "irrationality" of being Jewish even in America and to integrate it into their American lives, because they had either come to America as children (Kallen at age five) or had experienced Judaism as a living, intellectually exciting culture (as had Wolfson in Lithuania). Cohen possessed neither of these advantages, nor did he have any of the luck that facilitated the careers of Wolfson and Kallen (that is, their successful integration into the academic community without excessive self-denial). Cohen's career and his intellectual development in America is a more painful or, perhaps, radical version of that of his colleagues. It was, perhaps, closer in kind to that of the "sharp Jewish kids" described in such novels as Abraham Cahan's *The Rise of David Levinsky* (1917), Samuel Ornitz's *Haunch, Paunch and Jowl* (1923), or Michael Gold's *Jews Without Money* (1930). Although Cohen was exposed to the same squalid environment as the protagonists of these early American Jewish novels, he became neither a businessman, nor a lawyer and corrupt judge, nor a revolutionary. Instead he staked his life on culture and the rationalist capacities of the mind as Trilling would do an academic generation later.

If the Jewish intellectuals of Trilling's generation (born close to 1905) still struck Cynthia Ozick (born in 1928) as "self-conscious; they knew where they were and what they were,"[122] Cohen's relationship to culture and the (largely Gentile) academic life of the mind was even more brittle and uneasy. One of the reasons for Cohen's self-consciousness—which surfaced as ferocious intensity in his social interactions—may be, as David Hollinger suggests, Cohen's awareness "that many Jewish youths of the 1890s had absorbed [the unsavory], less refined aspects of [the New York] East Side life, and a related sense that his own hold on his chosen life was weak."[123]

Although Cohen left no philosophical heirs,[124] his life and work deserve examination for two reasons: Cohen's way of coming to terms with the transition from "bondage" to "freedom," from the Jewish shtetl in Russia to the American metropolis, appears to have been a straight flight into a universalism more radical and consistent than that which either Wolfson or Kallen had advocated in developing their respective consent communities. But a closer examination of Cohen's philosophy reveals the amazing (though upon further reflection not too surprising) fact that his reasoning was governed by the same concern as that of his two colleagues, namely, by an almost anxious attempt to strike and keep the balance between extremes. But while Wolfson and Kallen, in their endeavors to find a balance between apparent polarities, created new, third units, such as the community of philosophers or the consent community America, Cohen found no such answer. His solution to the problem of being Jewish in America consisted in nothing but the precise philosophical formulation of the problem itself, in his "principle of polarity."[125]

The second reason for considering Cohen in the present context is more external: through his position as professor of philosophy at City College of New York, Cohen had tremendous influence on the nascent group of New York Intellectuals. Hollinger even calls him "a consolidating agent in the formation of the secular, ethnically diverse, left-of-center intelligentsia that was to become institutionalized, by the 1940s, in the liberal-arts departments of several major universities and in many journals of opinion." But even for the thousands of immigrant sons Cohen taught who would not become intellectuals "he was a crucial exemplar . . . of what it meant to be an 'American intellectual.'" In short, as the first Jew to teach philosophy at CCNY and, as Hollinger claims, "the first Russian-born Jew to come to prominence as a public moralist and as a professional philosopher, Cohen was a pivotal figure in the accommodation of East European Jewry to American culture."[126]

Childhood in a Shtetl

Morris (Moshe ben Avraham) Raphael Cohen was born in Minsk, in either 1880 or 1881. The decision to adopt the earlier year was made in 1893, when Cohen ("Meishele") approached his religious majority, in order "to be on the safe side in regard to wearing phylacteries at morning prayers," one of the duties of a bar mitzvah.

> So I was called to read the Torah on the next Saturday, which was the Sabbath of Comfort, that is, the Sabbath on which the Haftorah or prophetic portion begins "Comfort ye, Comfort ye my people" (Isaiah 40). This circumstance and some remarks of my father would lead to the conclusion that I was born on the ninth day of Ab, the fast day which commemorates the destruction of the Temple and the beginning of the Exile (Golus). But as the ninth day of Ab is, according to certain traditions, also the appointed day on which is to be born the

Messiah who will release the Jews from bondage and lead them back to the Holy Land, I have concluded that my birthday must be on some other date. I chose July 25 because on that, or on some other day in the summer of 1892, my mother, my sister and I reached the harbor of New York and a new chapter of my life began (*DJ* 15–16).[127]

At the time of his bar mitzvah, Morris Cohen was already estranged from his religion. In the fall of 1892 he overheard a conversation between his father and an acquaintance from Minsk who challenged Abraham Cohen "to prove that there was a personal God who could be influenced by human prayers or deeds, or that the Jewish religion had any more evidence in favor of its truth than other religions" (*DJ* 69). His father's only answer, "I am a believer," deeply dissatisfied his son, who after some reflection found himself forced to conclude "that in all my studies no such evidence was available" (*DJ* 69). So far, these studies consisted in seven years of the Hebrew Bible (Tanakh) and probably some easier parts of the Mishnah, and in two years of Gemara. Cohen "learned" Tanakh and Mishnah in various frightful *hadarim* (Jewish elementary schools) in Russia. Most students who had gone through a heder education "were functionally illiterate in Hebrew, retaining only the most rudimentary vocabulary and a fuzzy or mangled understanding of particular texts."[128] But Cohen managed to pick up a thing here and there.

The first heder he attended as a malnourished and listless child of about three or four was, like so many of its kind, "crowded, noisy, unventilated, and conducted without any apparent rule or order." Cohen's descriptions bring to life the sordid reality depicted in the photographs of Roman Vishniac. "Our *rebbeh* [teacher] was a consumptive who coughed and spat extensively and occasionally shivered: in fact, he died the next year. Though we were in school practically all day, instruction was only occasional. The rest of the time we were either in the yard or sitting or walking about and talking in the classroom without any particular plan" (*DJ* 22–23).

The occasional instruction Cohen received did nothing to engage the interest of the outwardly inactive, but inwardly wide-awake child.

We were taught nothing at first but to recognize the letters of the alphabet with their vowel points. After an interminable time of this we were taught to read (that is, to pronounce) the words of the Hebrew prayer book, words whose meaning we were not told. This I later found was not merely a basis for future education but an immediate primary objective for most pupils, for it enabled them as good

Jews to fulfill their religious duty of reading or reciting their daily prayers and the longer ones on Saturdays and holidays. (*DJ* 22)

Fortunately, Morris Cohen's father, who in 1883 had left for America, was beginning to earn more money, so that his mother formed the plan of sending her sickly son "to her parents in Neshwies [Nesvizh] to take better care of [him] and incidentally, by paying three rubles a week for it, to help to support the old people, whose income was running very low" (*DJ* 23). Morris's father, Abraham Cohen, born in 1847, was one of those innumerable Jewish immigrants who came to America in the early 1880s with prayer shawl, phylacteries, eighty-five cents in his pocket (*DJ* 13), and no employable skills. He became a peddler, failed, and ended up in the garment industry. Abraham Cohen was lucky to find steady work in Rochester, New York, as a presser of boys' jackets. "Out of about five dollars per week that he . . . earned, he was able not only to save a little money to send home but also to lay aside a sum to enable him to return to Russia to rejoin his wife and children, after a painful absence of more than three years" (*DJ* 14).

When Abraham Cohen returned to Russia in the spring of 1887 he intended to stay. But the social and economic situation for Jews was so hopeless that he took his two oldest sons, who had been apprenticed to a shoemaker and a tailor, and left again for America a few weeks later (*DJ* 23). His wife and daughter remained in Minsk, while his youngest son was sent to his maternal grandparents in the countryside a few days before Passover in 1887.

The three years Morris Cohen spent in Nesvizh, in its hadarim and with his grandfather, were to have a "determining influence" (*DJ* 9) on his life. In 1887, Nesvizh, a town in Baranovichi oblast dominated by the Radziwill family, had slightly more than 10,000 inhabitants, about 54 percent of whom were Jews. The town was known for its talmudic scholars. Among those who had officiated there was Rabbi Yitzhak Elhanan, later the Kovno Gaon. But it had also been the hometown of Salomon Maimon, whom Cohen called "the greatest Jewish philosopher since Spinoza" (*DJ* 25) and who was buried after his death in 1800 outside a Jewish cemetery as a heretic. Nesvizh was also the home of Shomer (an alias for Nahum Meyer Shaikevich, 1849–1905), whom Cohen called "the Dumas of modern Yiddish literature" (*DJ* 25). Shomer was one of the first writers of Yiddish potboilers. His more than one hundred novels and plays, in which good always triumphed over evil, were avidly devoured by a steadily increasing Jewish reading public seeking refuge from their squalid lives in

Shomer's fantastic world of magic events. Despite Sholem Aleichem's ridicule,[129] Shomer insisted "that his books performed the valuable function of bringing ethical education to the Jewish masses whose general education had been neglected."[130]

Nesvizh itself was well equipped with educational institutions. The community had a yeshivah, a Hebrew school and kindergarten, and a Yiddish school, neither of which Morris Cohen attended. Instead he was put into the ḥeder of a melamed who "was exceedingly poor, had four children and was very much harassed." The immense pressures on the melamed worked slightly to the advantage of his pupils. "In his irritation, he omitted the usual ritual of deliberate punishment, the letting down of trousers and the application of the strap. Instead he lashed out his blows at the least provocation, and sometimes as in my case even without provocation, since I generally knew my lessons and had little energy for mischief" (DJ 30).

After two years in which Cohen learned to translate from the Tanakh into the vernacular Yiddish (DJ 30), he was transferred to another melamed, Reb Neḥemiah, a *maskil* (follower of the Haskalah), "that is, one who believed in bringing some of the beauty of Western learning into Hebrew studies." The new melamed seemed a little more enlightened.

> Indeed, he gave private lessons in grammar to advanced pupils who came to his house late in the afternoon or evening. . . . But we, the regular pupils, were taught nothing but the traditional curriculum, the Pentateuch with the Commentary of Rashi and a few other books of the Bible. Only in an occasional comment would our *rebbeh*'s learning open up for me glimpses of the great outside world of geography and history. I remember particularly his explanation of the origin and evolution of boats and of the Franco-Prussian War of 1870. One remark of his which later grew on me was his observation on the rich clothes and fine living of those who collected the charity money in the tin boxes dedicated to Reb Meier of the Miracle and found in every pious home (DJ 31).

The greatest influence on the child, however, was his grandfather. Hirsh Farfel "was turned loose from the parental home when he was about twelve years old" (DJ 10). This was not at all uncommon. He worked as an itinerant tailor and presser for many years until he had acquired enough money "to set himself up in his parental home as a tailor and even employ his father and another man as his helpers" (DJ 10). Although Hirsh Farfel knew a trade for which there was a certain demand, he was fantastically poor. Thus, his daughter, Morris Cohen's mother, was hired out as a field worker at age eleven. Nevertheless, she grew up to be a beautiful, spirited woman. As if having a daughter was not *shlimasel* (misfortune) enough (see Sholem Aleichem's stories about Tevye the dairyman), there had to be a cavalry regiment stationed near Hirsh Farfel's house. Not unreasonably, Hirsh Farfel "was afraid that some officer or soldier would seduce his daughter, and he sometimes spoke as if he intended to cripple her to prevent such a calamity" (*DJ* 11). Hirsh Farfel's educational methods had not changed since he had brought up his sons and daughter. He was a pious man, who believed literally in every word of the Bible, and was therefore convinced "that he who spares the rod spoils the child" (*DJ* 11). He beat Morris as he had beaten his own daughter, sometimes unjustly, which both experienced as humiliations driving them to the brink of suicide and which Morris, a sweet, docile child, resented bitterly (*DJ* 11, 36). Although a certain degree of erudition was a prerequisite for piety, Hirsh Farfel had never learned how to write. His daughter, however, whose earnings as a seamstress he kept, saved the occasional kopecks she received from him in order to pay a woman to teach her to write. "Reading prayers and sacred books was for men a religious virtue, but writing was a luxury—especially for women—and so in that effort my mother was ultimately defeated. But she made up her mind that when she had children she would do her utmost to see that they had the opportunity to learn to write as well as to read (*DJ* 11).

When Cohen lived with his grandfather, his mother remembered her frustrated efforts and insisted in a letter she paid someone to write that her son be taught how to write Yiddish. "To this my grandfather replied 'My dear daughter, I am giving your son Torah—the substance of life. The trimmings can come later.'" But this time his daughter prevailed and, eventually, "an old man was engaged to teach me and a neighboring boy how to write" (*DJ* 31). Although he could not write, Hirsh Farfel was knowledgeable in many other respects. He was one of the few Jews in town who spoke Russian fluently, and he could instruct his grandson in topics as diverse as the philosophies of Aristotle and Maimonides and Napoleon's Russian campaign (*DJ* 33). Although Cohen spent six days a week in heder, he later considered his grandfather his main educator in Nesvizh. After three years in a shtetl which Cohen later pronounced "unbelievably poor, dirty, criminally ignorant as to hygiene and altogether lifeless" (*DJ* 25), the boy wanted to return to Minsk. "When I left Neshwies my mind was full of anticipation of what I would do in Minsk. But it was not long before I realized my great fortune in having been sent to my grandfather in those crucial years of my life. Without that opportunity I could not have acquired the moral and intellectual interests which have been controlling in the course of my subsequent life" (*DJ* 39; cf. *DJ* 57).

Cohen's return to Minsk, which he had left as "a little animal" and reentered as "an Orthodox pietist" (*DJ* 41), was marked by an act that awaited most shtetl emigrants in America: when his mother saw that Morris's appearance was ridiculed by his friends, she cut off his *peyes* (side locks) despite the boy's mild protests and "obtained clothes for him like those worn in Minsk" (*DJ* 41). But (as was not true for Jewish boys in America), the effect of these actions was not immediately assimilative, "a chasm . . . continued to exist between me and the less piously indoctrinated boys of the neighborhood" (*DJ* 41). Again, Morris was placed in different hadarim. In one of them he was finally granted

> what I had desired in vain for several years—an opportunity to study Gemara. . . . We had an old Talmudic scholar teach several of us the Tractate Baba Kama, while others were taught Russian by a young man. After the Passover my mother hired a young Talmudic scholar who was living in a nearby synagogue and waiting for a call to serve as a *rov* [rabbi] to help me continue my Talmudic studies. I enjoyed that immensely but probably more from pride at attaining the heights of pious study rather than because of any inherent interest in the minutiae of the Law of Divorce (*DJ* 44).

Intellectually more important was Cohen's simultaneous discovery of the world of Yiddish—i.e., secular—literature, which was thrown open to him by Shomer's romance, *The Cohen*. Although Cohen's literary taste improved rapidly, he nevertheless resented Sholem Aleichem's harsh criticism of his fellow writer, because Shomer satisfied a deep emotional need. Much later Cohen would concede that Sholem Aleichem's "criticism may have been just, from a purely literary point of view, but it missed the fact that despite the cheapness of Shomer's novels he had a powerful educational and liberating influence on the Jewish people" (*DJ* 48). What Cohen in consonance with his own development called Shomer's "educational and liberating influence" was the result of the author's espousal of the Haskalah: Shomer "ridiculed the absurdities of the old superstitious fanaticism, and his young heroes and heroines who had taken up modern thought and education, were always superior personalities" (*DJ* 49); this was an attitude that Cohen soon came to share.

Living conditions in Minsk deteriorated again in the early 1890s and it was decided in 1892 that the rest of the Cohen family—Morris, his sister, and his mother—should emigrate to America. "Instead of going to America on a government passport my mother made arrangements with an agent who sold her a combination ticket from Minsk to New York, and this included an arrangement for the illegal crossing of the boundary into Germany. So many people were going to America that way that the enterprise was quite standardized" (*DJ* 59).

Cohen's father had used this route on his visit to Russia in 1890, and it was still in effect in 1906 when Cynthia Ozick's mother, Shiphra Regelson, then roughly Meishele Cohen's age, made the same trip with her mother. The wives with their youngest children were frequently the last to pack up and leave.[131] This very often meant strenuous dealings with the Russian authorities, as in the cases of Shiphra's and Meishele's mothers, and an initiation into the art of bribery. It also involved the closing of business affairs, dangerous because illegal travel to Germany—later recounted by innumerable *bobes* (grandmothers) as *di mayse fun dem grenets* (the story of the frontier)—and an exhausting steerage passage to America in overcrowded hulls with a number of small children, insufficient water and *treyf* (nonkosher) food.[132]

It has often been noticed that mothers loom large in early American Jewish fiction. Quite possibly the experience of their passage into the New World set free energies that afterward could no longer be reigned in. For those women who did not go to work upon their arrival in America (usually women with young children) running a household and a family was an insufficient outlet for the creative energies they had discovered in themselves; this was particularly true as housework had become much easier with the help of running water and gas stoves. "No more need for chopping wood, for making a fire in the oven or sweeping out the ashes" (*DJ* 67). The majority of immigrant women, however, contributed in some way to the family earnings. Daughters who worked outside the home during the pre-1945 period took positions as secretaries, bookkeepers, and stenographers—jobs they held until their marriages. "To be a private secretary was maybe the highest aspiration, a sign of status. And once they married, if they could then leave the work force because their husbands were doing well, then that, too, was a sign of status."[133] In any case, fewer Jewish women, particularly young women, accepted being told by their husbands how to run their business: "At first my father raised religious objections against lighting matches and using gas on Saturday. And though my mother's clever answers did not satisfy him, she prevailed. . . . In all other respects the old ritual observances remained in force" (*DJ* 67).

For Morris Cohen, the prayers and rituals became an empty shell the moment he overheard his father's unsatisfactory reply to another immigrant's challenge to prove the existence of a personal God and the exclusive truth of Judaism. Rather than being the immediate cause of Cohen's apostasy, though, this moment was the last in a series of experiences in America that alienated the boy from Orthodoxy. Among the first shocks had been his parents' unconcern about his neglecting Talmud studies. It was quite unlike the situation and the expectations in the Wolfson household. "There was no incentive and little opportunity for me to continue my Hebraic and Talmudic studies. There were no suitable books in our house and no one urged me to continue such study. It was taken for granted that in a few years I would join my father in some phase of tailoring, for I had no desire to become a rabbi. I did, indeed, once go to the synagogue on Norfolk Street where I found some tractates of the Talmud, but I lacked the ardor to engage in such study by myself long enough to surmount the difficult places (*DJ* 69).

Cohen's father insisted that as long as the son lived in his house he must say his prayers regularly, whether he believed them or not (*DJ* 69). His father's command reinforced in Morris Cohen the conviction that Orthodoxy was a rigid, mindless form of behavior, subjecting its adherents to an isolating, petrified physical and intellectual discipline governed by the demands of an antique and medieval superstition. Morris saw himself forced to obey until the fall of 1899, when he completely replaced his otherwise ineffectual father with a representative of culture, Thomas Davidson.

Adolescence in New York: Mood Swings

The seven years of Cohen's adolescence, between his arrival in New York in 1892 and his alliance with Davidson in 1899, were searching and troubled. He started public school in September 1892, and as soon as he had mastered English he began skipping grades, selling newspapers to support the family, and frequenting the Aguilar Free Library located on the third floor of the Educational Alliance (the former Hebrew Institute) (*DJ* 73). By the spring of 1895 he found himself eligible to take the entrance examination to City College. Contrary to his expectations, he passed with flying colors and won the gold medal for the best performance. "The medal made little subsequent difference, except that occasionally we were able to borrow a few dollars on it" (*DJ* 85). But his going to college, on which his mother insisted against all social and economic odds, "proved the best investment my parents ever made" (*DJ* 85).[134] For Morris Cohen, entering college ushered in a "great intellectual as well as physical awakening" (*DJ* 85). In September 1895, he enrolled in CCNY's five-year program, which he completed in 1900, the year Kallen entered Harvard College, while Wolfson was still studying at Slobodka Yeshivah.

> City College then, as in later years, offered a frugal though nourishing intellectual diet. Since the College was free, attendance brought no social prestige. Since admission was not limited by race, class, creed, or social status, it had to be limited by rigorous scholastic standards. Social life, sports, social polish, and the other superficial attractions of American college life were neglected. The consequence was that those to whom these extracurricular goals mattered found their way to other more congenial colleges and universities. . . . There was no need to preach to us the importance and value of scholarship, or to instill in our hearts a love of learning. That was why we were there. There was nothing else that we could hope to get out of the College. . . . Because the College made no effort to impose a single pattern of social behavior upon its graduates, its militarism was not tainted by totalitarianism. . . . The College thus, despite the mediocrity of its teaching staff in those days, embodied what has always seemed to me the essence of liberal education as opposed to dogmatic indoctrination. . . . The College was willing to ignore or forgive my defects in the social graces, as well as the unorthodoxy of many of my views. That the College tolerated me became, to me, a symbol of liberalism in education. It gave me a sound education in mathematics, languages, and the natural sciences and thus opened the gates to a wider intellectual world than I had dreamed of. (*DJ* 89–90)

This description, taken from Cohen's autobiography, which was written in the late 1930s and early 1940s after a lifetime at CCNY, speaks about the university with a peculiar mixture of gratitude and contempt. The first is grudgingly bestowed in recognition of CCNY's largesse. The second reflects Cohen's suppressed view of the superiority of Columbia University. The tone of controlled resentment and dutifully voiced appreciation in Cohen's description is, perhaps, the result of his impression that undergraduate studies at Columbia as well as later employment there had been denied him for nonacademic reasons, the first on account of his poverty, the second on account of his Jewishness.[135] Being forced to remain at CCNY, Cohen employed Hirsh Farfel's strategy and tried "to make a virtue of necessity and to find various reasons to glorify coarse bread." What Cohen said about his grandfather as educator was true for himself: "Continued calls on the endurance of hardships did not make him soft" (*DJ* 10–11).

For two years during his time in college, from January 1897 to January 1899, Cohen kept a diary. It reflects better than any other document the intense intellectual and emotional anxieties of a thoroughly deracinated youth whose maturation as an individual coincides with his attempt to break into a new culture. One of Cohen's assertions seems almost too much like an academic construction to be true. He claims that the two authors most important to him as an adolescent were the Benjamin Franklin of the *Autobiography* and the British self-help publicist Samuel Smiles. He turned to them to get a grip on himself and on the surrounding culture. Diary entries modeled on Franklin and Smiles not only outnumber but outweigh those inspired by other means of cultural reaffirmation to which Cohen fleetingly resorted, such as his readings of Gibbons and Graetz, his literary activities, his flirtations with socialism (as propagated by the Yiddish *Arbeiter Zeitung*), or his repeated resolutions "to renew [his] knowledge of Hebrew and especially of the Bible," or "to practice Jewish [i.e. Yiddish] writing and learn all things which may become useful so that [he might] have recourse to them whenever necessary in the future."[136]

What is most striking about the young Cohen's diary is that it appears to be a disordered but nonetheless exact formulation of the problems to which the older Cohen's philosophy provides a solution. Adolescent diary and mature philosophy appear as question and answer. Apart from statements of intellectual and emotional self-help in the manner of Franklin and Smiles, the diary is dominated by four moods: (1) a feeling of guilt for being a burden to his parents because as a student his time for earning money is limited; (2) a rebelliousness "merely for rebellion's sake" (P 16) against traditions, laws, and customs; (3) a feeling of being at sea "like a ship without a rudder tossed about on an angry ocean—no —sometimes on a calm ocean, but no land in sight" (P 21); and (4) a feeling of being split internally into opposing selves, with one self, for instance, being given to emotion, the other to reason" (P 21, 23).

These moods are in themselves contradictory: his guilt feelings vis-à-vis his parents arise from a sense of not complying with a filial duty, while his rebelliousness reacts exactly against such traditions; furthermore, while he flaunts his iconoclasm, he is worried about being outside an established culture and thus without guidelines of any sort. Cohen's cultural insecurity (surfacing as simultaneous reverence for and rebellion against tradition) is paralleled by his personal insecurity (expressed in contradictory statements about the 'true nature' of his Self). These insecurities would have been easy to resolve had Cohen simply decided in

63

favor of one of the terms, that is, latched onto one specific culture. But he chose not to do so. He wanted to be a thinker—not a Jewish thinker, nor an American thinker.[137] In Cohen's mind "the inadequacy of a thinker often turned out to be a function of parochialism. The most successful thinking thus became equated with cosmopolitanism, and the price of its achievement was heroic self-restraint: the supreme moral act of mind was to suspend judgment until everything had been considered."[138]

Consequently, Cohen had no simple solutions to offer, such as the espousal of Judaism, Americanism, Marxism, Zionism, or the like. Instead, he described the nature of the world in the abstract by formulating the principle of polarity. "As Hollinger explains, this term emerged in his formal metaphysical writings in the early twenties; it denoted Cohen's belief that the world ultimately consists of a series of polarities, of 'opposites' that require each other in order to be understood."[139] The heroic act and the task of the true philosopher was "to find and defend the virtuous middle way." His means of doing so were "the scientific method," logic, and reason. Comparing Cohen's adolescent diaries with his mature philosophy, it is difficult to dismiss entirely the idea that Cohen turned his own psychic disposition, kindly described by Hollinger as "the dynamic tension between total abandon and total restraint," into a description of the world. He made of his deracination (his being 'at sea,' lost between polarities, or between islands of parochial experience) the virtue of equipoise, the "middle way," or cosmopolitanism. Cohen had never "belonged" anywhere for a sustained period of time during his childhood and youth. Using a familiar strategy, he appears to have made a virtue of such detachment. As an adult he intensely "distrusted the concrete, the sensual, and the active"[140] because they required the immediacy of experience which was not only potentially chaotic and disturbing but also particular and thus limited and definite. The means for gaining equipoise and keeping the balance between polar extremes were logic and reason. In the diary, "the pressures . . . toward one polar extreme or the other" are not yet philosophically articulated as statements about the world. As is natural for an adolescent, they take the form of utterances about the self, such as "the struggle within me is that of *feeling* against the rooted sentiment of *Pure Reason*" (P 21). It seems not altogether impossible that Cohen's "at sea" image was inspired by one of the very few metaphors in Kant's *Critique of Pure Reason*: that of a seafarer lost on the ocean between illusions of stability (appearances).[141]

Of course, Cohen did not leap directly from his diaries to his later philosophy, but instead moved slowly, solving the problems pointed out above one by one. Apart from the pressing need to become financially independent, his strongest desire was to give his life a direction and thus to steady his mind. The following is one of many similar diary entries.

THURSDAY, AUGUST 19 [1897]

. . . In the evening I walked with S. K. [not identified]. We were telling each other of our respective troubles. I told him that the greatest trouble is to be a burden to someone who makes you conscious of it. I also told him how, being in childhood without the direct influence of a father and mother, and being often knocked around, my character became unlovable and somewhat hardened. At home I thought over to myself the influences that my early life has on my character. The first thing that strikes me is the bad neighborhood of our house. Then my being at first without any monitor, then under grandparents, then under loose control of parents then under no control at all. This I think made my mind unsteady (P 16).

Thus Cohen was ready to be picked like a ripe plum when the charismatic Thomas Davidson arranged a class about the educational problems of the twentieth century at the Educational Alliance in January 1899. Cohen, who at the time was participating in a Marxist reading circle at the Alliance, came to listen to Davidson because he had heard "that this class was an unusually large and enthusiastic one, and that Davidson was constantly attacking socialism" (DJ 104). Two things broke Cohen's rebelliousness and almost compulsive opposition: Davidson's frequent and easy references to "my friend William James," who for Cohen was "one of the Olympians, and it appeared almost unbelievable that an actual mortal should be on terms of familiarity with him" (DJ 104); and a warm gesture of Davidson's.

After one of the meetings, Davidson came over to me and said, putting his hand in a friendly way on my shoulder, "You have a fine mind. You ought to cultivate it." I was startled. It was years since anyone had paid me such a compliment. I asked, "What makes you think so?" And he said, "I am an old schoolmaster and I have never met anyone whose eyes are as far apart as yours who did not have a good mind." The remark pleased me more than I realized at that time. I told him that I was going to college and was trying my best to learn what the world was all about. Thereupon he invited me to visit him at his rooms on Stuyvesant Square (DJ 104).

Initially, Cohen was too shy to accept the invitation, but after a chance meeting in the street a friendship and correspondence developed which "caused a transformation in [his] life plans" (*DJ* 105). Davidson responded to the deep emotional needs of a youth who had confided to his diary on June 6, 1897: "I never have anyone point out to me my good points, my abilities" (*P* 13). Cohen was "almost intoxicated with joy at the warmth of [Davidson's] replies" (*DJ* 105). Cohen's diary ceases at the time he accepts Davidson "as a father" (*DJ* 121). This acceptance was all the easier since Davidson reinforced Cohen's intellectual trend away from the particular toward the universal. Davidson was the incarnation of the ideals of the Educational Alliance, with which Cohen had been associated since he had mastered English. The Educational Alliance emerged in 1893 from the reorganization of the Hebrew Institute and became "a wonderfully effective agency in the Americanization of the Russian Jews of the lower East Side."[142]

The directors of the Educational Alliance could have found no one more dedicated to saving working class Jewish immigrants from pessimism, parochialism, and political radicalism than the Scotsman Davidson. He believed that the best defense against "violence and barbarism" was culture, which he saw "as a preparation for all personal, domestic, social, and political relations; only a truly broad education could enable the breadwinners to enter into lofty personal relations, and to live clean, tasteful, useful, self-respecting lives."[143] Cohen surrendered unconditionally to Davidson's concept of culture and proved his subsequent devotion by spending more and more time teaching immigrants at the Breadwinners' College, an adult education program, after Davidson's death in 1899. Simultaneously Cohen taught as instructor in the Department of Mathematics at CCNY (after November 1902) and attended graduate classes at Columbia University, where F. J. E. Woodbridge and Felix Adler were among his teachers. The latter would soon succeed Davidson as Cohen's cultural father. In fact, the Hebraic tradition of Adler's Ethical Culture, which had a strong philosophical as well as social bent, suited Cohen even better than Davidson's Greco-Roman physico-intellectual notion of culture, which supplied the immigrants with the *Divine Comedy* in the original while reminding them that "high or stooping shoulders, a sidelong or rolling gait, a slow, ungainly movement of hands and feet" were not only unbecoming but that "they also go far to unfit their victims for skilled labor and efficient work."[144] But more importantly, Adler's Ethical Culture provided Cohen's move away from his father's rigorous ritualistic Judaism with a philosophical foundation; it rooted his individual action in thought and placed it within a larger cultural movement.

An Unlikely Father: Felix Adler (1851–1933)

Felix Adler came from Germany to America at age six when his father, Rabbi Samuel Adler, was called to succeed Leo Merzbacher as rabbi of one of America's first Reform congregations, Temple Emanuel in New York.[145] He attended Columbia Grammar School while being trained by his father in Jewish studies. He proceeded to Columbia College in 1866. After his graduation in 1870 he went to Europe to pursue his studies in Berlin, then the intellectual center of the Reform movement. The three years Adler spent at German universities transformed his thinking. When he returned to New York in 1873, with a Ph.D. summa cum laude from Heidelberg University, it was no longer possible for him "to deal with human affairs by mastering simply one historic tradition."[146] Adler did not want to succeed his father (who retired in 1874) as rabbi. This would have been difficult to engineer anyway because the son's lectures upset the community. But a temple trustee and friend of Samuel Adler's, the banker Joseph Seligman, liked the son's ideas and wrote a letter to the president of Cornell University on behalf of the young man: "Would Cornell wish to offer instruction in Hebrew and oriental literature in the context of world literature?"[147] At that time most other universities might have taken this offer for yet another example of Jewish "pushiness." But Cornell, founded in 1865 in pastoral isolation, was quite relaxed. In addition, it had a charter proscribing religious discrimination in the appointment of faculty. Cornell's president, the enlightened Andrew White, replied: ". . . Ours is one of the very first institutions ever established in this country on the basis of complete equality between men of every shade of religious ideas and of complete liberty in the formation and expression of thought. Dr. Adler, if I mistake not, is a man calculated by his lectures as well as by his influence in other ways to promote those studies calculated to break down all unfortunate barriers of creed which have so long afflicted mankind. And this it was that led me at the outset to take a real interest in the case."[148]

In the spring of 1874, Felix Adler began to teach at Cornell as Professor of Hebrew and Oriental Literature. His post was funded by Joseph Seligman and a few other contributors. In his inaugural address, Felix Adler described America as the realm of freedom in which opposites might be reconciled. The *Ithaca Journal* reports: "America, Adler concluded, has given a birthright of freedom prepared of the ripest fruit of the past. Here where 'individuals from all quarters of the earth are received into the community of the people, the true essential idea of this people rises above the national, is the idea of humanity itself . . . wherein may be consummated the union of the Aryan objective and the Semitic subjective . . . the union of the Real and Ideal of which the true manhood and womanhood will be born.'"[149] Such thinking proved unacceptable. When the endowment was considered for renewal, in early 1876, Seligman was told by Cornell's vice president: "The Executive Committee of the Cornell Trustees object to having professors nominated to them from the outside. . . . They, therefore, will not again accept any propositions for endowment where the choice of the incumbent is not left without restriction to the Trustees."[150]

This sounds like sensible university politics. Yet one of Adler's biographers, Benny Kraut, believes he has reason to suspect that the decision, ostentatiously made to preserve the integrity of the university, was actually made with respect to Adler. Kraut concludes that Adler simply was not wanted at Cornell.[151] The appointment of a Jew would have incensed part of the local Christian populace. But Adler had also disappointed those who had hired him as the son of a distinguished and widely respected rabbi and thus as a representative of American Jewry and Judaism. It turned out that Adler was not the Jew they had expected. As if Gentile anger were not enough, Adler had also upset the Jewish community; but here the real storm was still to come. A former student of Adler's at Cornell wrote: "Dr. Adler did not represent the Orthodox Jewish faith and was manly enough not to conceal it." He goes on to quote from an editorial in the *Cornell Review* of June 1874:

> We have no objection whatever to the establishment of a course of lectures in the university, however rankly it may savor of rationalism, provided it is so declared and understood in advance.
> In the case of the lectures now under discussion, it is an undeniable fact that this so called course of lectures upon Hebrew and Oriental Literature has been painfully calculated to develop in young minds, at least, strongly rationalistic views.[152]

It was precisely Adler's rationalism, which was heavily influenced by German neo-Kantianism, particularly as found in the works of Hermann Cohen, which fascinated Morris Cohen. Adler's appointment as Professor of Political and Social Ethics at Columbia in 1902 marked his reentry into the academy which he had left so abruptly in 1876. During the intervening period, a quarter of a century, Adler had devoted himself to the Society for Ethical Culture, which he had founded in 1876. Its orientation was radically anti-ritualist and anti-dogmatic. Adler's view of religion was that neither creed, nor sacrifice, nor prayer was fundamental to it. Religion, he claimed, "has its roots in the feeling of the sublime." The outer garb of religion was a consequence of "whether the feeling of the sublime is evoked predominantly by the mysterious, as in fetishism; by exhibitions of superhuman power, as in paganism; by vastness, as in Hinduism; or by the morally infinite, as in Judaism and Christianity."[153] Lectures comparing religions, cults, and rites made up a large part of the program of events at the Society for Ethical Culture. Its members subscribed to the essence of an ethical type of religion (as opposed to one believing in "the gods of force") without dogma, rite, or theology. "It were sad indeed," Adler said, "if morality depended upon the certainty of dogma. On the contrary it is true that all that is best and grandest in dogma is due to the inspiration of the moral law in man. . . . Dogma we will keep in abeyance—this is our point of departure, and the deed superior to the creed."[154]

Deed was the unifying element in the group's ethnic and religious diversity. One of the slogans was "Diversity in the creed, unanimity in the deed!"[155] What appealed to Morris Cohen in Adler and his Ethical Culture was the combination of two extremes to which he himself was prone: on the one side, Adler's abstractness, his rationalism, and indebtedness to Kant, and on the other side, Adler's emphasis on deed which manifested itself especially in his sincere interest in the "social mission of education." The combination of hard intellectual and hard social work, mainly educational, suited Cohen although it did not quite relieve the pressures mentioned in his diaries—foremost, that of justifying his academic pursuits in the face of other people's daily laboring. The conflict Cohen experienced is reminiscent of the discussion in the Talmud. Over a long period of time the Rabbis pondered the question of which takes precedence, study or work. Each alternative finds support:

> "And he that does not study is deserving of death." Or: "Greater is the study of Torah than the saving of lives." Or: "Study of the Torah transcends honoring father and mother."

> But it is also said: "Whoever occupies himself with Torah only is like one who has no God." Shemayah teaches: "Love work and hate lordship." And Rava used to say: "The goal of wisdom is penitence and good deeds; a man should not study Bible and Mishnah and rebel against his father and his mother and his teacher, or one who is superior to him in wisdom, as it is said 'The reverence of the Lord is the beginning of wisdom, a good understanding have all they that do

thereafter' (Psalms 91:10)—Scripture does not say 'to all those who study them [*lomdehem*]' but 'to all those who do thereafter [*ossehem*]'."[156]

At the bottom of Cohen's adolescent conflict and the extensive discussion of the rabbis is the question of the status, privileges, and obligations of the scholar—that is, his relation to society and its daily life. The Talmud does not suggest a simple solution, but instead relates the discussion itself. Diaspora history worked out an intricate system to sponsor penniless scholars: it ranged from "eating days" (on each day of the week a Talmud student would eat meals with a different family) to the obligation of a father to support his son-in-law and his family for a year after the marriage. This system, which had still functioned in Cohen's family in Russia and functioned for Wolfson in Lithuania and America, naturally disintegrated in a secular context. Its disintegration deprived Cohen not only of parental funding but also of the justification for prolonged studies, which had been the rationale for the support system in the first place.

Adler's solution to this dilemma, "the social mission of education," was not very original (the rabbis had, in fact, excluded it);[157] but it justified retrospectively Cohen's own decision (that is, his voluntary teaching at the Breadwinners' College). Adler approved of Cohen's development and gave his rationalist intellectual preferences a more definite direction; this was all Cohen expected of a father. In addition, Adler took Cohen on as an aide when he was denied a fellowship at Columbia University, and a short while later made available to him a fellowship from the Ethical Culture Society so that Cohen could finish his studies at Harvard University. Finally, he would take his place among the best.

Cohen at Harvard University

The two years Cohen spent at Harvard (1904–1906), rooming on Cambridge Street with Felix Frankfurter, hardly influenced his intellectual development. Unlike Kallen or even Wolfson, Cohen was not open to the Harvard experience. He was physically exhausted, which left him often ill and depressed, and intellectually preoccupied with the teachings of Davidson and Adler. Cohen showed his loyalty to his cultural fathers by lecturing before classes of Boston's breadwinners (adults pursuing a cultural education) and by leading the activities of the Cambridge Society for Ethical Culture.[158] Although he studied with most of the professors on Harvard's philosophical faculty, he eventually found himself caught between William James and Josiah Royce. The former he considered "the best friend I found on the Harvard faculty," the latter "the greatest teacher I had at Harvard" (*DJ* 132). In his adolescence Cohen's "intellectual world [had been] divided . . . into two camps, individualism or atomism on the one hand and absolutism on the other. I could not be at peace in either. I therefore fell into a slough of philosophic despond from which desultory reading and agonized efforts at original thought could not extricate me" (*DJ* 168).

Then, Davidson had come to the rescue. At Harvard, Cohen again found himself between two camps. Santayana, who would have been "sufficiently independent and formidable to have broken the polarity," was on leave for the whole two years Cohen spent in Cambridge.[159]

But Cohen did not waver for long. By now he was well enough equipped philosophically to make a decision and to feel at peace with it. He singled out James to become his "lifelong exemplar of passionate wrongheaded irrationalism" and "the representative of the ideas [Cohen] most wanted to destroy."[160] Cohen's opportunity to fly his philosophical flag came with his debut address before the American Philosophical Association in New Haven in 1909. In the ongoing generational conflict within the association, Cohen sided with the elders and the "old ideals of culture as the aim of college training" and criticized the philosophical revolt of the younger generation.[161] William James was the only philosopher over age fifty whom Cohen criticized. Cohen summarized his stance without mentioning names:

> To-day if anything is characterized as *experiential, functional,* or *dynamic,* that is enough to allow it to pass all the watch-dogs of philosophic criticism, and to characterize anything as *static* is to consign it to the lowermost depths from which no power can rescue it. I am not anxious to bring down the wrath of the gods by questioning the all-sufficient potency of such terms as *experience, evolution,* etc.; but may I ask what progress would mathematical physics have made if every time one approached a problem of stresses, he were frightened off by the warning that he must not for a moment entertain that most heinous criminal, the static point of view? I humbly agree with those who claim that the static point of view is mechanical and lifeless and, therefore, inapplicable to the entire universe, but I am quite sure that the dynamic point of view itself may be mechanical and lifeless.[162]

In the light of Cohen's biography it is hardly surprising that Cohen sided with those who upheld the "old ideals of culture" which he was striving to make his own, or that he rushed to the defense "of such classical sources of stability as disinterested reason, suspended judgment, logical order, and autonomy of the 'ought' from the world of actual experience." Cohen's view of the problem of the age as the need "to hold onto what was valuable about the inherited philosophical traditions of the West while moving toward new insights"[163] reflected very much his own personal needs: with his own world in permanent flux and himself at sea on "a wide and stormy ocean, the native home of illusion, where many a fog bank and many a swiftly melting iceberg give the deceptive appearance of farther shores," he was in search of stability, for the "land of truth," and "das Land des reinen Verstandes" (pure reason), where he could cast anchor. Unlike Kallen, who had counterpoised James's philosophy with Barrett Wendell's teachings about the Hebrew origins of the Puritan (and thus American) ideology, Cohen was not at all sure about his place in American society and thus could ill afford to make "flux" his philosophy. Instead, "his philosophy took form as a defense of certain wise, tried-and-true axioms." Cohen's contemporaries despised them as truisms. But as David Hollinger points out, "the leitmotiv of Cohen's career was the fear that these cosmic anchors were about to be washed away by a turbulence quietly building up within the intellectual and emotional preferences of the twentieth century."[164]

His anchor at Harvard was Josiah Royce, who reinforced Cohen's loyalty to culture and directed his dissertation on Kant. In a two-part series for *The New Republic*, entitled "On American Philosophy," in which he dealt almost exclusively with Royce and James, Cohen described what intrigued him most about Royce apart from his "mathematico-logical work." Cohen explained, "Royce's profound and loyal devotion to the ethical interests of humanity did not prevent him from regarding a question like that of human immortality as one to be settled by reason 'in precisely the same sense in which the properties of prime numbers and the kinetic theory of gases are matters for exact investigation.' In this way he continued to represent, against the growing tide of anti-intellectualism, the old faith in the dignity and potency of reason which is the corner stone of humanistic liberalism."[165]

James, Cohen claimed, was neither typically American in his philosophy, nor actually a philosopher (because he was deficient, as was Emerson, in his "mastery in logic"); Cohen portrayed James as Royce's exact opposite, as having "deep sympathy with common experience rather than with problems of the reflective mind." This may seem a little out of place in professional philosophy. "But the modern sophisticated intellect," Cohen continues, "is certainly tickled by the sight of a most learned savant espousing the cause of popular as opposed to learned theology, and by the open confession of belief in piecemeal supernaturalism on the basis of spiritistic phenomena."

Cohen concluded his portrait with an acerbic remark that can hardly be called ambiguous: "Unlike any other philospher, William James was entirely devoid of pride of the intellect. He was willing as Jesus of Nazareth to associate with the intellectual publicans and sinners, with the denizens of the intellectual underworld."[166]

Cohen's almost compulsive vision of the world—philosophy, politics, and so forth—as split into polar extremes was counterpoised by his persistent efforts to achieve a reconciliation between such extremes, for instance, by defining them as interdependent. In that way, Cohen might well be described as a centrist who finds himself between extremes and attempts to hold them together by a grand effort of the reasoning mind assisted by his highly developed dialectical skills. To prevent the disintegration of the world of culture was Cohen's primary concern. On the personal plane, affection for the cloister and his "intense self-absorption which stands in the way of disintegration,"[167] are related phenomena.

Cohen's insistence on the preservation of the old and known hampered his creativity. It obstructed the synthesis of his views into a vision. His mind was sharply analytical, but creative only in a talmudic way: in the reconciliation of (apparent) opposites. Cohen was painfully aware, as Sidney Hook writes, "that he lacked the creative gifts of so many thinkers to whom he felt intellectually superior."[168] But by making the short critical essay and the book review his characteristic genres he turned his analytical skills into an asset—much to the chagrin of the reviewees. Hook calls Cohen "the most incisive and formidable critic of the time."

> He had an unerring eye for the weakness of any position, and since all positions on fundamental questions have weaknesses, Cohen always had something to say that was unfailingly right. . . . Cohen, in addition to possessing a highly developed sense for contradiction and a superb dialectical skill, had a keen eye for what was left out, for what received too much or too little emphasis. He was death on the monisms and absolutisms and reductionisms of his time. . . . Dewey once remarked that the only thing he had against Cohen was his undue fear lest someone agree with him.[169]

All of what has been said so far about Morris Cohen came to culmination in his classroom performances. Unlike that of his colleagues, Wolfson and Kallen, Cohen's importance did not rest on his written work but on something as apparently ephemeral as undergraduate lecture courses. But the time and place at which he taught were such that what and how he taught had a lasting, often devastating, effect on this specific student body.

A Jewish Socrates at the City College of New York

After his return from Harvard to CCNY, Cohen was thoroughly disappointed to find that his application to be transferred from the Department of Mathematics at CCNY to that of philosophy had been denied. It was not until Harry Overstreet became head of the philosophy department (in 1910) that the appointment of a Jew became at least a possibility. In 1912 Cohen was transferred and promoted from instructor to assistant professor. He was made full professor in 1921 and professor emeritus in 1938.

Until the time of World War II, the number of Jewish students at CCNY remained disproportionately high (in 1918 it soared to 78.7 percent). Cohen was aware that "as a son of immigrant parents I shared with my students their background, their interests, and their limitations" (*DJ* 145). Therefore, he felt particularly obliged to educate, form, and direct these youths from the vantage point that his longer life and philosophical studies afforded him. "My students," Cohen reminisced, "were, on the whole, relatively emancipated in social matters and politics as well as in religion. They did not share the Orthodoxy of their parents. And breaking away from it left them ready and eager to adopt all sorts of substitutes" (*DJ* 145).

Cohen considered it his main task to demolish these substitutes. The students accepted him "as one of themselves" and as one who had "made good," therefore they tolerated his harsh treatment.[170] Cohen's teaching goal was to free the minds of his students from any preconceived notions, from any ideology they might have absorbed while growing up, and "to cultivate their powers of critical reflection so that they would become more intelligent members of the community rather than technical philosophers" (*DJ* 147). Although he was intellectually demanding, he was modest regarding his vocation, academic philosophy. Too modest, perhaps.

> I did not make the mistake of thinking that because [philosophy] was the thing I could best teach, it was the only important thing in life. Civilized life demands a division of labor. It would be enough if I could lead pupils out of the Egypt of Bondage into the Desert of

Morris Cohen.
Archives of City College of New York

Freedom and leave them there. I had faith that they would enter the Promised Land without me. Though I am liberally skeptical I have firm faith that if you remove certain obstructions the free mind will thrive by its own energy on the natural food which it can gather from its own experience. (*DJ* 146–147)

In his refusal to qualify somehow "freedom," Cohen's solution to the ḥarut/ḥerut problem was as radical as it was cruel and doubly naive. It was cruel because Cohen, better than anyone else, knew about the pain involved in being "free," in being lost in vastness. And it was naive to believe that the minds of twenty-year-olds could be remade into tabulae rasae. Furthermore, this view was naive in light of Cohen's own philosophy, which saw polar extremes as interdependent and not as absolutes. Freedom (ḥerut) needed its counterpart, bondage/obligation (ḥarut). Cohen had still other metaphors in store.

It seemed to me that one must clear the ground of useless rubbish before one can begin to build. I once said to a student who reproached me for my destructive criticism, "You have heard the story of how Hercules cleaned the Augean stables. He took all the dirt and manure out and left them clean. You ask me, 'What did he leave in their stead?' I answer, 'Isn't it enough to have cleaned the stables?'" (*DJ* 146)

75

Only years later could his student Sidney Hook think of a rejoinder: "Of course! But Hercules was no philosopher! A philosopher, you have led us to believe, is full of—wisdom."[171] Cohen knew that this teaching goal "exposed [him] to the charge of being merely critical, negative or destructive" (*DJ* 146). In fact, his negativism was not only destructive but was experienced as cruelty.[172] This was due in part to the method by which Cohen tried to achieve his goal. It was the Socratic method: teaching by means of searching and provoking questions (*DJ* 144). There was nothing wrong with the Socratic method as such, as Sidney Hook explained:

> Primarily negative in impact, the Socratic method is ideally designed to undermine the dogmas, convictions, and assumptions that one has inherited from tradition and from the surrounding milieu without recognition of their alternatives or awareness of the grounds of belief on which they are founded. . . . The Socratic method, skillfully used, can and should be a propaedeutic to a genuine liberal education: it gives students a feeling of evidence, an awareness of what follows from what, and it instills a healthy wariness of easy generalizations, a skepticism about "what everyone knows," and an intellectual distrust of panaceas.[173]

But Cohen's method entirely lacked Socrates's courtesy. It was essentially "the method of treatment by shock" which Cohen considered "the most effective way of leading students to appreciate the nature and dimension of ignorance" (*DJ* 148). His student Sidney Hook described the classroom situation:

> If a problem was being considered, Cohen would deny it was a genuine problem. When he restated the problem, every answer to it was rejected as vague, or confused, or ill informed if not contrary to fact, or as leading to absurd consequences when it was not viciously circular, question-begging, or downright self-contradictory. The students' answers, to be sure, were almost always what Cohen said they were while he dispatched them with a rapier or sledgehammer—and usually with a wit that delighted those who were not impaled or crushed at the moment. Cohen enjoyed all this immensely, too. There was no animus in this ruthless abortion of error, of stereotyped responses, and of the clichés and bromides that untutored minds brought to the perennial problems of philosophy. And although the students soon felt that whatever they said would be rejected, they consoled themselves with the awareness that almost everyone was in the same boat. When they were not bleeding, they enjoyed watching others bleed.

Occasionally Cohen would let up on a student who had the guts and gumption to answer back; if, ignoring the laughter of his fellows, he insisted on his point in the face of Cohen's mounting impatience, that student was subsequently treated more gingerly. Or when Cohen had the answer to a moot point—an answer he was holding in reserve to trot out after he had gone through the class beheading one student response after another—he would occasionally skip the student who he suspected might supply that answer. Some of us who felt the call of philosophy and had avidly read Cohen's published articles could sometimes anticipate what he had in mind. He let us alone in class but we had our egos properly pinched in private sessions with him.

Cohen's class was often an exhilarating experience. We became logical hygienists and terrorized our friends and families, and especially other teachers, with the techniques, and sometimes the pungent expressions, that we picked up observing Cohen in action. His method was not merely a form of logic chopping, or splitting hairs pointlessly, or of talmudic exegesis with which many of his students had some familiarity. We acquired a salutary skepticism of authority in intellectual matters and were able to free ourselves of the hypnosis of the printed word in disputed matters.[174]

A generation of students later, Cohen's teaching methods had not changed. Irving Howe, whose first two years at CCNY coincided with Cohen's last years there as a professor of philosophy, gave the following account of Cohen in the classroom:

It was an experience of salutary terror, listening to this master of the cleansing negation. Like Ronald Colman in one of those movies where he played an elegant Britisher taking on the natives with a gleaming sword, Cohen would take on students to his left, students to his right, ripping open their premises, cutting down their defenses. You went to a Cohen class in order to be ripped open and cut down. The tough-spirited boys who took his classes—many didn't have the courage —knew Cohen meant nothing personal when he said one of them had been speaking foolishly; he said it to adults, too. The students who adored and feared him knew that he cared mostly for an honest struggle in behalf of truth and just a little for the vanities of dialectic. Socrates may also have been a bit of a showman.[175]

In fact, Cohen's method was not that of Socrates but that of a "secularized counterpart of a *rosh yeshivah*."[176] Cohen had never attended a yeshivah and had not studied Talmud except as a child. But it seems reasonable to assume that Cohen's sharply analytical mind and his dialectical skills were first trained in the Russian ḥadarim and further developed during his life of cultural transitions. He wanted his students to have a better start: he wanted them to enter "these blessed United States" (*DJ* 58) as free people, unbound by beliefs or prejudice, so as to be able to fully participate in America's "promise of freedom" (*DJ* 227). But toward the end of his life he had to admit:

> None of us are self-made men and those who think they are, are generally no credit to their makers. The language in which our thinking moves, the ideals to which we are attuned in the formative years of our childhood, our habits, occupations, and pastimes, even our gestures, facial expressions and intonations, are so largely the social products of generations of teaching, that no man can understand himself and his limitations unless he understands his heritage; and it is very difficult to understand one's heritage, or anything else, unless one approaches it with a certain amount of sympathy.[177]

Only late in life was Cohen capable of that sympathy. Although he was "never . . . ashamed of being born [Jewish]" (*DJ* 4), he took no special pride in it. Growing up Jewish entailed the danger of succumbing to a particularist ideology which needed to be overcome. Yet Cohen did not consider himself an assimilationist. Here, too, he tried to devise a middle way. He thought it a matter of course that "everyone living in this country and seeking to share fully in its life and in the responsibility of citizenship must try to assimilate American ways of earning a living, dressing, eating, recreation, newspaper reading, and use of the English language" (*DJ* 223). This, however, did not mean "that Jews should give up as quickly as possible all those characteristics which distinguished them from their non-Jewish neighbors" (*DJ* 222). Cohen quite agreed with Kallen when he said "we can make the most effective contribution to civilization by being our own selves and not mere slavish copies of others". And: "Whatever our beliefs, we are Jews by descent. . . . It is not only vain but incompatible with self-respect to try to appear other than we are".[178]

But what *was* the self of a Cohenian nonobservant rational Jew? What was the distinctive "something" that Cohen expected him to contribute to the "general fund of [America's] spiritual goods" (*DJ* 223)? Cohen, who called himself a "pluralist" (*DJ* 226), again agreed with Kallen that the "cause of liberal civilization will not be served by wiping out the cultural values of any minority" (*DJ* 226). Yet Cohen's answer, to beware of all ideologies and to opt for reason in the search for truth, was not the particularist answer of the pluralist who knew that he also contributed his own self to plurality. It rather resembled that of a person who was afraid of pluralism, unless plurality could be coordinated, and thus controlled, by reason. Cohen's answer reflected what had enabled him to make sense of his culturally pluralistic experiences, namely, "the subordination of material things to spiritual values" (DJ 224), that is, "high respect for, and internal interest in, the intellectual life for its own sake" (DJ 223). To be Jewish was for Cohen to lead a life of pure reasoning. This capacity of "the Jews" Cohen considered "a valuable influence mitigating the American acquired habit of glorifying narrowly practical values" (DJ 223).

Rationalism versus Zionism: Cohen versus Lewisohn

When the Nazis came to power in Berlin in 1933, Cohen realized that mere sympathy for his heritage was not enough. He called for "an effective intelligence service for the Jewish people in their fight against the forces which would degrade them and deprive them of their human rights" (DJ 241). Out of the handful of people who met in June 1933 at the New School for Social Research grew the Conference on Jewish Relations. Among its first members were such illustrious men as Albert Einstein, Harry Wolfson, Felix Frankfurter, Isaac Kandel, Edward Sapir, and Salo Baron. The conference tried to battle anti-Semitism and similar violations of human rights with academic means by compiling studies, filing petitions, and joining protests. Cohen describes its early work.

> One of the first problems to which we turned was the problem of bringing before the world's conscience the character and dimensions of the German assault upon Jewish, and therefore upon human, rights. . . . One of the first . . . studies, embodying materials compiled for a petition to the League of Nations, was the volume, *International Aspects of German Racial Policies*, published in 1937. . . . In 1938 we published, under the title *A People at Bay*, Professor [Oscar] Janowsky's report to the Conference on the situation of Jews in Eastern Europe. At the same time we undertook a series of studies of the problem of multinational states, with particular reference to minority rights. We hoped that these studies, directed at the history of Switzerland, Belgium, and other multinational states, would throw important light not only on the problems of Europe but also on the central problem of Palestine. (DJ 243–244)

Six years after the establishment of the conference, its endeavors led to the founding of the journal *Jewish Social Studies*. As did Kallen, Cohen considered enterprises such as these to be the Jewish contribution to America, as his chapter heading "Jewish Social Studies: A Contribution to American Democracy" (*DJ* 237) indicates. Yet throughout his post-1933 Jewish activities, Cohen retained his secular, cosmopolitan, and essentially assimilationist stance. His biographer David Hollinger states it succinctly:

> It was an abstract liberalism that Cohen employed to justify his participation in Jewish affairs. His concern for "Jewish survival" was always a defense of Jews, as human beings, against genocide, persecution, and discrimination; it was never an attempt, consciously at least, to perpetuate Jewish identity. Cohen believed it was inevitable that the Jews would eventually cease to exist as an identifiable racial, religious, ethnic, and cultural group, simply because "no one can reasonably suppose that the present divisions of mankind will last forever." He professed his willingness to accept, "in the end," total assimilation.[179]

It is therefore hardly surprising that despite his knowledge of the Nazi threat to the survival of European Jewry, Cohen remained adamant on the question of Zionism. Twenty years after his 1919 battle with Kallen in the pages of *The New Republic*, Cohen saw himself compelled to reiterate his arguments in much sharper form in a review of Ludwig Lewisohn's book, *The Answer: The Jew and the World—Past, Present and Future* (1939). Lewisohn suggested that it would be a solution to the Jewish problem to "remove the Arabs from Palestine and Transjordania, over a million of them . . . and put in their place a majority of the Jewish population of the world." This struck Cohen as being in blatant opposition to the economic, political, and cultural facts of the region. But then, he added, "urban idealists who want other Jews to go back to the land are not interested in the facts of rural economics."[180] However, Cohen was not an anti-Zionist on principle.

> I have the deepest admiration for the brave and wise efforts through which Jewish pioneers have rescued the soil of Israel from centuries of neglect and abuse. I should like to see the racial or religious discriminations with which the British exclude Jewish immigrants and restrict Jewish land ownership broken, just as I should like to see similar discriminations in our own land broken. I should, above all, like to see Hebrew University become a beacon of light throughout the world. . . . I have hoped that all these things may be accomplished without introducing into the political structure of Palestine discriminations against non-Jews which would undermine the struggle of all oppressed minorities for freedom and equality. (*DJ* 226)

He was deeply "disturbed by the concept of a Jewish State" and posed questions which fifty years later have lost nothing of their naiveté and nothing of their appositeness.

> Is a Jewish State a racial state based on mystic ideas of "blood and soil"? Will all non-Jewish inhabitants have equal rights in such a state? Will it be possible for non-Jews to hold public office? Will a Moslem, for example, find no legal obstacle to becoming President of the Republic? If Jews are permitted to immigrate will Arabs be excluded from immigration on equal terms? Certainly I could never bring myself to support efforts to establish a Jewish State which would not be in accord with the democratic principles of separation of Church and State and equality of civil, religious and economic rights to all inhabitants regardless of race and creed. Perhaps Zionists will some day devise a Constitution and Bill of Rights that do not violate the conceptions on which Jews throughout the world base their claim for equal status. (DJ 227)

Lewisohn's book confirmed Cohen's worst misgivings about the Zionists. "Not only are Mr. Lewisohn's ideas hazy, confused, and disdainful of the facts, but his major premises are indistinguishable from the current anti-scientific racial dogmas which threaten to destroy liberal civilization."[181] Cohen recognized the cruelty in linking "such an ardent Zionist as Mr. Lewisohn with Hitler and Mussolini, even ideologically."

> But the fact is that he does agree with them not only in their dogmatic racial fatalism but also in one of the conclusions that they and others draw from it, and that is that the democratic liberal regime of emancipation and toleration has not only failed but cannot and indeed ought not to succeed. . . . By implication [Lewisohn] is committed to the view that one born a Jew cannot enter completely into English, French and German culture. . . . Thus he adds another justification for the quotas which American higher educational institutions set up to prevent the entrance of too many Jews.[182]

Cohen traces Lewisohn's "illiberal" and "irrational" views to his complete immersion "in the romantic reaction against the liberalism of the eighteenth century which set up reason and science above privileged prejudice masquerading as faith, intuition or what not, and valued our common humanity above all the particularisms which divide us." Since Cohen identified Lewisohn as a convert "to Martin Buber's form of Judaism," one is reminded here of the old strife between mitnagdim and ḥasidim. That "Mr. Lewisohn is a Freudian and comes close to identifying Judaism with Freudianism" did not make him more attractive in Cohen's eyes, because with the publication of *Moses and Monotheism* Freud had just recently proved himself to be "an opinionated crank who is more interested in his tortuous speculation than in getting at the verifiable facts." Cohen was put off by Lewisohn's "humorless and rigid sense of self-importance that is so often found in his native Prussia" (which, by the way, Cohen had never visited). And he was angered by the empty Judaism of Lewisohn's book, which "is like that of Martin Buber, a misty cloud of modern European romantic phrases. It arises out of emotional dissatisfaction and impatience with the rational demands of Western scientific culture but is quite alien to the substance of historic Jewish realities."[183]

Cohen, a true liberal and adamant rationalist, lived long enough to see another sort of irrationalism triumph in the country of Kant, the country of pure reason, and to see "Western scientific culture" employed to reduce the best of Jewish culture to bones and ash. Cohen died in 1947 without a comment on the Holocaust. In 1948, even he might have welcomed the creation of the state of Israel.

4   Men of Letters

LUDWIG LEWISOHN'S ASCENT TO COLUMBIA (1882–1903)

Morris Cohen's uncompromising rejection of Lewisohn's version of Zionism reflected the deep disdain of the Jewish rationalist for the Jewish romantic. In 1939, on the eve of the Shoah (Holocaust), when the age-old discussion of who was a Jew was ended by Nazi Germany with a cynicism unique in world history, and in Europe all doubt ceased about what it meant to be a Jew—a vermin exterminated with a disinfectant—the debate of what was or was not Jewish raged on among American Jewish intellectuals. In the unfolding spectrum of opinion, the Eastern European rationalist Cohen and the German romantic Lewisohn found themselves at opposite ends. Both men had discarded their earlier indifference (if not antipathy) toward Judaism in favor of a more sympathetic attitude, and were serving on the editorial boards of Jewish magazines;[1] but in their thoughts about the nature of Judaism, Cohen and Lewisohn differed radically.

Most likely, however, Cohen would not have objected to some of the ideas in Lewisohn's first, fairly liberal, Zionist book. In *Israel*, published in 1925, Lewisohn praised the efforts of the early settlers in Palestine, because he thought it "necessary to normalize the situation of the Jewish people: to establish a peasantry on the soil of Eretz Israel [land of Israel], to create for the Jew that blending of native land and native speech which is the mark of other national cultures."[2]

Lewisohn considered "the upbuilding of Palestine" important for diaspora Jewry. "Palestine has healed thousands of souls, it has spread the sense of national and human dignity to the remotest regions of the dispersion, it has given us recognition as a people and a place in the councils of the nations. It is self-recovery; it is salvation. The upbuilding of the land is the historic task of the Jewish people of this age" (*I* 158).

But in 1925 Lewisohn was still hesitant to embrace the idea of a Jewish state in Palestine, unless its constitution granted Jews, Arabs, and Christians equal rights (*I* 209) and guaranteed cultural pluralism even among its Jewish population. Although Lewisohn favored "the establishment of Hebrew as the language of Jewish Palestine," he thought it imperative that "the Palestinian Jew . . . be bi-lingual not only in fact but on principle. I was frightened by the many little children who could speak Hebrew only" (*I* 219). What frightened Lewisohn was the singlemindedness of the cultural Zionists rooting for an "autochthonous cultural folk-life in Hebrew" (*I* 216) and the romantic basis of their ideology (*I* 216–217).

> The Hebrew idealists have let the arguments of the Central European folkists and nationalists get under their skins. . . . The analytically minded Jewish man of letters who everywhere strengthens the hands of the liberals, pacifists, rationalists is a better friend not only of Israel but of mankind than the most exquisite of folk-poets with the mentality of the romantic soldier, hangman, priest.
>
> Hebrew is established as the tongue of the land of Israel and as the unifying factor of the Jews who live in the land. With this inevitable fact it would be foolish to quarrel. My criticism is directed against an attitude toward that fact which involves dangerous implications. The most dangerous of these implications is, in effect, a denial instead of an affirmation of our history and character, a dream that we shall gain health as a people by becoming like other peoples, by reintegrating ourselves wholly with earth, myth, legend and thus recovering the naiveté and the naive creativeness of other folk-groups who have never lost that touch with earth, myth, speech. (*I* 217–218)

Lewisohn objected to the creation (or "revival") of a Palestinian Jewish "patriotic tradition" not simply because he considered all patriotic traditions "but a survival of old fears and barbarous instincts" antedating the use of reason by the Greeks as well as the discovery of those moral concepts by the Jews "that first measured the state not by its power, but by its usefulness to the citizen and changed the sullen tribal slave into a free man" (*I* xii). Lewisohn objected mainly because he considered the nationalism of the cultural Zionists an atavistic return to tribalism which negated what distinguished the Jewish people from all other peoples.

For Lewisohn, the Jews were not only "the people of reason and peace" (*I* 219), but "the most modern of peoples" (*I* 221), the people whose history embodied the ultimate modern experience. First of all, their history taught them to transcend a nationalism based on the unity of race, culture (language), and soil, and to discredit the belief that "varieties within a national culture are evil" (*I* 223). Diaspora history demanded "mental and cultural flexibility" (*I* 221) and hence had created a people whose essential national features were, paradoxically, cultural pluralism and cosmopolitanism, and whose individual members were "liberal, pacifist, humanitarian" (*I* 277). If the Jews were to succumb to Hebrew nationalism inspired by the example of the "Central European folkists" it would "rob us of clear advantages and reduce us, for the sake of fancied and romantic goods, to the status of a Near Eastern peasant people" (*I* 221). About thirty years later a young Canadian Jew would leave his kibbutz for exactly that reason: it dawned on him that minus the rhetoric of the "Hebrew nationalists" he was nothing but a Near Eastern peasant; and this was not what he wanted to be. He returned to Canada and eventually became a professor of literature in the United States.[3]

The second feature of Israel's[4] modernity emerges from the summary of Lewisohn's argument against Hebrew nationalism: "In brief, the romantic idealists in Zion plan to substitute national assimilation for personal assimilation. We are to go to Zion and be a folk like other folks. Precisely the contrary is to be striven for. We go to Zion to be ourselves. The function of those who go to Zion is to teach the eternal and necessarily eternal masses in the Galut [diaspora] to be themselves. Self affirmation as a people and as individuals must be our aim. We do not desire renationalization in the romantic sense" (*I* 218).

Lewisohn suggests that another "modern" achievement of the Jewish people is the substitution of the individual for the collective, that is, the emancipation of the individual and his or her needs from the demands of the collective or nation. It did not occur to Lewisohn that this liberation had been precisely the achievement of St. Paul some nineteen hundred years earlier, with disastrous consequences for the Jews. But around 1925 Lewisohn had just encountered the works of Sigmund Freud and found himself encouraged to declare the emancipation of the ego from the superego.

Whereas Lewisohn's first claim regarding the essential modernity of the Jewish people—its cultural pluralism—is easily acceptable within the framework of Jewish thought, his second claim—the precedence of the individual over the collective—is not. Lewisohn's enthusiasm for Freud induced him to modify his view of Judaism. This modification was not caused by the difficulties Lewisohn encountered when he attempted to integrate Freudian views into the ideology of normative Judaism, which focused on the collective, but rather, it stemmed from a more personal confusion. Lewisohn had discovered almost simultaneously two apparently exclusive ways of rooting himself: the return to the collective via Zionism, and the exploration of the self via Freudianism. He could never quite make up his mind whether the Jewish collective or the individual self was more important for him. The tension between the two poles would inform much of Lewisohn's literary criticism after 1925. Surprisingly few critics have commented on it. One was Granville Hicks, who as an American and a Marxist could be sensitive to that tension.[5] As we shall see, the pull toward the subjective proved stronger for Lewisohn. In his second Zionist book, *The Answer: The Jew and the World—Past, Present and Future* (1939), which Morris Cohen reviewed, Lewisohn's liberal notion of a democratic, culturally pluralist Palestine accommodating the modern people par excellence (combining the cosmopolitan and the individual) had given way to a sentimental reinterpretation of Zionism that favored only one of the terms, namely, the subjective. It is not surprising then that Cohen, as an advocate of the Enlightenment—which emphasized the collective rather than the subjective—should criticize Lewisohn's romantic Zionism for precisely the reasons that caused him to object to Lewisohn's Buberism and Freudianism. Cohen disliked any overemphasis of the subjective. Moreover, Lewisohn's self-indulgence was simply too much for Cohen.

Lewisohn's life can be seen as a sequence of apparent turnarounds: from Anglo-Americanism (its Southern version), to Germanism, to Zionism, to Freudianism, to hasidism. But these "conversions" do not involve changes in the structure of Lewisohn's thinking. All that changed was the vocabulary with which Lewisohn expressed his thoughts. The structure, or grammar, of his thinking remained the same. At its center was an ardent desire for self-realization. Lewisohn became a champion of the subjective and individual, whereas Cohen remained firmly committed to the objective and communal.

But the two men shared a tendency to translate their individual problems and idiosyncrasies into statements about the universe. Cohen checked this inclination by subjecting his thoughts to the control of logic and reason. Lewisohn, by contrast, permitted this tendency to develop freely. It grew into a weltanschauung which allowed him "to write the history of literature as the history of Ludwig Lewisohn."[6] It was this unchecked narcissism, rather than (as is often assumed) his romantic Zionism and late-found religiosity, or even, as Gordon Hutner intimates, the latent anti-Semitism in American literary criticism, which caused the rapid fall of the literary critic Lewisohn, from high esteem in the 1920s to irrelevance in the 1930s and near-oblivion thereafter.[7]

A German Jewish Childhood in the South

The most incisive assessment of Lewisohn and his achievements is still that which the twenty-seven-year-old Alfred Kazin formulated in 1942. Kazin, on the move from Brownsville, New York, into literary America, is clearly conflicted about his not entirely genteel precursor. Kazin identifies major issues and presents Lewisohn in a nutshell.

> The passion with which he insisted upon the elementary facts of the creative process singled him out immediately at a time when cynicism and apathy could easily be taken for tragic sense. This is not to say that he was averse to the extravagances and inanities of contemporary critical thought. On the contrary, he was the most frenzied apostle of them, since he carried the postwar discovery of sex and the calumny of the past to the point of self-ridicule. But Lewisohn was never a "simple" figure, and his worst qualities represented the exaggerations of a mind which was in itself indispensable to the growth of a mature criticism in America. Few critics in America have ever, indeed, had so moving an ideal of the critic's function or kept to it so stubbornly. It was merely unfortunate that the very intensity with which he insisted with an almost religious conviction upon the nobility and the universal significance of creative expression—"Art is the life-process in its totality"—tricked him into saying too much.
>   . . . Inevitably, he conceived a function for his criticism that was oracular rather than didactic. More strikingly than any other in a generation of critics who wished to write like artists, he was a tormented and imaginative writer who carried over into his criticism the tensions of his novels. At the same time he was an oversensitive alien who had been lacerated by Know-Nothingism in the Middle West during the war, a Jew who raised the loneliness of the Jewish mind to a historical principle, and a humorless lover-hero of the Freudian epoch who translated his domestic difficulties into pompous dicta for everyone at large. As the future was to prove, Lewisohn's criticism was thus not merely creative, but also a form of martyrology.[8]

It is tempting to link Lewisohn's gradually evolving view of himself as a perpetual victim (as Jew, German, husband, artist, academic, and so forth) to his childhood in a country whose refined, alienated (that is, assimilated) bourgeois Jewry became the incredulous victim of a murderous mass-society without offering any resistance. But this is not the place to sound this abyss or to explore the nooks and crannies of Lewisohn's psyche.[9] Instead, I will delineate the rather simple pattern in Lewisohn's seemingly diversified life and work.

Ludwig Lewisohn was born in Berlin on May 30, 1882, to "Jews of unmixed blood and descent who had evidently lived for generations in the North and North East of Germany."[10] His maternal grandfather, clean-shaven and attired stylishly, "performed rabbinical functions to scattered congregations in East Prussia" (US 15). Family anecdotes ascribed to him "much rabbinical learning, but a whimsical contempt for the ritual law." He could afford to cultivate "something dangerously like incompetence in worldly things" (perhaps the only vestige of orthodox behavior), because his wife kept the pots boiling. "It was she who had run the primitive little factory that turned cotton into wadding for the greatcoats needed in the severe winters on the Russian frontier; it was she who had toiled early and late that her sons might have an academic education" (US 15).

Not much is known about Lewisohn's paternal grandparents because their poverty forced them to turn over their "oldest child at age five to childless but wealthy relatives" (US 16). Thus Lewisohn's father grew up in cosmopolitan Berlin, in an atmosphere of leisure and affluence that contained the seeds of his subsequent failure (US 19, 20).

Lewisohn's mother, a first cousin to his father, had come to Berlin at age twelve from "the bleak East Prussian village of her childhood" (US 21). Her education within the narrow confines of a *Höhere Töchterschule* (finishing school) taught thoroughly what it chose to teach (French, literature, music, manners), but could not satisfy the young woman's emotional and intellectual needs (US 20). She was not permitted to embark on a professional career because the family did not need the money. In Berlin's Jewish society, the laws of the Torah had been replaced by the even stricter laws of Gentile etiquette. Lewisohn's parents, Jacques and Minna, conformed to the roles of lady and businessman, but eight years into their marriage reality cracked open their fragile bourgeois shell and compelled them to seek refuge in exile (US 20). In 1890, Jacques Lewisohn's business collapsed and the family left for America.

Lewisohn grew up as the only child of parents who compensated for their displacement first from Jewish into German and later from urban German into rural American society by cherishing desperately what seemed to provide a spiritual home: Deutsche Kultur. Their son's subsequent firm belief that the "characteristic modes of thought and feeling of the North German and those of the Jew who has discarded his archaic Orientalism are profoundly alike,"[11] has its origins in his parents' almost religious attitude toward—*faute de mieux*—German culture. Like the majority of Berlin's bourgeois Jews, "they were Germans first and Jews afterwards." Lewisohn's description of his parents reflects his appreciation for their way of life. "They were not disloyal to their race[12] nor did they seek to hide it. Although they all spoke unexceptional High German they used many Hebrew expressions both among themselves and before their Gentile friends. But they had assimilated, in a deep sense, Aryan ways of thought and feeling. Their books, their music, their political interests were all German" (US 17).

In other assimilated, German Jewish, middle-class families, such as Gershom Scholem's, even "linguistic Jewishness" was not tolerated. Scholem recalls that in his home "there were only a few perceptible relics of Judaism, such as the use of Jewish idiomatic expressions, which my father [born in Berlin in 1863 and thus Jacques Lewisohn's junior by three years] avoided and forbade us to use, but which my mother gladly employed, especially when she wanted to make a point."[13]

In such families the high holidays, Rosh Hashanah and Yom Kippur, were usually observed only by the most conservative members, often only by the maternal grandmother. Jewish families in Berlin such as the Lewisohns, Scholems, and Benjamins celebrated Christmas.[14] "It was asserted that this was a German national festival, in the celebration of which we joined not as Jews but as Germans."[15] That a childhood in an assimilated, German Jewish middle-class family in Berlin around the turn of the century was not at all ideologically determining is illustrated by the fates of the four Scholem brothers: Reinhold, "displaying even stronger assimilationist tendencies than my father," became a nationalist; Erich joined the Democratic Club; Werner became a communist; and Gerhard, or Gershom, developed into a Zionist and a scholar of Kabbalah.[16]

Lewisohn left Germany at age eight, too young to take anything with him but sensory impressions and the memory of Berlin's "homely and familiar comfort" (US 1). Thus preserved, northern Germany and its people would always compare favorably to the land of "Puritan barbarism" (US 237) that was to become Lewisohn's home in exile. When Jacques Lewisohn's business failed, the decision to go to America was made on the slender basis of some letters his wife Minna had received from her youngest brother, Siegfried, who had apparently prospered there. When the three Lewisohns arrived in St. Matthews, South Carolina, in 1890, they were in for an unpleasant surprise.

> My uncle had sent the [St. Matthew's] Herald to Berlin and my father, who did not understand the art and vocabulary of town-booming nor the society items of an American village newspaper, assumed that [St. Matthew's] was a town of some importance and my uncle a prominent citizen. And here he had come to a squalid village, the guest of a man well-enough liked by his fellow citizens but wretchedly poor. My aunt, moreover, though a woman of some kindly qualities, was a Jewess of the Eastern tradition, narrow-minded, given over to the clattering ritual of pots and pans—"meaty" and "milky"—and very ignorant. (US 41)

For Ludwig's father, the change was a liberation (US 42). But for his mother it brought "profound spiritual isolation" (US 44). Although most of the town's ten Jewish families, all of whom were recent immigrants, were quite prosperous and well liked by their Gentile neighbors, the Lewisohns made no attempt at becoming friendly with them. "We saw a good deal of my uncle and his family and their friends. But culturally we really felt closer to the better sort of Americans in the community . . . " (US 44). The "better sort" were the members of the Methodist church. They "were, upon the whole, more refined, had better manners than the Baptists and were less illiterate" (US 42). However, it took even the Methodists a while to discern that the Lewisohns "were of a different mental type and of different antecedents from the other Jews in [St. Matthews]" (US 43). A certain suspicion planted by Mr. Lewisohn's unorthodox behavior had to be overcome: "He did not perform the external rites of the Jewish faith and upon entering a fraternal life insurance order, he smiled and hesitated when asked to affirm categorically his belief in a personal God" (US 43).

Although he was not unaware of the disturbing effects the social fall had on his parents, Lewisohn enjoyed the change. Landscape and climate awakened in the Prussian boy "an almost massive joy in nature." In his memoirs he recalls the exuberance of his first summer in the American South. "I had been used to the cool, chaste, frugal summers of the North. Here the heat smote, the vegetation sprang into rank and hot luxuriance—noisome weeds with white ooze in their stems and bell-like pink flowers invaded the paths and streets. I felt a strange throbbing, followed by sickish languor and a dumb terror at the frequent, fierce thunderstorms. Both my intelligence and my instincts ripened with morbid rapidity and I attribute many abnormalities of temper and taste that are mine to that sudden transplantation into a semi-tropical world . . . (*US* 39).

Whereas the squalid shtetl of Nesvizh had transformed the seven-year-old Moishe Cohen from a "little animal" into a well-behaved Jew within three years, the equally squalid village of St. Matthews transformed the seven-year-old Ludwig from a well-behaved Prussian into, alas, a little animal. The intense enjoyment of nature, to which the mature Lewisohn attributes the child's simultaneous intellectual and sexual awakening, sought expression in an adequate medium. Since sex was not yet a pleasure in the boy's paradise, he indulged in the next best thing: the production of art. "Suddenly, upon a day amid the steady radiance of that Southern summer a blind, imperious impulse took hold of me. [He gathers some tools and begins writing.] The prose and verse were mixed indiscriminately, assonance sufficed in place of rime [*sic*], all I felt was an intense inner glow. It was all instinctively done in German" (*US* 48–49).

The child was also susceptible to other aesthetic pleasures. The beauty of the church and "the familiar hymn-tunes" (*US* 51) drew him into the Methodist Sunday school, where Lewisohn felt "a spirit and faith not wholly unlike that of the primitive Church. . . . I accepted Jesus as my personal Savior and cultivated, with vivid faith, the habit of prayer in which I persisted for many years" (*U* 50–51). The positive emotional experiences in the village of St. Matthews in the 1890s lead the mature Lewisohn to the conclusion that "there lingered in that village . . . something of that honest simplicity, that true democratic kindliness which we like to associate with the years of the primitive Republic" (*US* 54). Lewisohn's childhood experience of nature in its double aspect of arousal and decay, eros and thanatos, his ecstatic experiments in creating art, his embrace of the sentiments of love and faith in the "primitive Church," and his feeling at home in the brotherhood of the "primitive Republic" are all aspects of a fundamental sense of Oneness, of an accord between self and surrounding world. This sense of the world is the privilege of a child (or of the naive Romantic). Lewisohn's description of his childhood presents an intriguing portrait of a world before the Fall. Yet to accept the fragmentation of this Oneness is a sign of successful maturation. The narcissist in Lewisohn, however, would always mourn its disintegration. He tried to restore the world's wholeness, through Zionism, Freudianism, and, finally, ḥasidism.[17]

The fall from paradise occurred all too soon. In 1892, Lewisohn's parents moved to Charleston, South Carolina, in search of better economic opportunities. In 1800, Charleston had been home to the largest Jewish

The young Ludwig Lewisohn in
Charleston, South Carolina.
Courtesy American Jewish Archives.

community in America. Until the Civil War, the South, rather than the
North, had been the center of American Jewish life. And it was in the
South that "the Jews first experienced the freedoms for which the United
States would become a bastion. Virginia, South Carolina, and Georgia
were the first states to grant Jews political equality. The first Jewish vote
in America was cast in South Carolina."[18] But the Lewisohns saw "invisible barriers" rise up around them (*US* 57). The upper-class Protestants
would not have them and "it was clear that my parents could find no
friends among the humbler Catholics or Presbyterians. . . ." But neither
did the Lewisohns want to be friendly with the German Jews. "They saw
no reason for associating with North German peasants turned grocers
(although they had the kindliest feelings toward these sturdy and excellent people), nor with rather ignorant semi-orthodox Jews from Posen.
They had not done so in Berlin. Why should they in America . . ." (*US*
58–59).

In the right to associate with the social group they preferred, the
Lewisohns saw "the precise virtue of America, the fundamental spiritual
implication of American life!" (*US* 59). Their social attitude resulted in
"utter friendlessness." The adult Lewisohn blamed his parents' isolation
on the failure of the Americans to live up to the "American idea." This has
a touch of the absurd. But in 1921–22, when Lewisohn wrote the major
part of his autobiography, his frustrating experiences at Columbia col-

ored his memories. By that time American exclusivity had also become a political reality. Anti-Semitism infested society and quotas regulated the access of Jews to all major social institutions, as well as to the country itself. Life for Jews in the South around 1890, however, was still a relatively relaxed affair.

In Charleston the ten-year-old Ludwig pursued the romantic course on which he had first embarked with his simultaneous discovery of creation in the forms of nature, sex, and poetry. Next, he encountered Sir Walter Scott, Charles Dickens, and Roman Catholicism. The ritual of the latter "touched to the very quick my sense of beauty. I was powerless before it as I am before beauty still. . . . I went to Mass every Sunday. . . . The services became my great passion. I went to Vespers, and more and more it seemed to me that to be a priest of this Church would be a calling that would satisfy every instinct of my nature" (US 62, 63).

But the principal of the Charleston high school, which Lewisohn entered in October 1893, managed to reclaim him for the Methodist church (US 67). Finally, in his third year of high school, Lewisohn made a fateful discovery while translating Virgil: "I had a gift for literature! I knew it now; I never doubted it again" (US 68).

At thirteen, Ludwig was a boy "throbbing with a passion for poetry that I still think was rare and not ignoble" (US 69). On his thirteenth birthday, on the shabbat after which Jewish boys are called to the Torah, Lewisohn was given a three-volume set of Thomas Babington Macaulay's essays. "I was intensely happy. I needed nothing more that whole summer" (US 70). He decided to shift his future priesthood from the religious to the secular realm and "to become not only a poet but a scholar and a man of letters" (US 70). By the end of high school he had given his aspiration a name: "I meant to be . . . a professor of English literature" (US 79). By that time he had discovered sex. But unlike his comrades he was also a young gentleman (US 74) and thus refrained from indulging himself. At fifteen he "was an American, a Southerner, and a Christian" who cared for only one thing, "supremely—the poetry of the English tongue" (US 77).

He buried "the rebellious things" in him "deeper and deeper—sex and doubt" and went off to college in Charleston. There he gave his Americanization the finishing, aristocratic touch by cultivating a deep reverence for England and its literature. It culminated in an "Ode to England" written when he was eighteen (US 87). As Werner Sollors points out, "Lewisohn's mental southernization was intense," inducing him to contribute some unenlightened statements to the *Charleston News-and-*

Courier.[19] He was "a Pan-Angle of the purest type" (*US* 87), by which he may have meant nothing more than that he loved all things English and Anglo-American. Only when it came to the writing of poetry was Lewisohn of two minds. On the one hand he was dissatisfied with his mentor, his professor of English, Lancelot Minor Harris, a Virginia aristocrat who wrote poetry in his spare time. "Since art means passion and since all passion has a touch of wildness, he was ever too much of a gentleman to be an artist" (*US* 83). On the other hand it was clear that wildness, even a touch of it, was out of the question for a future professor of English. Finally, Lewisohn dropped wild poetry and chose Matthew Arnold as the subject for his master's thesis. Arnold had been "the object of my latest and deepest enthusiasm in college" (*US* 93). His Victorianism was then the ticket into the academy. (This would still be the case thirty years later, when Lionel Trilling tried his luck at Columbia.) Parts of Lewisohn's thesis on Arnold were reprinted in *The Sewanee Review* of 1901 and 1902.[20] Lewisohn's personal preference for Romantic "wildness" and abandon is clearly noticeable, but he recognizes the virtues of the classical poets' restraint. "The quality, the rare and beautiful quality, in a poet's character which such a restraint points to is saneness, a control of the emotions by the intellect, a treatment of life with one's soul, not with one's prejudices; with mind, not with passion."[21]

This sounds like Lewisohn's own program to bring about his metamorphosis from Romantic poet to professor of English. His "Study of Matthew Arnold" is a remarkable achievement in scholarship, style, and critical method, designed to prove that the author had, indeed, succeeded in rooting his "being in the cultural tradition of the Anglo-Saxon aristocrat" (*US* 95–96). Determined to become a high priest of literature, Lewisohn suppressed his "very powerful instinct of sexual selection," renounced the girl he had chosen (*US* 96), worked hard, and after his graduation from Charleston College applied for fellowships at Harvard and Columbia (*US* 101). Although he was admitted as a graduate student to Columbia, he received no financial aid. But he was not discouraged. He would borrow money. In proper aristocratic, rather than Jewish immigrant fashion, "the notion of working my way through the graduate course never occurred to me. For I was not concerned with text books or, primarily, with degrees, but with a life to be lived, an absorption and dedication to be accomplished. And this never presented itself to my mind as possible upon any terms but those of a complete release from sordid preoccupations" (*US* 101).

Ludwig Lewisohn as a student at Charleston College.
Courtesy American Jewish Archives.

Lewisohn at Columbia University

Ludwig Lewisohn's arrival in the big city at age twenty much resembles Hawthorne's Robin Molineux in search of his kinsman: he came to Columbia with inappropriate expectations and equipment: "I had no social adroitness but the most quivering sensitiveness and pride. I was passionately Anglo–American in all my sympathies, I wanted above all things to be a poet in the English tongue, and my name and physiognomy were characteristically Jewish. I had ill-cut provincial clothes and just money

95

enough to get through one semester" (*US* 103). But the British restraint of Morningside Heights did not agree with him. He was frustrated and unhappy until he discovered the works of modern German literature in the university library.

> I read them with joy, with a sense of liberation, with a feeling that no other books in the world had ever given me. I struggled against that feeling; I seemed to myself almost disloyal to the modern English masters, to the very speech that I loved and which I hoped to write notably some day. But a conviction came upon me after some months with irresistible force. All or nearly all English books since Fielding were literature. This was life. All or nearly all the English literature by which our generation lives is, in substance, rigidly bounded within certain intellectual and ethical categories. This was freedom. (*U* 112)

The new reading matter helped Lewisohn to rediscover and accept his wild, romantic self, of which he "had been ashamed and which [he] had tried to transmute into the correct sentiments of [his] Anglo-American environment." The works of modern German literature, Lewisohn claimed, "made me free; they set me on the road of trying to be not what was thought correct without reference to reality, but what I was naturally meant to be" (*US* 114). In his autobiography, written twenty years after this experience, Lewisohn again links intellectual and sensual maturation. He presents his intellectual liberation as coinciding with his acceptance of sexuality as "natural," that is, morally neutral. Released into freedom, "all the defences of my soul broke down" (*US* 117). The repression of his adolescence gave way to "a blind and morbid passion. . . . I committed every extravagance and every folly" (*US* 116). He emerged from it with the insight that would inform all his later critical and creative writings, except his Zionist work. "The passion of love [read: sex] is the central passion of human life. It should be humanized; it should be made beautiful. It should never be debased by a sense that it is in itself sinful, for that is to make the whole of life sinful and to corrupt our human experience at its very source. Love is not to be condemned and so degraded, but to be exercised and mastered. . . . Natural things are made sinful only by a mistaken notion that they are so" (*US* 117, 118).

The American attitude toward sexuality, particularly as Lewisohn had witnessed it in the South, where women were pure and marriage hallowed while "all the men and youths slunk into the dark alleys" (*U* 118), seemed to him one of untenable "ethical dualism." He considered this dualism "the chief and most corrupting danger of our life as a people" (*US* 118).

It is hardly surprising then that in his major critical work on American literature, Lewisohn sees Hester Prynne as "the bearer of the spirit of liberty." He also praises Thoreau's "great and central and tonic doctrine of independence," although he intensely disliked Thoreau's asceticism.[22] But the American reality, as Lewisohn saw it, stifled individual self-realization. Sexual repression and the resulting moral hypocrisy were symptoms of a fundamental ill: America was dominated by the Puritan ideology, which emphasized the tribal, despised personality, outlawed the "natural," and was to blame not only for America's philistinism but also for the creation of a professoriat whose chief features quite apart from the expected display "of that infinitely curious, characteristic American trait—the easygoing, kindly, disastrous dislike of clean-cut individual convictions" were "its cowardice and its effeminacy of mind" (US 169). The barely forty-year-old autobiographer harbored no illusions about the academy. His twenty-one-year-old subject, however, had not yet arrived at these insights. What had become clear to the young Lewisohn was that if he could not be an Anglo-American for social or temperamental reasons, he wanted to be an epigonic German Romantic. The irony of it was that he would leave Columbia without his doctorate because he was a Jew.

In 1903, the year Horace Kallen became an instructor of English at Princeton, Lewisohn received his master's degree from Columbia and applied for a fellowship. It was not granted. When he inquired why he had not been considered, a man he later calls "Brewer" answered him.[23] "It seemed to us . . . that the university hadn't had its full influence on you" (US 120). Lewisohn protested and Brewer tried to calm him by saying that the department had recommended him for the next academic year. Lewisohn felt at a loss. "The truth is, I think, that Brewer, excessively mediocre as he was, had a very keen tribal instinct of the self-protective sort and felt in me—what I was hardly yet consciously—the implacable foe of the New England [i.e. Puritan] dominance over our national life. I wasn't unaware of his hostility, but I had no way of provoking a franker explanation" (US 120).

Writing to Brewer from his home in Charleston during the summer vacation, Lewisohn finally elicited the explanation he sought, as Brewer replied: "It is very sensible of you to look so carefully into your plans at this juncture, because I do not at all believe in the wisdom of your scheme. A recent experience has shown me how terribly hard it is for a man of Jewish birth to get a good position. I had always suspected that it was a matter worth considering, but I had not known how wide-spread and strong it was. While we shall be glad to do anything we can for you, therefore, I cannot help feeling that the chances are going to be greatly against you" (*US* 122).

Lewisohn was crushed. This he had not expected: to be excluded from the American academy which professed "freedom and equality and democratic justice" (*US* 125) because he was a Jew. What sense did that make? It only confirmed an earlier insight into the "Anglo-American mind." His rejection was an instance of "precisely that strange dualism of conscience which I had discovered there in the life of sex" (*US* 125). In the passage best known today from all of Lewisohn's forty volumes, he compares the covert American anti-Semitism with its overt German counterpart which, safe at home in Charleston, he much prefers.

> We boast our equality and freedom and call it Americanism and speak of other countries with disdain. And so one is unwarned, encouraged and flung into the street. With exquisite courtesy, I admit. And the consciousness of that personal courtesy soothes the minds of our Gentile friends. . . . It will be replied that there are a number of Jewish scholars in American colleges and universities. There are. The older men got in because nativistic anti-Semitism was not nearly as strong twenty-five years ago as it is to-day. Faint remnants of the ideals of the early Republic still lingered in American life. But in regard to the younger men I dare to assert that in each case they were appointed through personal friendship, family or financial prestige or some other abnormal relenting of the iron prejudice which is the rule. But that prejudice has not, to my knowledge, relented in a single instance in regard to the teaching of English. So that our guardianship of the native tongue is far fiercer than it is in an, after all, racially homogeneous state like Germany." (*US* 124)

The 1939 appointments of Lionel Trilling at Columbia and Harry Levin at Harvard are generally taken to be the first appointments of Jews to tenure-track positions in American English departments. Lewisohn's assessment is often quoted to support statements about the prevalence of anti-Semitism in the academy. But perhaps one should be cautious, if not skeptical. Lewisohn tended to consider the events in his life as fully representative of American history in general. And while Lewisohn may not always have erred, the situation of Jews at Columbia certainly deserves to be investigated from a more objective angle. The following section describes the relation between Columbia University and the Jews until the First World War. After this excursion the portrait of Lewisohn will be continued and concluded.

COLUMBIA UNIVERSITY AND THE
JEWS AT THE TURN OF THE CENTURY

During the last decades of the nineteenth century, those in power at Columbia University planned to transform their institution into "the center for the training of the nation's future leaders." These future leaders were selected from the upper and upper-middle classes and entered Columbia after thorough screening by their respective preparatory schools for traits like "poise," "character," and "ability to lead." Since the real selection process took place before the students entered college, the university implemented administrative reforms between 1890 and 1910 that would facilitate the admission of this desirable, pre-selected group to Columbia College. Until 1905 hardly any of the academic officials were concerned about the ethnic and religious composition of the Columbia College student body. The masses of impoverished immigrants arriving in New York during the 1880s were not considered a threat. Few Columbians believed "that more than a handful of immigrants would ever perceive that anything of value took place on Morningside Heights."[24] They were mistaken. Even before the end of the first decade of the new century, the Columbians realized that they had a "Jewish problem" and that their dream was about to collapse. It took them another decade to come up with a "refined" screening method which effectively prevented the admission of too large a number of society's less desirable elements without being blatantly anti-Jewish. Eventually, Columbia's administrators developed a masterpiece of refinement compared to which President Abbott Lawrence Lowell's straightforward quota system for Harvard looked quite boorish. A 1931 study concludes:

> Columbia's machine for regulating the flow of Jewish students through its classrooms is one of the most elaborate ever devised. Armed with its eight-page blank, its talk of scholarship standards, its personal interviews, psychological tests, physical examinations, and passport photograph requirements, Columbia can select exactly the applicants it desires, keep the Jewish quota down to the fractional percentage it may determine, and defy any one to slip by unnoticed. With this minute sifting for good material and testing for young scholars of promise, if Columbia fails to produce the bulk of the nation's future leaders, it will be a discouraging blow to human foresight.[25]

Although Columbia's anti-Jewish bias did not influence the official admissions policy of the college until after World War I (by 1921, only 22 percent of the College's entering class was Jewish[26]), discrimination against

Jews was almost a matter of course in other areas of university policy, such as the selection of trustees or the hiring of faculty. This had not always been the case.

The history of Columbia College begins in 1754, with a charter granted by George II to the King's College. In 1776 its quarters were requisitioned and the college's activities were suspended. It was revived in 1784, when the surviving governor of King's College petitioned the state legislature to make the college a university and grant a new charter. The legislature complied, adopting an elaborate scheme for a state university with the old King's College at its core, and changing the name from King's to Columbia College. In 1787, the school reverted to private auspices but held on to the charter granted three years earlier by the Regents of the State of New York, who ruled that each religious denomination should be represented by a regent on the board of the college. In 1787 the enlightened board of trustees consisted of twenty-four members: "two Anglican divines, a Presbyterian minister, the pastor of a Dutch Reformed church, a rabbi of a Hebrew synagogue, nine lawyers, five physicians, several politicians and at least one merchant."[27] The rabbi was the Sephardi Gershom Mendes Seixas, the first American-born rabbi. He served as trustee of the college from 1784 to 1814.

In 1810, after a riot caused by the appointment of a Scotch Presbyterian to a professorship, a new charter was adopted which stated that "no religious tenets should prevent admission to any privilege or office of said college."[28] The replacement of positive inclusion by the apparently less discriminatory nonexclusion soon began to have the opposite effect. When Gershom Mendes Seixas retired, he was not replaced by another Jewish trustee. Although New York's Jewish community grew considerably in number during the nineteenth century and gained enormously in stature with the economic success of the German Jews who came to the United States about 1850, New York's Jews did not feel comfortable and secure enough to press for fair representation in the administration of the city's educational and recreational institutions until quite late in the century. But by the 1890s, their economic power, which made them an elite within American society, gave them the self-confidence that their Sephardic predecessors had drawn from their distinguished history. Some of America's most generous philanthropists were second-generation German Jews. Jacob Schiff, for instance, contributed liberally not only to Barnard, the women's college affiliated with Columbia, but also to a fund for the payment of Columbia's debts. But not until 1891 did he try to elicit from Seth Low, who was Columbia's president at the time, a commitment to nominate a

Jewish trustee.[29] When Schiff repeated his request more urgently in 1900, President Low answered him sincerely. The warm, relaxed, and gracious tone of Low's letter shows the writer to be a true representative of the best Columbia tradition. He called Schiff's attention to "his appointment of four Jews to the University faculty, an achievement which Low thought unmatched in any other university, as an indication of his personal sympathies," and continued: "If no such trustee has yet been chosen, it does not indicate, I am sure, an illiberal spirit, but the fact that when vacancies have occurred other considerations have prevailed." He told Schiff that he believed Columbia to have "shown itself so liberal that it ought to be free from misinterpretation, because in one direction it has not moved along these lines."[30]

Low did, in fact, press his trustees to consider the election of a "representative Hebrew" and suggested Isaac Newton Seligman, the son of banker Joseph Seligman (Felix Adler's sponsor), for one of the two current vacancies. The reasons he gave in support of his suggestion were designed to impress the trustees: Seligman "would bring Columbia 'into closer touch with the business community,' and would 'secure the hearty support of this element by giving it representation on the Board of Trustees.'"[31] Low's recommendation was not followed. The reasons for the trustees' stalling were essentially the same as those that had led to the discrimination against the elder Seligman, when the leading hotel in a resort that was no longer top drawer tried to enhance its status by excluding one of America's wealthiest Jews. Harold Wechsler observes about the trustees: "Columbia's trustees considered themselves members of New York's upper class; they considered the Board to be 'the highest honor that a man can receive in that line.' But, in reality, they were a cut below the top. Instead of conveying prestige to the Board by their service, they derived prestige from that service. This fact made them highly status-conscious, which in turn led to a social snobism [sic] that had a definite ethnic cast."[32]

As in the case of the Saratoga Springs hotel (which was ruined by the ensuing counter-action of American Jews) the trustees and other members of the large group just below the top were not mistaken in considering the Jews a dangerous threat to their precarious social status. Elite Jewish families such as the Adlers, Guggenheims, Loebs, Schiffs, and Seligmans "would not defer to the leadership of such men [as the trustees] or to the social system they represented."[33]

After much discussion and some financial pressuring, the university board finally elected a Jewish trustee in 1928. Benjamin Cardozo, scion of a Sephardic family and a distant relative of the first Jewish trustee, Gershom Mendes Seixas, was one of the most distinguished lawyers in the United States. The year before, in 1927, he had been elected chief judge on New York's Court of Appeals; in 1932 he would become a justice of the Supreme Court of the United States. Another lengthy discussion preceded the election of the next Jewish trustee, Arthur H. Sulzberger, the publisher of *The New York Times*, in 1944. But thereafter the election of Jews as trustees or high-ranking university officers was no longer problematic.[34]

On the faculty level, the exclusion of Jews was by no means as strictly practiced, but neither was their appointment a matter of course until after the Second World War. President Seth Low considered his appointment of four Jews before 1900 "unmatched in any other American university." This might have been his honest impression, but it misrepresented the facts. President Charles William Eliot of Harvard was similarly liberal-minded, and even Yale had hired a number of Jews. But only rarely did these appointments lead to tenured professorships; and if so, this was more likely to happen at Harvard than at Yale, and more likely in the sciences than in the humanities. In any case, neither the university nor the appointee wished to emphasize the appointee's Jewishness; so that Low's impression was probably shared by the public at large. One of Columbia's preeminent professors, the anthropologist Franz Boas, was as infrequently identified as a Jew by the public as was Harvard's Hugo Münsterberg. If they were considered outsiders at all, it was because they were thought of as Germans. Boas's work, which did much to enhance Columbia's reputation, certainly discouraged thinking in racial terms, as did Felix Adler's. The latter had been appointed professor of political and social ethics at Columbia in 1902, the year Nicholas Murray Butler succeeded Low as president. With the changing of the guard at Columbia and Harvard (where Lowell succeeded Eliot in 1909) what little liberalism there had been toward the Jews rapidly disappeared. Butler and Lowell were both destined to play the part of the villain in the drama, "The Jew and the Academy."

On the Columbia faculty, matters became unpleasant when James Speyer, a wealthy Jewish businessman, presented his friend President Butler with a tricky gift. Unlike the Trojans, the Columbians had no Laocoön who could sense the danger in the gift of the Greeks. In 1905, Speyer endowed an exchange professorship "under the terms of which a distinguished American professor would lecture for a year in Prussia." In return, the United States would be visited by the Kaiser Wilhelm Professor funded by the German Ministry of Education. Speyer added that he "wished Butler and the trustees, as administrators of the Theodore Roosevelt Professorship, to make an effort to appoint regularly a Jewish scholar to the post."[35]

Butler was unwilling to include this stipulation in the formal document establishing the professorship, just as Cornell University thirty years earlier had declared it would "not again accept any proposition for endowment where the choice of the incumbent is not left without restriction to the Trustees." But because Speyer was more insistent in 1905 than Seligman was in 1876, he and Butler reached an informal agreement that Speyer summarized in a letter to Butler in 1910. Butler, Speyer writes, had conceded "that no discrimination should be shown, either in theory or practice, as to the religious belief of anybody to be nominated for that Professorship, and that from time to time, say every third year, if possible some suitable person of Jewish belief should be nominated. You told me at the time that it was better not to put this in the deed, but that you could consult with me, and that we could no doubt arrange it in some way."[36] At first, Butler was as good as his word. Punctually, in 1908, he insisted on Felix Adler's appointment against the objections of "important German academicians." But in private he agreed with the first Roosevelt Professor, John Burgess, that "it is simply absurd for us to send a German Jew as Roosevelt Professor" when the Germans desired "genuine Americans of the old stock as representatives of American culture and not German Jews."[37] As sponsors, however, the Jews were all right; that was what they had always been. Three years later, in 1911, Speyer pressured again for a Jewish appointee. This time, Butler referred the matter to the board of trustees. Its powerful Committee on Education[38] answered Speyer in much the same way in which the Cornell committee had replied to Seligman: "It is the wish of the Committee, as it is of the Trustees as a whole, to make every possible recognition of your friendly and generous support. It is, however, quite beyond the power of the Committee or of the Trustees to make the religious tenets of any appointee a condition of his appointment. The charter of the College and the unbroken traditions of the Trustees for more than a century and a half require that there shall be absolutely no discrimination made on account of religious belief."[39]

The sincerity of the moral *stand taken by the trustees is flatly contradicted by the plan to appoint "genuine Americans of the old stock," but the high-minded wording of the letter made it impossible for Speyer to accept the trustees' offer to return his gift. The outbreak of World War I and the discontinuation of the exchange program between Germany and the United States relieved Speyer of the unpleasantness of further pressing the issue.

Three years after the éclat surrounding Adler's appointment, the only Jewish professor of literature on the Columbia faculty, Joel Spingarn, was fired. However, the facts do not permit a reading of this incident as a further example of Butler's anti-Jewish bias. Spingarn might have been the first Jewish professor of non-Semitic literature in the United States. (Leo Wiener was a linguist rather than a literary critic.) But when used to describe Spingarn, the term *Jewish* refers to nothing but an accidental detail of his descent. Jewishness played absolutely no role in Spingarn's life—the only monograph on the critic does not even mention the fact.[40] There is no hard biographical evidence that would allow one to question the apparent unimportance to Spingarn of his Jewishness. It is quite possible that those around him were not aware of it and therefore left him alone (although an exception will be mentioned later). What surprises, however, is the fact that Spingarn's intellectual preferences, the sharp dichotomies dominating his life, resemble so strongly the intellectual grammar and structures found in other "alienated" Jewish academies of the time. Of course, it would be absurd to claim that an infatuation with form as perfected in the Renaissance, and a simultaneous enthusiasm for the Romantics' rebellion against form and repressive social norms, as well as an obsession with the dichotomies derived from this paradoxical combination (art vs. life; form vs. flux; that is, harut vs. herut; society vs. individual; morality vs. aestheticism; Hebraism vs. Hellenism) are peculiar to Jewish intellectuals trapped in the American academy. Yet a preference for thinking in stark oppositions is clearly noticeable among all of them. To what extent, however, this feature is related to an awareness of being Jewish in a Gentile world is impossible to determine. Spingarn, for instance, showed no sign of social uneasiness. Except for his political views, which were extraordinary for an academic in his time, he was the perfect Columbia gentleman.

THE CASE OF JOEL ELIAS SPINGARN
(1875—1939)

Spingarn came very close to being Lewisohn's dream of himself come true. There was never a doubt in Lewisohn's mind that Spingarn was a "New Yorker and a Jew."[41] But unlike Lewisohn, Spingarn overcame these designations of origin by entering culture for the sake of culture, while the young Lewisohn *used* culture as a means to achieve status or recognition in the consent community his parents had chosen, and thus he preserved an awareness of his distance from that community. Lewisohn was never quite at ease in American society, because unlike Spingarn, he did not take its culture and society seriously. A sketch of Spingarn's biography may provide an illuminating foil for the analysis of Lewisohn's life and work. Compared to the grace and ease with which Spingarn moved in the realm of culture, Lewisohn's deliberate attempts at becoming a man of letters appear all the more willful and pained.

Spingarn was born in New York in 1875 to immigrant parents. His mother was from northern England, while his father had been "swept from his Austrian home as a mere boy by the political and economic upheaval of 1848."[42] At fifteen, Joel ran away from home to Philadelphia, where he assumed the name Juan de Lara, invented a romantic biography to go with it (that of an orphan cheated out of his rights), and fell in with an alcoholic writer who was "really" the scion of a wealthy Southern family. Joel was recaptured by a private detective who retraced a letter in which the boy had prosaically asked his parents for new clothes. Back in New York he continued his exotic adventures in writing and attended the City College of New York. In 1893 he was admitted into the junior class at Columbia College, where he formed the plan (never executed) to edit the complete works of the Renaissance dramatist John Lyly. He graduated from Columbia with honors in 1895, and left for Harvard University. There he studied with such notable philologists and scholars as Francis James Child, George Lyman Kittredge, Charles Eliot Norton, and Barrett Wendell, and also with Lewis Gates, who introduced him to German Romanticism in a course on "English Literature in Its Relation to German Literature, 1790–1830." By this time the two poles to which Spingarn would be equally drawn had made their appearance in his life: the Renaissance, with its emphasis on society and form; and Romanticism, with its emphasis on the individual and sensation. Although there is a certain amount of overlap between the two intellectual worlds (the Renaissance brought about the emancipation of man from the dominance of the Church and gave rise to man as a creator who vies with God; while Romanticism maintained enough respect for society to subject the individual's sensations to the demands of social decorum, which then became the source of suffering), one may still note that an infatuation with the Renaissance *and* with Romanticism are not easily reconciled in the psyche. But in his theory of art, Spingarn would attempt to do just that.

After a year at Harvard, Spingarn returned to Columbia in 1896 and enrolled in the comparative literature program. Here he discovered his two inspiring teachers, the person of George Edward Woodberry and the writings of Benedetto Croce.[43] Spingarn received his doctorate in 1899. In the same year he published his dissertation *A History of Literary Criticism in the Renaissance* with Macmillan in New York. The book brought him, at the age of twenty-four, fame and personal letters of praise from renowned scholars and an appointment as assistant in comparative literature to Woodberry. He became chief assistant and tutor in 1900, then adjunct professor of comparative literature upon Woodberry's resignation in 1904, and finally full professor in 1909; he was fired on March 6, 1911, not as a Jew but as an aesthete who opposed President Butler's "corporate efficiency" (D 47). The professoriat was pleased. With Spingarn's dismissal, order was restored: the department of comparative literature "established by President Seth Low to help keep Woodberry's war with the English professors (especially Brander Matthews) under control" (D 161) was abolished, and Woodberry's rebel-disciple, who had dared to defy the profession in his public lecture entitled "The New Criticism" in March 1910, was punished and exiled, although for the wrong reasons.

In the eyes of the guild, Spingarn's crime was his declaration of independence for art in 1910. Spingarn saw art as an expression of the creative spirit which called into being its own terms of reference. Art was neither religion, nor history, nor politics, nor rhetoric, although these were the materials for art. Out of these materials the primary imaginative activity made "something else which we call poetry, or literature, or art" (D 86). The act of imagining was more than just a preparatory step in the creation of art; it was already the transformation of these materials into "something else" and was hence identical with "expression."[44] The equation of imagination and expression linked content and form but removed the whole unit, the art object, from the grasp of the critic as (material) analyst. Just as the act of imagining resisted reductive analysis, similarly conceptual categories could not be applied in the criticism of its products. Art was, as Croce claimed, "independent of conceptual analysis" (D 90). Art was in a category by itself and as such was neither religious, nor historical, nor moral, nor political; it was not a reproduction of life, but—if anything—a creative criticism of it. In brief: art was art, and could only be "criticized" according to its own laws.

Spingarn's stance called into question the critical activities of the profession and was understood as a direct attack. His exile from the academy did not silence him. With the publication of his *Creative Criticism* in 1917, the debate flared up again and Spingarn predictably had to contend with a most formidable foe, Irving Babbitt of Harvard University.[45] But not only did Spingarn's radical aestheticism offend the profession; its practical consequences also obstructed what President Butler most cared about, namely the efficiency of Columbia's administration. Butler was about to transform "a school of a few hundred students into a university of twenty-five thousand" (D 46). Spingarn refused to conform and function. On November 23, 1910, he wrote to Butler: "I confess that my heart sickens at the very thought of administrative tasks for which I have neither capacity nor inclination, and I do not propose to have the leisure for productive scholarship interfered with by any additional burdens of this kind; but certainly every manly and high-minded scholar in the country would sympathize with my refusal to perform such tasks whenever they conflict with my knowledge of my own capacity or my devotion to my own scholarly ideals."[46]

Spingarn's refusal to cooperate in the administration of the department and his comments on the firing of a colleague in December 1910 induced the Committee on Education to recommend Spingarn's own dismissal as of March 6, 1911. Spingarn retired to his country home, Troutbeck, in Amenia, New York. He bought the *Amenia Times* and became involved in the local affairs of his county as well as in the larger affairs of the National Association for the Advancement of Colored People (NAACP) in which he was active until his death in 1939.

It is one of the curious facts about Spingarn that his extreme aestheticism was always counterpoised by a keen interest in politics. Spingarn's aesthetic theory fused some of the aspects that intrigued him and that he found expressed in cultures and literatures as different as Renaissance and Romanticism. But his solution of the tension in the pure appreciation of an absolute art had a major disadvantage. Although it fused the Renaissance appreciation of art as form and the Romanticist infatuation with the appreciating eye (or I), it widened rather than closed the gap between life and art, between the individual and the community, or *civitas*, as Spingarn preferred to say. The completion of the Renaissance revolution in Romanticism (in which the emancipation of man evolved into the emancipation of the individual) split the creative man, who like Lorenzo di Medici, il Magnifico, had been sovereign creator (as artist *and* politician). With the transition from Renaissance to Romanticism art shifted from the realm of the public eye into that of the individual I.

Seen from a European perspective, Spingarn's obsession with the fusion of Renaissance and Romanticism, or more precisely, with an epigonically Romanticist reception of the Renaissance, was not at all original. The Renaissance was a fashionable obsession in fin de siècle Vienna, from the painter Hans Makart to the writer Hugo von Hofmannsthal.[47] Hofmannsthal's early drama *Der Tod des Tizian* (1892), for instance, makes artistically Spingarn's theoretical point: the late Romanticist appreciation of art (*the* product of the Renaissance) leads to an extreme aestheticism (understood as the contemplation of life through the medium of art). The young rebel-hero in Hofmannsthal's drama feels the hollowness and insincerety of aestheticism and yearns for the real thing: life in all its vulgarity. However he does not have the energy or the courage to leave the academy on the hill and to descend into the city.[48]

Spingarn, however, counterpoised his academic life on Morningside Heights with baths in the masses. "In 1908 [he] ran for Congress as the Republican candidate from New York City's traditionally Democratic Eighteenth District" (*D* 23). An act of defiance? A signal to the masses that he was different from them? He wrote to Woodberry about this experience:

> But surely you will want to hear something of the "crowded hour of glorious life" which he only knows in our peaceful democracy, who is a candidate for office. The sense of life which the experience gave me is beyond my academic style to picture. Be a candidate, I abjure you, dear Mr. Woodberry, before you die! Defy your "illusionaries," break faith with Nietzsche and Anatole France, send rainbows shooting through their mists, by being a candidate!
> . . . I spoke every evening, scarcely ever less than four or five times, once as many as eight, whirling from place to place as fast as gasolene [*sic*] could speed me. . . . I have felt no results from this unusual burden of work, except possibly a heightened sense of physical well-being, and a temporary ennui at the contrasting tameness of the academic life. (*D* 24)

In 1912, a year after his dismissal from Columbia, and again in 1916, Spingarn was a delegate to the national convention of the Progressive Party in Chicago; he enlisted in the army in 1917, became co-founder of Harcourt Brace & Co. in 1919, made speeches for Franklin D. Roosevelt in 1932, and remained active for the NAACP from the time of his dismissal in 1911 to the time of his death in 1939. And all of this went on while he elaborated and refined his aesthetic theory of creative criticism.

Spingarn's "political sense"—his view that only "the sense of relation to a civitas" could be the source of an individual's identity—and his "aesthetic sense," which perceived (as did the Viennese fin de siècle aesthetes) in a great work of art "a vision of reality,"[49] were equally strong and theoretically irreconcilable. The first thrust him into life and con-

Joel Spingarn.
Courtesy National Association for the Advancement of Colored People.

nected him with the community, while the second isolated him. It was perhaps only in Spingarn's American patriotism that the two senses were fused. "Spingarn was deeply involved in the American tradition of examining the American psyche, prescribing for its ills, and defining its mission" (D 37). As a man of vision in Emerson's sense, he fought a double battle against American materialism in the academy as well as in political life *ad maiorem patriae gloriam.*

Nevertheless, Spingarn was attacked by Stuart Sherman as un-American. (Sherman was one of Lewisohn's philistine Goliaths, and was a first-rate foe of both Jewish Davids, Spingarn and Lewisohn). Marshall van Deusen summarized neatly the highlights in Sherman's chivalrous defense of American "Belles Lettres."

> Stuart Sherman charged that Spingarn was an "alien-minded" critic, whose theories, "imported from beyond the borders of Anglo-Saxonia," and elaborated by "the quick Semitic intelligence," in a "supersubtle Italian fashion," were part of a revolt being conducted by writers "whose blood and breeding are as hostile to the English strain as a cat to water." Spingarn's distinctions were such as "Charles the Second would have understood," and they were designed to liberate us "from Puritanism and from Democracy." But the liberation would only extend "the ordinary man's preoccupation with sex"—"serving sensual gratification and propagating the curiously related doctrine that God cares nothing for the Ten Commandments or for the pure in heart." Invoking the authority of what every "American schoolboy knows," Sherman concluded that the divorce of "beauty from her traditional associates in American letters . . . has left her open to seduction"; for "Beauty, whether we like it or not, has a heart full of service." (*D* 110)

And of such innocence, the "lusty" Jew took advantage, raping not only poor Belles Lettres but also the Virgin Land in toto. The stereotype underlying Sherman's critique was not very pronounced in the history of European anti-Semitism. But in America, where fear of miscegenation was well established, it resurfaced. The fact that Lewisohn, after encountering Freud in the 1920s, became obsessed with America's sexual liberation, of which he was to be an agent, and the fact that the sexual attraction of the Newark Jew to "the real McCoy" was to play such a prominent role in the creative explosion of American Jewish fiction after the Second World War (as, for instance, in the work of Philip Roth), should not only be understood as a desire for assimilation, or (from a different perspective) as a rebellious violation of tribal taboos, but also as a self-confident challenge to a vicious stereotype. The extent to which the nonmarital union of Jew and Gentile was taken up by American Jewish authors is a measure of their self-confidence. The extent to which this theme stopped being titillating or threatening to Gentile readers is a measure of their acceptance of Jews.

In Spingarn's work, America's sexual liberation, the move from "Puritanism to Democracy" in Sherman's words, was not yet the prominent theme it was to become in Lewisohn's work. This was what Lewisohn disliked about Spingarn. He was completely in accord with Spingarn's dictum "that 'every work of art is a spiritual creation governed by its own laws'" and he found it "extremely handsome and refreshing when Spingarn wrote: 'It is not the function of poetry to further any moral or social cause, any more than it is the function of bridge-building to further the cause of Esperanto.'" But he strongly disagreed with Spingarn's suggestion "that the work of Euripides and Dante, of Milton and Goethe, even of Shelley and Whitman is not the expression of the poets' moral and metaphysical being, but only of an abstract aesthetic functioning." Lewisohn considered this to be "factually and intellectually quite on the level of Babbitt's 'art without selection' or 'expression triumphs over form.' An empty aestheticism was opposed to an empty moralism."[50]

For Spingarn, the moral and metaphysical belonged to the realm of history, from which the realm of art was completely separated. The facts of history, Spingarn argued, were generated through the development of the human spirit. But the determining factors underlying these facts were "the great generating forces, religious and ethical, which move men to transform circumstances into a new life."[51] The separation of the realm of art and the realm of history (which includes what there is of rabbinic metaphysics) along the lines of time is in keeping with what has become normative Jewish thought. It would be absurd to claim that Spingarn developed his theory of art as a Jew. His aestheticism would most likely qualify as straightforward idolatry. But it seems worthwhile to point out that the fundamental structure of his worldview—his strict separation of the realms of time and timelessness—is perfectly compatible with rabbinic thinking.

A Different Perspective: Jacob Zeitlin (1883—1937)

When Ludwig Lewisohn studied at Columbia, Edward Woodberry was the god of the undergraduates ("we liked to believe that he had no equal") and Spingarn was his prophet.[52] Yet neither of the two is mentioned in Lewisohn's autobiography. Lewisohn always found it hard to accept other gods; and he found it equally difficult to deal with intellectual and personal resistance in others. He expected to be pampered by the world as he had been by his doting, lonesome mother. Lewisohn's picture of Columbia's anti-Jewish bias was put into proper perspective by Jacob Zeitlin, a professor of English at the University of Illinois, who reviewed Lewisohn's *Up Stream* for the *Menorah Journal*.

Zeitlin, a Russian Jew of almost exactly Lewisohn's age, entered Columbia's graduate school a year after Lewisohn "and encountered substantially the same advice from Professor 'Brewer'" that Lewisohn had, namely, to drop his plan of becoming a professor of English literature. But in his review, speaking about himself in the third person, Zeitlin

> feels it his duty to acknowledge that he was aware of no personal hostility or racial ill feeling behind this advice, which he ascribed rather to a praiseworthy candor in facing things as they were. To warn the Jewish aspirant of what he might reasonably expect in the quest of academic employment, of the many doors that would be inexorably locked to him, of the barriers he would be called upon to overleap . . . was not the dictate of an unkindly spirit. When the student advisedly undertook to risk the outcome, no further obstacles were put in his way. If he did not meet with the same encouragement and cordiality as his fellows, he at least had no great reason to complain of injustice. Disappointment he might excusably feel, in proportion to his naive anticipations of a world free from sentimental prejudices, but to make his disappointment a ground of pique and resentment against either institutions or persons argues him incapable of the philosophic detachment of a critic.[53]

For professors in American English departments to alert Jewish students to the difficulties they would in all probability encounter should they insist on becoming professors of English themselves remained fairly common practice for another three decades.[54] By the time the generation of Sidney Hook and Lionel Trilling entered Columbia, what had shattered Lewisohn's academic aspirations had become a normal feature of Jewish life at the better universities. Hook describes the experience of his generation.

> It would be wrong to say that Columbia was overtly anti-Semitic in its practices or that we experienced the atmosphere as perceptibly anti-Semitic. For us it was normal atmospheric pressure. We had no difficulty in getting glowing recommendations from our teachers for posts elsewhere. When nothing materialized, in some disciplines we could even understand the reasons why, without feeling any bitterness about it. . . . The English departments and the German departments seemed closed territory to those who were not indigenous to their tongue and culture. I have the impression that Clifton Fadiman, who would have made a brilliant teacher, was discouraged from continuing graduate studies by one of his Columbia teachers. At about the same time one of the most outstanding students of German was told by a professor in the German department that as a Jew his chances of an appointment were very slight (he went on to Columbia Law School and years later ended up as a teacher there).[55]

Nonetheless Columbia, which by the 1920s employed a few Jewish professors,[56] had a better record than New York University, for instance, whose University Heights division, "then considered the citadel of the University, was *Judenrein*, not only in philosophy but in almost every other department." Hook would become "the first appointed instructor known to be Jewish" at the Washington Square College of NYU.[57]

Although the majority of Jewish students, who were soon to enter the colleges and universities, would react to these "obstacles" in the way that Zeitlin recommended, his insistence that things were not really so bad if you took them in the right spirit and his disparagement of Lewisohn —who interpreted these obstacles as a personal insult—were part of an attitude that was common among men of Zeitlin's generation, and particularly in his career. They were steeped in a "cult of gratitude."

Jacob Zeitlin was born in Nizhny Novgorod and came to the United States in 1892 as a nine-year-old boy. In 1898 he graduated from a New York public school and won a Pulitzer scholarship, which he held until 1906. In his will, Joseph Pulitzer, publisher of the *New York World*, had allocated funds for scholarships "to enable poor boys of ability to enter the professions and overcome the handicap of poverty which might otherwise prevent their achieving success." The competition was for graduates from the New York public schools only. It is not surprising then that many of the Pulitzer winners were Jewish and chose to go to Columbia.[58]

The Pulitzer scholarship enabled Zeitlin to obtain his secondary schooling at "desirable" places. He was "prepared" at Horace Mann and DeWitt Clinton high schools, and entered Columbia as a "polished" Jew in 1901. He received his bachelor's degree in 1904, his master's in 1905, and his doctorate in 1908. His dissertation was designed to show his mastery of his adopted culture: it was called "The Accusative with Infinitive and Some Kindred Constructions in English." The last year of his doctoral program he did not spend at Columbia, because he had already been appointed as instructor in English at the University of Illinois in 1907. There he advanced quickly in his career (associate professor in 1910; full professor in 1916) and died suddenly of a heart attack in 1937.

Too little is known of Zeitlin's personal life to permit sweeping conclusions. Newspaper clippings in the archives of the University of Illinois at Urbana-Champagne show the photograph of a dark-complexioned man with Mediterranean-Jewish features. His academic as well as occasional journalistic writings show him to be entirely comfortable in the American academy. In 1928 he edited the essays and, in 1929, together with Homer Woodbridge he published *The Life and Letters of Stuart P. Sher-*

man, the genteelly anti-Semitic foe of Spingarn and Lewisohn. Whatever may have motivated Zeitlin's recommendation of acquiescence and his ridicule of Lewisohn, his overall assessment of Lewisohn's "case" was right on the mark: "There can be no doubt that in his choice of a career he was handicapped by his double alien origin, and there is much undeniably in the American outlook to exercise the critical intelligence, but after all his complaints are weighed, we cannot help feeling that the root of Mr. Lewisohn's unhappiness lies in his own spiritual organization."[59]

There was a certain toughness to Zeitlin, which is also noticeable in the students of Hook's generation. It is a toughness vis-à-vis adversity —particularly that encountered in the Gentile world (which is always expected)—which developed during centuries of persecution in Eastern Europe. This toughness supplemented by a stubborn insistence on survival became part of the Eastern European Jews' outlook on life. It induced Zeitlin to ridicule the German Jew's "naive anticipations of a world free from sentimental prejudices," and it enabled him—despite "Czar Nicholas" (as Columbia's president Butler was jokingly called)[60] and his administrative entourage—to become probably the first tenured Jewish professor in an American English department. Lewisohn lacked such toughness and the self-discipline that goes with it. He did not fight back, but vented his anger in rashly written books in which lack of control over his emotions impaired his judgment. His treatment of Columbia's anti-Jewish bias in his autobiography is a case in point. As Zeitlin indicated, Lewisohn did "damage to his statement of the fact by exaggerating the rigor with which Jews are excluded from certain university seats."[61] Lewisohn was not a man of moderation. Once he was released (involuntarily) from the genteel restraint of the academic world, he always preferred the wild outcry to the low-keyed statement, even if the outcry ruined his reputation.

LUDWIG LEWISOHN'S DISSENT FROM COLUMBIA (1904–1955)

When the Anglo-American-minded Southern Christian gentleman Ludwig Lewisohn was turned away from Columbia University as a Jew, a world collapsed. "And for the first time in my life my heart turned with grief and remorse to the thought of my brethren in exile all over the world" (*US* 123), reminisced the Lewisohn of 1922. But the Lewisohn of 1904 was not yet very Jewish-minded. The next six years would be hard for him. A Columbia professor helped him find a position on the editorial staff of Doubleday, Page & Co., a job Lewisohn soon disliked because the house "did not consciously or purposefully publish a line for its literary or scientific value" (*US* 129). Two years later, in 1906, he was ready for his downfall. He married Mary Crocker Childs, an English-born Gentile divorcee, many years his senior and mother of four grown children.[62] Lewisohn settled with her in Charleston, where he had found refuge after quitting his job at Doubleday. His mother, Minna Lewisohn, "kept the pot boiling and paid the rent" (*US* 137) while her son tried his hand at writing. He turned out stories that were accepted eventually by *Smart Set, Uncle Remus,* and *Town Topics,* the latter a New York weekly, but which were rejected by the more literary magazines. Lewisohn's first novel met with equally hard luck. The domestic situation in Charleston deteriorated to such a degree that Ludwig and his father borrowed money to give the younger Lewisohn a second start. "I had . . . to fight my own man's battle" (*U* 138).

He returned to New York, settled in Washington Heights, and "wrote and sold six serials against every human and artistic instinct of my nature" (*US* 141). Meanwhile, he peddled his novel. Finally, Theodore Dreiser, who read it for B. W. Dodge & Co., recommended it for publication. "True, Dreiser had no style. Neither had Balzac." But Lewisohn admired Dreiser nevertheless because "he has seen life more largely and truly than any other American novelist. And he has let life interpret itself upon the basis of its eternal facts. He has let life mean—life! Not some moralistic crochet that is the weapon of his own intolerance" (*US* 142). The book Dreiser recommended was rather conventional.[63] Although *The Broken Snare* (1908) is filled with domestic unhappiness, marital strife, an elopement, pregnancy, accidental abortion, and other strong stuff for turn-of-the-century readers, the values it advocates are conservative: marriage is necessary because "free love" leads to suffering and religious guilt.[64] The novel lacks intensity in spite of its subject matter, and the author's marked misogyny is particularly annoying because there is so little to distract the reader.

It is hardly surprising that the novel "didn't sell. It didn't sell at all" (*US* 145). But with his first novel just gone to press, Lewisohn wrote another one "without one touch of the sensuous beauty of the first—a bare, plain, austere transcript from life, holding within itself, because it is of the very core of reality, a massive moral implication" (*US* 145). It is more than likely that this book, too, dealt with Lewisohn's intense marital problems at the time.[65] It must have contained some strong stuff for the time because Anthony Comstock, "that human symbol of the basic lies of our social structure," confiscated the printed copies and destroyed the plates in his crusade against vice. Lewisohn was desperate. "I was beaten, broken, breadless. I was a scholar and forbidden to teach, an artist and forbidden to write. Liberty, opportunity. The words had nothing friendly to my ear" (US 145).

Lewisohn was not prepared for the existential insecurity that came with "liberation" from academic and genteel restraints. In 1910 the poet William Ellery Leonard, who was a friend from Columbia days, came to the rescue. He persuaded the head of the German Department at the University of Wisconsin to offer Lewisohn an instructorship.[66] Although Lewisohn considered this an entrance into college teaching through the back door, "the sense of both liberation and security which my first academic position gave me" (US 152) triggered a spurt of scholarly activity that continued after Lewisohn left Wisconsin and joined the German Department at Ohio State University in Columbus. He edited a volume on *German Style* (1910), edited and translated the works of Gerhart Hauptmann (seven volumes, 1912–1915), translated works by the dramatists Hermann Sudermann and Georg Hirschfeld, the novelist Jakob Wassermann, and the by now almost forgotten writers Soma Morgenstern and Jacob Picard. During this busy period Lewisohn also wrote his critical studies *Modern Drama* (1915), *The Spirit of Modern German Literature* (1916), and *The Poets of Modern France* (1918). This time Lewisohn's "liberation" (US 152)—and there would be a few more—was not only from economic hardships; it was above all an intellectual, almost spiritual liberation. As professor of German literature, he could drop all pretense of being a "civilized" Southern Christian gentleman with an Anglo-American mind and profess openly what he felt most at home with, German paganism (the so-called *Naturalismus*). Lewisohn himself considered the advocacy of German *Naturalismus* morally superior, for example, to an infatuation with American literature, because modern German literature and civilization embodied "the widest moral and intellectual liberty and tireless spiritual striving."[67]

German Liberty and American Bondage

Lewisohn's reversal of the protagonists standing for ḥarut and herut— his condemnation of America as the land of bondage and his praise for Germany as the land of liberty, which take up the last third of his autobiography *Up Stream*—may sound peculiar at first, but it is based on a striking perception. What appealed to Lewisohn in German literature written between 1880 and 1910 was an intense physicality, a preoccupation, if not obsession, with the is-ness of things, an obsession which soon became intensely spiritual (when the literary mood shifted from naturalism to symbolism). God was dead and the established religions were discredited as a path to truth. Therefore the only way to arrive at *nuda veritas* or the naked truth (a key term of fin-de-siècle culture) was through an exploration of the phenomena. Experiencing the is-ness of things, one might arrive at the meaning of life. Each object could at any moment open a vista into the spiritual realm.[68] In each object the physical and the spiritual were fused.

What distinguished this modern symbolism from that of the Catholic Church and its medieval handbooks, which gave the spiritual meaning of each phenomenon in creation, was that the connection between the physical and the spiritual realm (between object and meaning, between the literal and the spiritual sense) could no longer be systematized and proclaimed ex cathedra as a set of equations explaining reality and the meaning of the world. Augustine's *De Civitate Dei* could still do that. But in modernity the connection between the physical and the spiritual realm, between object and meaning, depended solely on the experiencing eye/I and was established and valid only in the moment of vision.[69] This subjectivization, the transfer of control over this connection from the "objective" authority of the Church to the subjective authority of the experiencing eye/I, had been undertaken by the Protestants almost four hundred years before the rebellious Joyce would reinvent it.

For Lewisohn, an important consequence of this dependence on the immediacy of experience for access to the spiritual world was that it made a generally binding moral code impossible. Morality presupposes distance from experience and certainty about a stable connection between the physical and the spiritual realm, that is, between the worlds of action and meaning (reasonable certainty, for instance, about the relationship between act and reward or punishment). The original guarantor of the stability of this connection was the Catholic Church, which defined the meaning of words and deeds. But its authority was broken and the morality it advocated discredited.

What Lewisohn's "modern German literature" celebrated was the fusion of the physical and the spiritual in the moment of experience. Thus, experience becomes identical with meaning. This fusion is not constrained by morality (which Lewisohn takes to be the evaluation of an act imposed upon the actor by the authority in control of the relation between physical and spiritual realm). The supreme authority in this world is the individual. It determined what was "moral" as it determined the "meaning" of things.[70] Consequently, modern German literature proclaimed an orgy of subjectivity, culminating in the union of all Germans in an ecstasy of spiritualization.[71] "Yet the young poets in Germany who are listened to by thousands and thousands—Franz Werfel and Walter Hasenclever and many others—are crying out for more inwardness, not less, for spiritualization and conquest and absorption into the mind of all things and all men; for a suspension of all moral judgment, all strife and for the remoulding of the world through love" (US 211). Whether the Germans listened indeed by "thousands and thousands" to these poets is difficult to ascertain. But their longing for ecstatic union and spiritualization was certainly satisfied ad nauseam in the pompous heyday of the Führer who, suspending all moral judgment, undertook the remolding of the world through terror. Familiarity with Lewisohn's biography makes it easier to understand why the union of body and spirit and the attendant emancipation of the individual from all externally imposed rules of behavior (morality) should appeal so strongly to him. "Modern" German literature, as Lewisohn read it, celebrated the liberation of the individual from all those external forces (rules of constraint in the academy and in marriage) which dominated much of his life, and it declared that a fully realized self unified sexuality and intellect, fused body and mind—a claim that expresses Lewisohn's experience and perception of his own self since early childhood.

What irritated Lewisohn about America was precisely what had upset the Catholics about the Protestant revolution, namely the dissociation of the physical from the spiritual realm (the resegregation of immanence and transcendence, which is a basic tenet in Judaism). One consequence of this development had been a new appreciation for and appraisal of the material world in the sixteenth and seventeenth centuries, which had triggered a burst of scientific activity. Centuries later, Lewisohn deplored the decadent materialism of a "society which, as a whole, venerates Edison more than Emerson." Such a society could take little pleasure in the spiritual realization of the self (through the intoxicants "*Wein, Weib und Gesang*," or drink, sex, and music) and hence generated a repressed, enslaved people, the heirs of the early Puritans. "One knows the type: thin-lipped, embittered by the poisons that unnatural repression breeds, with a curious flatness about the temples, with often, among older men, a wiry, belligerent beard. You have seen them with their shallow-bosomed, ill-favored wives—stern advocates of virtue—walking on Sunday self-consciously to church. The wine they have never tasted, the white beauty they have never seen, the freedom of art they have never known—all their unconscious hungers have turned to gall and wormwood in their crippled souls" (*US* 186–187). Lewisohn was considerably less charitable than was Sherwood Anderson who, writing in 1915–1916, granted the emotional cripples of small-town Ohio at least the stature of "grotesques," of men and women whose psychic deformity was a consequence of some crucial failure in life, "whose humanity has been outraged and who to survive Winesburg have had to suppress their wish to love."[72] In Lewisohn's vindictive description, Anderson's "grotesques" are reduced to caricatures.

Organized in such groups as the "Lord Day's Association" or the "Society for the Prevention of Vice" (*US* 187), some Americans terrorized their countrymen. "We are helpless against any irresponsible person who shouts: Morality, Purity, the Home" (*US* 187). Lewisohn saw America enslaved by an excessive materialism producing an "appalling mental vacuity" (*US* 188) and by a stern moralism repressing all physical pleasures. "The result is dumb misery and perversion and the sickening putrefaction of the impulses of will and sex" (*US* 187). America was a country caught up in the exploitation of the material world at the expense of the truly spiritual sphere (that of the self), and in which the individual was tightly controlled by a group of unfulfilled materialists who claimed to have the right vision.

Thus Lewisohn came to the inverted conclusion that Germany was the land of liberty and America the land of bondage: in the former, self-realization was possible and resulted from the union of the physical and the spiritual realm; in the latter, the separation of the two realms prevented the liberating fusion and thus enslaved the self. Lewisohn's experiences in Ohio during the First World War seemed to confirm this view. He saw the anti-German outbursts of his fellow Americans, as he saw the American war fever in general, as the explosion of a valve that had been kept closed for too long. "When psychical explosions come, they necessarily take the form of war, hate, persecution, lynching. Degraded by the oppression of Moralty [*sic*] and Purity and the Home—in their current meanings—men summon the evil passions bred by their degradation to defend its instruments . . ." (*US* 187).

Lewisohn shared the fate of his honorable colleague at Harvard, Hugo Münsterberg. He was attacked as a poisonous pro-German influence, on the evidence of his book, *The Spirit of Modern German Literature* (1916). He was denounced by a real-estate broker as a German and had to appear before the district attorney (*US* 217). Lewisohn's was not a singular experience. Nor did he exaggerate in *Up Stream* the fanaticism of the cult of loyalty which came to the surface in America in 1914, intensified until 1917, and continued at about the same pitch until well into the 1920s. In a classic study, Richard Hofstadter and Walter Metzger write about the "crisis of 1917":

> All over the nation, patriotic zealots on boards of trustees, in the community, and on the faculties themselves, harassed those college teachers whose passion for fighting the war was somewhat less flaming than their own. Suddenly, the gains for academic freedom that had painfully and gradually been won . . . were swept aside. With frightening quickness, the hard-to-learn manners of tolerance yielded to crude tribal instincts of taboo. The academic profession . . . confronted the almost total collapse of the moral and institutional safeguards that had been wrought in the slowness of time.[73]

In 1917 Lewisohn thought it time to run for cover. He applied for a leave of absence from Ohio State University. He would never return. From the beginning, the German persona, which Lewisohn embraced as his 'real' self after his rejection as a Jew by the academy, had been adopted as a stance of opposition against America. Behind the many personae with which Lewisohn chose to mask his Self during his life—Southern Christian gentleman, German, Zionist, Freudian, Buberian—a common impulse can be discerned: to define himself as different from and in opposition to his environment. Lewisohn perceived himself as Dissent incarnate and thereby, curiously, he affirmed an American tradition. American ideology developed precisely through repeated acts of dissent. At the end of *Up Stream*, upon leaving Ohio State University, Lewisohn smugly sums up what is probably the only constant in his definition of self: "And I, in my own small and dusty way, was the eternal outcast, rebel, the other-thinking one—guilty before the herd, guiltless in the dwelling-places of the permanent, breaker of taboos, creator of new values, doomed to defeat on this day in this little grimy corner of the universe, invincible and inextinguishable as a type" (*US* 215). His German persona, adopted in defiance of American society, was a declaration of solidarity with his parents who, he thought, had been rejected by America. This German persona was a curious mixture of sex, soil, and spirit, and expressed an intense but somewhat abstract longing for rootedness. When Lewisohn's father died in 1917, "his mind unbalanced by the wretchedness into which his wife's death [in 1912] had cast him,"[74] his son was devastated that he had not managed to live up to his parents' expectations and had been unable to compensate for their failures with his successes. But the loss of his last parent was also a liberation of sorts. Lewisohn dropped his German persona. He turned to American culture and to the investigation of his personal misery; that is, he eliminated the "soil" component from the matrix of his self and found the remaining two elements in a sad state of disarray.

Trapped in New York: *Don Juan* and *The Case of Mr. Crump*

For the next seven years Lewisohn lived in New York, five of which, from 1919 to 1924, he spent at the drama desk of *The Nation*. During that time he produced five books: the first was *A Modern Book of Criticism* (1919), an anthology of American and European criticism which condemned in its introduction Paul Elmer More and the humanists, and spoke out for the liberation from morality. "I need no hierarchical moral world for my dwelling place, because I desire neither to judge nor to condemn. Fixed moral standards are useless to him whose central passion is to make men free. . . . More wants to damn heretics . . . I do not. His last refuge, like every absolutist at bay, would be in the corporate judgment of mankind. Yes, mankind has let the authoritarians impose on it only too often."[75] Two other books, *The Drama and the Stage* (1922) and *The Creative Life* (1924), were collections of critical pieces Lewisohn had written for *The Nation*; only *Up Stream* (1922) and *Don Juan* (1923), the first volume of his memoirs and the first of Lewisohn's deliberately autobiographical fictions, were original compositions. They started the long train of his personal outpourings. This burst of creativity was apparently triggered by a change in Lewisohn's life. In 1921 or 1922 he entered into his long liaison with the then-twenty-year-old singer Thelma Spear. Mary Crocker, Lewisohn's much older wife, refused to grant him a divorce. The strict divorce laws of New York State left Lewisohn no further recourse. The impossibility of dissolving his marriage caused great pain to all parties concerned. But the way in which Lewisohn turns the civil law of New York (by which he had agreed to be married) into another example of the American discrimination against Jews in the second volume of his autobiography, *Mid-Channel* (1929), is farcical. (It should be remembered that Lewisohn's return to Jewishness occurred about four years before the publication of *Mid-Channel*.)

> The laws of the state of New York are based on the Christian assumption that marriage is a sacrament whereby the corruption of nature is curbed and bridled, that it ought to be permanent and that the only offence against it that can lead to its dissolution is an act involving

"moral turpitude." . . . I would not dream of giving offence in either Vilna or Jerusalem by eating *trefe* food. But the human disgracefulness of assimilationism is illustrated by the fact that the Jewish community of New York, the most powerful and numerous in all history, has not demanded, has not dreamed of demanding exemption from laws that have no relation to its instincts, its tradition or its reason [which Lewisohn then goes on to explain]. But we American Jews, supposedly free citizens in a free state, submit to an outraging of our innermost susceptibilities which the Colonial powers of Europe will not inflict on subject and semi-barbarous populations. (*MC* 27–28)

Although his personal misery, which the state of New York refused to alleviate, would be treated in extenso in a number of Lewisohn's fictions, the author was after bigger game. He wanted to match what he deemed Dreiser's achievement in *Sister Carrie:* "There is no profounder illustration than the character of Hurstwood in all literature of the great saying of Goethe that every concrete thing, if it perfectly represents itself, becomes a sufficient symbol for all" (*US* 142). The "concrete thing" which from then on Lewisohn would represent (though perhaps not perfectly) is, of course, his own self. His fiction, criticism, and journalism became the confessional expression of a representative man. This view is summed up in the prologue to *Up Stream:* "For both the novelist and the philosopher [i.e. critic] is only an autobiographer in disguise. Each writes a confession; each is a lyricist at bottom. I, too, could easily have written a novel or a treatise. I have chosen to drop the mask. . . . There are thousands of people among us who can find in my adventures a living symbol of theirs and in my conclusion a liberation of their own and in whom, as in me, this moment of history has burned away delusions to the last shred" (*US* 9–10). As did Schopenhauer and Freud before him, Lewisohn considered sexuality the real common denominator of all mankind. Given his personal situation, the shift of emphasis from "soil" to "sex" in this stage of his self-realization was a natural one. But it also helped Lewisohn to make three claims: (1) that the advocacy of enjoyable sex implied the right to habeas corpus, to each man's control over and possession of his own body, which was exactly what his wife and the state of New York denied him; (2) that the advocacy of sex (identical with his claim to physical freedom) put him immediately in opposition to Puritan morality. This added the "oppositional" ingredient essential to Lewisohn's self-definition; and (3) that the advocacy of sex integrated him into the fate of mankind, whose representative man he considered himself to be. Concerning this phase in

Lewisohn's intellectual development, Leslie Fiedler is right on the mark with his observation that "the only subject to which Lewisohn responds in his fiction with real fervor, the single spring of his creative work, is his own sex life desperately projected as typical."[76]

Appropriately enough, Lewisohn reentered the world of fiction (abandoned in 1908) with a novel called *Don Juan* (1923). He wrote it under unfavorable circumstances within twenty-nine days, probably in the summer of 1923, with his "world and life" dancing "feverishly on the point of a spear" (*MC* 66). Although he calls himself a "wretched introvert," he proclaims five lines later that "all art is lyrical or self-expressive in its original motivation and drive" (*MC* 66). *Don Juan* is only a mild precursor of Lewisohn's best, most vicious, and most self-expressive novel, *The Case of Mr. Crump* (1926). The earlier novel deals with a man locked in an unhappy marriage, in love with a young woman who is not his wife. The civil law of the state of New York does not grant divorce except on the grounds of adultery. The unfortunate man cannot strike a deal with his wife, nor does he wish to compromise his lover, who comes from a small town in New England. When the pressure from the Puritan environment and the conventional family on the offending Don Juan increases, he contemplates suicide, finds release in intellectual conversations with characters representing Dreiser and H. L. Mencken, and in a sexual relationship with a "liberated" woman. But eventually, he escapes to Europe, leaving behind both his wife and his lover. The protagonist's dilemma is a result of his own conservative values: he can neither accept love without marriage ("liberated" women are only tolerable for a short time), nor endure his marriage without love; and marital love seems to require the wife, as one of Lewisohn's critics pointed out, "to be completely without demands, more an idol-worshiper than a human being."[77]

Don Juan was a very limited artistic achievement. But writing it proved to be doubly liberating for Lewisohn. He discovered the relieving effect of writing autobiographical fiction, as would Philip Roth some fifty years later. But for Lewisohn writing was not yet what it would become for Roth: a means of coming to grips with himself. For him it was never, not even after his discovery of Freud in the mid-1920s, a means of exploring the self. At most, it was a means of disseminating accumulated pressure. He could achieve distance from upsetting events by committing them rashly to paper and by insulting his adversary. Thus writing provided brief, temporary relief. Roth, by contrast—who found himself in a marital deadlock similar to Lewisohn's—seemed to aim at, or at least to hope for, a deeper therapeutic effect. This may not yet be the case in *When She*

Was Good, in which he dealt with the social environment and circumstances that formed his wife.[78] But novels such as *My Life as a Man* seem to take the therapeutic (perhaps psychoanalytic) possibilities of literature seriously.[79] The pleasure of revenge, however, which injured Narcissi gain from their confessions, is equally strong in both Lewisohn and Roth.

The Case of Mr. Crump, written three years after *Don Juan*, presents Lewisohn's life as a man. It is a thinly veiled account of his disastrous marriage to Mary Arnold Crocker. The psychological penetration of the subject matter is not the book's forte. (Lewisohn thought Flaubert had a "comparatively limited mind," *MC* 161.) Its chief literary merit is the portrait of the perfect bitch, which in "its bitterness, its frankness, and its almost brutal directness" far surpasses Roth's vicious portrait of Maureen.[80] Joseph Wood Krutch was the first who did not read the novel as a case history:

> It is upon the portrait, physical and spiritual, of Mrs. Crump that the novelist centers his effort, and it is indeed her book. Beginning with a description in a tone of half-detached irony of her and her antecedents, it gradually increases in power and ferocity as it describes the increasing sluttishness of her personal habits and the increasing meanness of her soul. No disgusting detail of her physical decline is omitted and no aspect of the torturous process of her mind is left unanalyzed, until she at last stands forth a figure at once monstrous yet credible.[81]

She is, as a line canceled from *The Waste Land* manuscript has it, like all women a creature of "unreal emotions and real appetites."[82] How Lewisohn could persuade the fastidious Thomas Mann to write a preface to this "novelistic document of a life, of the inferno of a marriage," which description already "exhausts the book's horrifying and infuriating subject matter,"[83] remains an enigma.

Lewisohn claimed that "in a strictly philosophical sense, *The Case of Mr. Crump* is a work of the severest moral idealism in which again and again definite concepts of good and evil are brought into confrontation" (*MC* 170). But the United States Post Office department disagreed: "The views of men of letters, contemporary or otherwise, are entitled to due respect, but this office must be governed by the views of the Federal courts as to what constitutes obscenity within the meaning of Section 211 of the Federal Criminal Code in passing upon matters coming before it" (*MC* 169–170). *The Case of Mr. Crump* was not deemed fit to be distributed by the post office. American publishers refused to print it because they feared libel suits; the book finally appeared in Paris in 1926. Lewisohn asked Theodore Dreiser to review it. But Dreiser declined, because he thought that Lewisohn had not been "far enough removed, in time, from the actual events about which this book is written, to approach them with the clear, uncolored, unemotional viewpoint which any writer must have when fictionizing that which lies nearest his heart." He disliked the book's "harshness, the vulgarity, the bitterness, the one-sided-ness, the psychological astigmatism," but he had praise for its "vivid, incisive style." He recommended that Lewisohn "wait a little while and then rewrite it."[84]

But patience and self-criticism were not Lewisohn's forte. He thought himself distanced enough from the events to "transmute experience into art" (*MC* 163). Two years after the beginning of his liaison with Thelma Spear, he had left for Europe (1924). Unlike his fictional protagonists Lewisohn took his lover with him. He toured the continent widely, and become a convert to Zionism (in 1925). In 1926 he discovered "that in the detachment and peace which I found in Paris things that had been working themselves out and ripening primarily in my subconsciousness for years, reached the point of condensation or precipitation" (*MC* 163). At this moment, *The Case of Mr. Crump* simply surfaced, and "wrote itself" (*MC* 163). The novel was not a painful coming to grips with the disaster of a marriage to an older, lower-class, Christian woman who rallied the forces of sex and public morality against desertion by her "victim." Nor was it a serious investigation into the couple's psychodynamics which had made this disaster inevitable. And it certainly did not undertake to reassemble the man's shattered self. Coming to grips, investigating, reassembling are essential features in Philip Roth's remarkably similar novel, *My Life as a Man* (1974). Lewisohn's *The Case of Mr. Crump*, by contrast, was a simple striking out against an enemy he had already deserted.

Lewisohn saw himself (as he saw his protagonist, Herbert Crump) as the victim of America's social conventions and public morality, which induced him (as they did Roth's Peter Tarnopol in the 1950s) to be "nice" and not to desert a woman in need, and which then condemned him to stick it out. Looking back from *The Case of Mr. Crump* to Lewisohn's previous books, these polemics against American puritanism and morality, much as they were the fashion of the age, turn out to be pleas on his own behalf. This then solves the seeming paradox of the authorial voice in Lewisohn's fiction and criticism, which speaks out constantly against "Morality, Purity, the Home" (*US* 187) but at the same time holds ultraconservative, pre-modern views on women (*MC* 220), music (*US* 191), and literature.[85] Moral liberation was good only when it served Lewisohn's purposes, that is, when it supplied the frustrated husband with a lover or a divorce. In the same self-serving way Lewisohn would put Freud's ideas to use in his American literary history, *Expression in America* (1932).[86]

Refuge in Europe: Leaping into the Heart of Israel

In 1924, Lewisohn moved from New York to Paris, where he kept away from literary circles. He thought he "had little in common with the 'expatriates'" (*MC* 164), and socialized only with a select few of them. "Mr. James Joyce, a man of commanding gifts and erudition," for instance, who "works heroically long hours in order to propound a series of coldly calculated philological puzzles," (*MC* 43) was not among the favored few: "I found and find myself, to sum the matter up, in my modest way a little remote from the 'quarter' as such. Its preoccupations are not mine; its ways are not mine. I find that I want more bourgeois responsibilities, not fewer, more order and dignity of life even in external things, not less. I thrive and my work thrives under these conditions. I want to be more bound—so the bonds be rationally chosen—never less" (*MC* 166–167).

Lewisohn had hardly settled in Paris with his lover, Thelma Spear, and gotten used to his liberated self, when he began to cast around for new bonds, for something more tangible than "freedom" by which to define his self. Europe offered him three alternatives: the tribal (Zionism), the ego-universal (Freudianism), and the tribal-universal (Buberism). Each alternative emphasized a different element in Lewisohn's tripartite matrix of self, formed by soil, sex, and spirit. Lewisohn decided not to rush things, and to content himself with redefining the expatriates' "exile" as *galut* (*MC* 167). This renaming not only had the advantage of touching on an element common to all three alternatives—Zionism, Freudianism, and Buberism were, after all, three responses of Jews in exile to the pressures of their environments—but moreover, the renaming and hence reidentification also furnished Lewisohn with what he was most in need of after his escape from American puritanism: a formidable foe against which to define himself. By understanding himself not as in exile but as in galut (that is, by defining himself as a Jew), he would from now on have to count among his foes much of Europe's respectable bourgeoisie.[87]

A visit to Berlin convinced Lewisohn that "this city and its cool Northern charm . . . could never become for long an abiding place for me." Hence the element of "soil" in his matrix was free and could be shifted.

This happened almost immediately: "strangely, vividly, though yet un-seen, I had a vision of palms and tawny hills and the dark Mediterranean tide upon the shore of Palestine . . ." (*MC* 85–86). Lewisohn was fortu-nate. His former employer asked him "to travel to Poland and thence to Palestine [to] write a series of articles for *The Nation* on the Palestinian experiment of colonizing Jews upon their ancestral soil" (*MC* 54). He published an account of these travels in a book called *Israel* (1925), which he wrote in Vienna (*MC* 133). His Austrian environment had as great an impact on the book's argument as the travel experiences themselves, be-cause Freud's city harbored the two great foes against whom Lewisohn conceived his book (and simultaneously his new Zionist self): anti-Semitism and assimilation. From now on Lewisohn would call himself a Jew and devote the rest of his life to the ever-more perplexing discovery of what that word meant.

Unexpectedly, Lewisohn's early education as a Southern Christian gen-tleman, which had prepared him to embrace the epigonic Romanticism of "modern German literature," proved to obstruct the process of his re-Judaization. The radical rationalism of the Pharisaic tradition (which became what Harold Bloom calls "normative Judaism") was entirely for-eign to his thinking. It advocated just the opposite of what had been Lewisohn's most cherished ideas. Having accepted the separation of tran-scendence and immanence as the basic feature of its weltanschauung (bridged only by God's rare revelations in history), the Pharisaic tradition focused on the material world (the notorious Jewish this-worldliness), and consequently banned all investigation into man's subjectivity. Yet de-spite Deut. 29:28, intense scrutiny of the world of phenomena was not only permitted but desirable.

Jewish rationalists such as the Gaon of Vilna, an accomplished mathe-matician and Talmud scholar, could display a double-track mind like Sir Isaac Newton; or, like Freud, whose "identification with Judaism was aggressively secular," could concentrate completely on the world of phe-nomena. Posing to himself the question "how the Jews had acquired the character peculiar to them," Freud gave a mitnagdic answer: "In the first place there is the this-worldliness of the view of life and the overcoming of magical thinking, and the rejection of mysticism."[88] The rejection of mysticism is precisely what constitutes the iconoclastic character of Freud's own work: he looked at the realm sacred to all mystics, Christians, and Romantics—man's soul—with the unblinking eye of the church mouse for whom the wafer is just a biscuit. He subjected the self to a radical scientific investigation and, by finding a technical language for its structure and dynamics, objectified the subjective, and thus turned man inside out.

Much as Lewisohn found himself in agreement with Freud's views on the importance of sexuality, Freud's rational vivisection of the self was decidedly not to Lewisohn's taste; nor, for that matter, was the ego-less weltanschauung of the earlier, less secular Jewish rationalists. The mitnagdic views of both the Vilna and the Vienna gaon were incompatible with Lewisohn's concept of self-realization, which had developed out of his Christian and Romantic education. Therefore, Lewisohn had to move outside the Pharisaic tradition if he wanted to integrate his former understanding of self-realization with his new desire to be part of the Jewish people.

Two solutions to this problem had already been developed in Europe: Theodor Herzl's Zionism and Martin Buber's ḥasidism. The first integrated the "tribal" (Morris Cohen's phrase) and the self: that is, Herzl applied the example of Christian nationalism to the Jewish people, whereas the second integrated the universal and the self: that is, Buber applied Christian universalism to Jewish thinking. The development of Zionism and the discovery of ḥasidism by assimilated Jews are ideologically and psychologically related phenomena—both are rooted in a desire for the rebirth of Judaism.[89] The concept of self-realization is central to both. The telos of Herzl's Zionism is the union of all Jews in Zion; the telos of Buber's ḥasidism is the *communio* with God of the unified (or simple) self (*Einfalt*). The blending of the physical and the spiritual realm in both views appealed to Lewisohn. Neither as Zionist nor as Buberist would Lewisohn have to restructure his thought; he could remain self-centered and still be a Jew. And a combination of Zionism and Buberism would cancel out the last of the oppositions, that between tribe and self, and bring Jewish bliss on earth.

In his writings on Jewish subjects over the next twenty-five years, from *Israel* (1925) to *The American Jew* (1950), Lewisohn tried to achieve precisely this combination.[90] His writings became increasingly intense in their appeal, shrill in tone and tortured in their effort to reject assimilation and to advocate the development of an authentic self; for Jews, Lewisohn claimed, this would be identical with a Jewish national self. Taken together, these writings amount to a Romantic theory of Jewishness, which Norton Mezvinsky has analyzed in some detail. Here he summarizes its development:

Martin Buber and Ludwig Lewisohn, Brandeis University, 1953.
Photograph by Ralph Norman. Courtesy Harry Zohn.

In 1950 Lewisohn published *The American Jew: Character and Destiny*. With this work the course of philosophical development was completed, as Divine will and supernatural intervention became the sole reasons for the uniqueness of the Jewish people. The Jews were a distinct nationality, argued Lewisohn, because God ordained them such in the Bible. In *Israel* the Bible was taken as a secular expression of Jewish nationality. In *Mid-Channel* he had viewed the Bible as an expression of universal religious truths but kept this apart from his theory of Jewish nationality. Finally, in *The American Jew: Character and Destiny* he evolved directly from the Bible a unified religious and nationalistic concept of the Jewish people.[91]

Lewisohn's turn to religion in general—which occurred at some point between the end of *The Island Within* (1928) and the writing of *Mid-Channel* (1929)—and to ḥasidism in particular was predictable, because this romantic version of Judaism not only de-emphasized the particularities of history, about which Lewisohn never cared very much,[92] but also dissolved all troubling dichotomies, such as the distinctions between tribal and individual self, physical and spiritual world. Furthermore, romantic Judaism lent itself to an elaboration into a grand vision of a unified *Israel*. This was the destiny Lewisohn had in mind for American Jew. Whether women too were to be included in this destiny is not entirely clear, because Lewisohn always uses the male pronoun when he writes about the American Jew. He was to be liberated from the bondage of American freedom into the freedom of Jewish bondage. So far, the existence of the American Jew had been inauthentic. He was "a slave in body and in soul, imprisoned in the cold and empty hell of a self-created *Galuth*." But he could be redeemed by "reidentification . . . with his Jewishness at the deepest level of consciousness." At this moment, he will not only be able "to *see* with an utter certainty of vision, irrespective of opinion or content, that ear-locked Hasidim on Avenue A and 3rd Street, dancing with holy joy on *Simchat Torah*, are free men," but he will also "*spontaneously desire to practice the Mitzvoth. He will seek to re-incarnate the Torah by what it is.*"[93] This is Lewisohn at his highest pitch: The basis on which ḥarut can be read as ḥerut is the ecstasy of the self, the moment of apotheosis in which the enslaved soul of the American Jew becomes *Jew*.

Lewisohn envisioned a similar apotheosis (a term in complete contradiction to Jewish thinking but quite apposite in this context) for the Jewish nation as a whole. It is depicted, for instance, in a sentence that moves in breathless crescendo from Zionism to Divine Will. "For Zionism is that central aspect of the Jewish faith, based on the witness of all history, that the Jewish people, the suffering servant of mankind described by the prophet, must survive as a religio-ethnic entity elected to exemplary form and sanctification as the immanent trend of the historic process determined by the Divine Will."[94]

It is not necessary to present here Lewisohn's intellectual development leading up to his apotheosis in 1950. After the introduction of the religious element, which surfaced first in his vilification of Pauline Christianity in the last part of *Mid-Channel*, Lewisohn's argumentation remained structurally the same. He no longer strayed from his destined path as an American Jew, but headed directly toward his haven. In fact, *Haven* was the title of the third volume of his autobiography, published in 1940.

Lewisohn's turning point can be precisely located in his fiction. His best novel, *The Island Within* (1928), which portrays the progress of a large Jewish family from eighteenth-century Eastern Europe observance to twentieth-century American assimilation, ends with the protagonist's cautious return to the Jewish fold.

In his perceptive review of the novel for the *Menorah Journal*, Irwin Edman, a professor of philosophy at Columbia University, thought two things wrong with the protagonist's solution to his personal problems. First of all, "Judaism sentimentally returned to, as Arthur sentimentally returns to it at the end of the book . . . is not an escape from the perplexities of the modern world." And second, "neither Mr. Lewisohn nor anyone else has made it clear what the Judaism is to which one is to flee. . . . What is that Judaism to be—a neo-mystical piety, a social clannishness, a sophisticated revival of a naïve Jewish culture?" Edman politely called Lewisohn "a romantic Jew as many unbelieving Catholics, like Joyce, are romantic Catholics,"[95] perhaps because he refused to believe that a rebellious "modern" like Lewisohn could become seriously intrigued with romantic religion and with hasidism at that. But with the writing of *Israel* in 1925, Lewisohn had begun to devise ways in which to blend his Christian and romantic ideology of self-realization with a culture to which he belonged by descent. Step by step, Lewisohn sought to reclaim his lost Jewish heritage. But he did not see that in the process of reclamation he transformed what he found, according to the needs of a self that was structured on an ideological pattern antithetical to that of the culture he was reclaiming. Instead of connecting him to his people, Lewisohn's idiosyncratic romantic Judaism exiled him to an island within.

The End

Lewisohn returned from Europe to America in May 1934.[96] He, his companion Thelma, and their son James (born in Paris in 1933) arrived in Montreal and immediately moved to Burlington, Vermont, into the home of Thelma's mother. From there, Lewisohn went on the lecture circuit but had to avoid New York State because of an impending lawsuit filed against him by his wife. In 1935, Thelma's mother died and Thelma inherited the house. It was sold and the money became the basis of the financial settlement Lewisohn made with Mary Arnold Crocker who finally, in 1937, granted him a divorce. In September 1937, Lewisohn and Thelma Spear moved to New Rochelle, New York, where Lewisohn began to work for a Zionist organization. He began to write for *The New Palestine* in 1940 and served as the paper's editor from 1943 to 1948. Between January 1944 and August 1945, Lewisohn wrote at least 106 unsigned editorials and eighteen book reviews for *The New Palestine*. One of his biographers claims that "during the years as editor of *The New Palestine*, his writing was unambiguously for the collective, even though privately the old war over self was still waging."[97]

In late 1938, he began to write his worst novel, *Forever Wilt Thou Love*, which was published early in 1939. It was reviewed in the *New Palestine* in April 1939. It was not "written after the end of Lewisohn's alliance with Thelma Spear" but its "unusual bitterness"[98] was definitely supposed to be "a warning to her" (Saiger). Thelma liked the novel and in an undated letter to a friend praised it as "noble *and* sexy."[99] In August 1939, Lewisohn and Thelma Spear decided to part; they moved into separate apartments on October 1, 1939. A long and terrible custody battle followed, which was covered by the sensationalist press, such as New York's *Daily News*. Thelma kidnapped her son on December 8, 1939. But Lewisohn, who early in 1940 had married Edna Manley, was awarded custody on March 4, 1940. On April 23, 1941, the decision was reversed and custody awarded to Thelma Spear. Lewisohn stopped paying child support and had to move away from New York City. He lived in Arizona, New Mexico, and Rochester, New York, where the Manley family home was. Thelma seemed to have neglected and abused her son, which encouraged Lewisohn to contest the court decision and he regained custody in June 1944.[100] Meanwhile he had "divorced" Edna Manley and "married" Louise Wolk in 1944, events which formed the basis for his regaining custody. The facts seem to be that the divorce from Manley did not go through until 1947. He married Wolk in February 1948. She was the beautiful woman with whom Lewisohn arrived at Brandeis University, where he had been appointed a professor of comparative literature in 1948. He was appointed university librarian in 1955, and he died of a heart attack in Miami, Florida, the same year.

Brandeis University, where Lewisohn ended his days as a spiritual Zionist, was an odd place during the first two years of its existence. Founded five months after the state of Israel—in October 1948—and headed by the shrewd and energetic Abram Sachar and a board of eight Jewish trustees, of whom only three had college degrees but all of whom believed in the American Jewish dream of success through education, Brandeis had probably the nation's most bizarre faculty. It was a collection of intellectual outcasts and oddballs, "radicals, semiradicals, pseudoradicals, and ex-radicals."[101] They were German and Austrian refugee academics, Russian emigrés, and literary mavericks, who had found a haven in this camp down the road from classy Harvard. The university bristled with pioneer spirit. Irving Howe describes Brandeis in those early days.

[It was] a remarkable place mixing college, political forum, and kibbutz, where the abundant energies of Jewish intellectuals—some of them free-lancers from New York and others refugees from Germany —found bread, speech, and audiences. Innocently, shrewdly, Brandeis didn't hesitate to hire bright (sometimes merely eccentric) people who lacked Ph.D.s or had European credentials little honored in the United States. Frank Manuel taught history, Philip Rieff and Lewis Coser sociology, Abraham Maslow psychology, Herbert Marcuse his version of Marxism. Gifted composers like Arthur Berger and Irving Fine headed the music department. The atmosphere was intense, unstarched, impudent.[102]

In 1953, Irving Howe went to Waltham, Massachusetts, for a job interview at Brandeis and encountered a "miscellaneous faculty committee."

Around the table sat Simon Rawidowicz, a historian of Jewish thought; Ludwig Lewisohn . . . Joseph Cheskis, a professor of French with a thick Yiddish accent; and several scientists. Just as I had no conventional credentials, so they had no conventional questions. The session lagged, it began to look bad, until I mentioned casually that I was working with the Yiddish poet Eliezer Greenberg on an anthology of Yiddish stories in English translation. Faces broke into smiles. Rawidowicz began "correcting" my overestimation of Peretz; everyone started talking Yiddish. I relaxed happily, sure I was going to get the job.[103]

Howe's anecdote is typical of something Arthur Schnitzler sarcastically called the "ä soi" ("oh, I see") effect—an instantaneous relaxation and opening of the upper shirt button, so to speak, as soon as the visitor has been identified as one of *us*. It is a touching testimony of the habitualness of fear of *them*. This fear does not vanish entirely but is greatly reduced when the stranger turns out to be able to speak the family language. What made Brandeis "home" for Lewisohn was less the heymishkayt of Yiddish than the reduction of the element of other, which he had permitted to dominate his life as the element against which he had to define himself. At Brandeis he could let go, and consequently he became extremely self-absorbed. This is best illustrated by an anecdote told by Professor Barbara Herrnstein Smith, who was one of those Brandeis students whose accomplished papers, Irving Howe confessed, made "a kind of terror pass through me."[105] In 1955, a few months before Lewisohn's death, she was the first student to receive a master's degree in English literature from Brandeis University.

The way the exam went, as many exams of this kind do, is that you have a list of texts that you have to know, forty or fifty titles, or whatever it was. All of my professors were in this room. My major teacher at that time was J. V. Cunningham. Irving Howe by then was a friend as well as a teacher. I was brought in, and I expected to be asked questions about texts on the list. I was a very good student, had studied hard and was confident. Out of respect for his seniority, the chairman said: "We'll begin the questioning with Dr. Lewisohn." So Lewisohn began. He said: "Well, tell me who wrote this. . . ," and he quoted some lines that I did not recognize. I said: "I am sorry, Dr. Lewisohn, but I don't know that." "Well, what about this . . . ," and he quoted some more lines. And it went that way for about ten minutes, with him reciting lines and my saying over and over again, "I am sorry, I can't identify that." Then he stopped, and J. V. Cunningham asked me some historical questions, which I answered, and then Irving Howe asked some interpretative questions, and everything was fine. At the end the chairman came to where I was waiting and said, "You have just passed the exam, with distinction." I said: "Well, I am glad to hear it. But how can it be with distinction since, for the whole first ten minutes, I didn't recognize anything?" Then he said: "We didn't know how to let you know, but everything Lewisohn was giving you was garbled, mostly versions of his own poetry, mixed with Byron, mixed with whatever."[106]

Barbara Herrnstein Smith's rather harsh report of her teacher as irresponsibly self-absorbed is not corroborated by others who also knew Lewisohn during his last years. But while their picture of a mellow old man might be colored by the pieties of the imperative *de mortuis nil nisi bonum*, the judgment of his student might have been exacerbated by a fundamental incompatibility of temperaments. It is, indeed, difficult to imagine two personalities more at odds with each other than the self-indulgent, narcissistic Lewisohn and his tough-minded, anti-sentimental student. She opposed her teacher's chauvinism (by passive resistance rather than open confrontation) on the basis of the same rationalism that fifteen years earlier had informed Morris Cohen's attack on Lewisohn's "tribalism."

But there is more to Barbara Herrnstein Smith's rejection of Lewisohn than the traditional opposition of the rationalist to the pietist. By 1955, a generation of future Jewish academics began to leave the colleges feeling comfortable with being Jewish in America. These students could take for granted a degree of integration into and acceptance by America's Gentile society that would have struck the immigrant academics as simply miraculous. This new generation, born in the late 1920s and the first half of the 1930s, considered Lewisohn's defense technique of offensive defiance, euphemistically called "self-realization," absurd and reflective of a faulty notion of the self. The notions of the young were more genteel. A cultural chasm had opened between the immigrant academics born around 1880 and their grandchildren born around 1930. They were separated by the term *American*, which had become part of the latters' definition of self. Over the din of the word *American* neither Wolfson and Glazer at Harvard nor Lewisohn and Herrnstein Smith at Brandeis could understand each other.

When the immigrant academics thus far presented came to America between 1887 and 1903, they came as Jews without a qualifier (except perhaps for Lewisohn, who considered himself a *German* Jew). Six decades later an *American Jewish* culture had come into existence, which had little to do with the American culture that the immigrant academics found here upon their arrival and even less to do with the Jewish culture they had brought with them. As in many multi-ingredient concoctions, the individual elements lost their specific flavor. Combined, they formed a new, yet unnamed thing. In a notorious quip, Harold Bloom denigrates this new creation. "'American Jewish Culture,' considered merely as a phrase, is as problematic, say, as 'Freudian Literary Criticism,' which I recall once comparing to the Holy Roman Empire: not holy, not Roman, not an empire; not Freudian, not literary, not criticism. Much that is herded together under the rubric of American Jewish Culture is not American, not Jewish, not culture."[107] But elsewhere Bloom compares American Jewish culture to that of the Jewry of Hellenistic Alexandria; an Israeli scholar has made the same comparison.[108] It suggests the reconciliation of opposites separating Jewish and Gentile culture, which is (of course) undertaken by the smaller group. Hellenistic Jewry found itself between idolatry and monotheism, between aestheticism and the Second Commandment, the cult of seeing and the culture of hearing,[109] whereas American Jewry had to devise ways of reconciling community-centeredness with individualism, the god of history with the oversoul, and text-centeredness and urbanism with an admiration of nature.[110]

The reconciliation of these opposites was not easily achieved. By all appearances, the passage from the Eastern European shtetl into the American metropolis was accomplished within two (or at most, three) generations. Yet despite the claim of the former Talmud student David Levinsky in Abraham Cahan's famous novel that "the very clothes I wore and the very food I ate had a fatal effect on my religious habit," and that "a whole book could be written on the influence of a starched collar and necktie on a man who was brought up as I was,"[111] it took more than lunching on BLT sandwiches and milkshakes to transform those deep-rooted intellectual structures (which I call "intellectual grammar") developed over centuries of segregated living and concentrated study.

Even though the children and grandchildren of immigrant rabbis or ordinary observant workmen would no longer keep the sabbath or accept the dietary laws, their cultural interests and mode of perception would remain shaped to some extent by their ancestors' intellectual grammar. This is true for the generation of Jewish intellectuals intervening between the generation of immigrant intellectuals—the Wolfsons, Cohens, and Kallens—born around 1880, and that of their grandchildren—the Fishes, Blooms, and Alters—born around 1930, who today hold professorships in all departments of the most prestigious universities.

That intervening generation—the Trillings, Hooks, and Schapiros —born around 1905, which became the first generation of the so-called New York Intellectuals, seemed ages removed from their fathers' study houses. Yet their mode of thought, the thrust of their intellectuality linked them more often than not to the mitnagdic tradition of their forebears. Theirs was a generation of transition in which certain intellectual and cultural features of their fathers' world were still preserved, and yet they concluded their parents' conquest of urban America. This includes the American academy and the last bastion of Anglo-Saxon culture: the Ivy League English departments. Lionel Trilling, son of an immigrant of roughly Horace Kallen's age, became Columbia University's first Jewish professor of English literature. His success brings the story of the Jewish folly of embarking on academic careers in the humanities against the double odds of anti-Semitism and economic hardships to a happy end.

5   A Professor of Literature

LIONEL TRILLING (1905–1975):
REPRESENTATIVE MAN

To call Lionel Mordecai Trilling, whose life and work have come to represent the entry of Jews into the world of Ivy League English departments, a man of two minds is a commonplace in literary criticism. It is less trite to note that criticism itself is subtly but surely of two minds about the man. Depending on the critic's relation to American culture, Trilling is either seen as pioneer (Morris Dickstein), representative man (Mark Krupnick), "dead end" (Cornel West), or cultural apocalypse: "the Jew as last man of letters" (Daniel O'Hara). The variations in the critical assessment of the young lion whose storming of Morningside Heights one hundred and fifty years after the fall of the Bastille was his only revolutionary act before he settled like the ancient Mordecai into life at the Gentile court, depend on whether the critic's ancestors were stormers or defenders. For the former he signals a beginning, for the latter an end. Trilling's representations in criticism, his transformation into a Christ figure by Christians, a representative man by Americans, and anything from assimilationist to *ilui* (learned luminary) by Jews would deserve a study of its own.

Here it will suffice to point out that for Jewish students, who became part of the next generation of critics, Trilling was an important social and intellectual role model. For Jews such as Morris Dickstein, for instance, who grew up in an Orthodox Eastern European family, Trilling's "constitutional ambivalence is related to his ordeal of being Jewish in a Gentile world, of teaching English literature in a *gentile* university."[1] For them Trilling was a pathfinder on terra incognita and his criticism provided charts for their movement from ḥarut—be that Dickstein's Jewish or the critic Eugene Goodheart's Stalinist orthodoxy[2]—to ḥerut. Wrote Goodheart, "Trilling represented for many Jewish students at Columbia in the forties and fifties . . . the possibility of entering into a world of letters and cultivation not to be found in the boroughs of New York where we grew up."[3] For them he was a pioneer.

That he was Jewish helped these students overcome the emotional ambivalence that was building up during "one of the longest journeys in the world," that is, the journey "from certain neighborhoods in Brooklyn to certain parts of Manhattan."[4] The uneasiness that tempered their exhilaration at the discovery of the "free" world of literature was caused, as the writer Phillip Lopate put it, by "the feeling I got at Columbia . . . that the world I had come from was being dismissed."[5] Columbia was troubling because it clothed itself somewhat self-consciously in the garb of a foreign world. Like its counterpart at Yale, the Columbia English Department cultivated a certain "Oxbridge" style of restraint and sophistication which was alien to the youths growing up in the close-knit, impudent intimacy and liberating chaos of Jewish immigrant households. "The Anglicized reserve between faculty and students, the teas, and the subtle, bewildering code of manners . . . could be quite painful to a scholarship student like [Phillip Lopate] from the Jewish and Puerto Rican slums of Williamsburg, Brooklyn." Therefore, the discovery of a Jew in the department, and one of eminence and distinction to boot, was encouragement, consolation, and the source of a certain "malicious satisfaction." Encouragement because Trilling's prestige proved that one could "make it" and become a professional of high culture even as a Jew; consolation because he hadn't been struck dead yet even though he certainly wasn't donning his tefillin; and malicious satisfaction (1) because Trilling's presence made Morningside Heights captured territory for Jews and (2) because knowledge of his Jewishness undermined his authority. Trilling was a "cousin." He was family; never mind his WASPish appearance. But more important, for Jews like Goodheart, Dickstein, and Lopate, Trilling signified the possibility of ḥerut without bad conscience.

For Jews such as Mark Krupnick, with weaker ties to their descent culture and fewer scruples about living in America, Trilling "emphasize[d] the self's freedom to make anything of itself regardless of the past." They saw an "American Trilling, in the line of Emerson,"[6] who created himself

Lionel Trilling, 1964.
Courtesy Columbia University.

as well as his culture and in such cultural newness and innocence became their representative man. In Krupnick's case, moreover, the earlier generation's experience of Trilling as cicerone on the way from community- to individual-oriented thinking was repeated. The slightly older Eugene Goodheart had relinquished his Stalinism under Trilling's tutelage at Columbia in the early fifties.[7] Krupnick, after turning away from the "Romantic socialism" of the sixties, that is, from the "libertarian socialist dream of a community of redeemed selves in the real world,"[8] and from his inspired attacks on Trilling in the seventies, discovered in the late eighties Trilling as a critic who "wants to reawaken the liberal intellectuals to the idea of the individual's free will and consequent personal responsibility."[9]

The present discussion of Lionel Trilling will neither trace the familiar profile of an assimilating American Jew nor delineate Trilling's spiritual biography while analyzing his criticism.[10] Instead, it will approach Trilling from the perspective of his descent culture. This is not to "Judaize" Trilling. He would have resented that, as he resented any labeling. For him, a writer was a writer.[11] The triumph of enlightened America was precisely that this statement had become possible for Jews.[12] Yet to see Trilling as a descendant of Europe's rationalist Jewish culture and hence in the tradition of the academics studied here helps to explain some of his odd preferences: his limited interest in poetry, his refusal "to define authentic moral experience in terms of a transcendent religious perspective," his refusal "to explore deeply the demonic side of the psyche,"[13] his championship of William Dean Howells and George Orwell against the intellectual fashion of the day. These and other positions are hardly surprising in a man of mitnagdic sensibility.

Trilling combines traces of a variety of his Jewish antecedents in the academy. With Joel Spingarn he shared an inclination—though it was a brief one for Trilling—to flirt with the idea of autonomous art. With Morris Cohen he shared a fascination with the principle of polarity, a notebook full of self-doubt, a tendency to oscillate between self-loathing and self-affirmation, and the conviction that the irrational should be subject to reason. A first cousin to this conviction was Trilling's preoccupation with the form of the novel and with the "great practical sanity" of the English novel in particular, which "gives the impression of absorbing all extremes, all maladjustments and contradictions into a normative view of life."[14] The novel, with its social concerns, was the vessel that contained (and thus domesticated) the destructive energy of the creative power originating in the dark recesses of the self.

Trilling shared with Lewisohn a need to explore the self. But while in Lewisohn's world this need was a legitimate part of one's intellectual pursuit, such indulgence went against the grain of Trilling's culture. Both Lewisohn and Trilling, however, employed Freud for cultural criticism rather than (auto)psychoanalysis; both wrote "autobiographical" fiction and criticism; that is, each turned self-preoccupation into representative critical writing transforming his complete oeuvre into a confession or spiritual autobiography;[15] and each, after much investigation, finally grounded the self in "biological fact." It was their last means to prevent the disintegration of the (Jewish) self under the pressures of modernity.

Such similarities are less interesting, however, than the differences. Lewisohn had a truly romantic temperament; he was self-centered and given to indulgence in extremes, whereas Trilling, peering into the abyss of romantic creativity, was held fast by a rationalist tether. Yet he was curious about this abyss. Despite his "strongly antiutopian" sensibility, "he felt an undeniable attraction to the extreme, the romantic, and the apocalyptic."[16] But he did not abandon himself to it. Unlike Lewisohn, Trilling desired "to avoid the extremes of divine presumption and demonic deflation inherent in any experience of the sublime." Instead, he tried to anchor the self in the ordinary, and to locate himself on the "middle ground of commonplace."[17] For such a mind, the subversive, shocking, extraordinary nature of art could be a problem. As his student Morris Dickstein observed, Trilling belonged entirely "to the party of gentility, the camp of the superego. But an especially strong personal pressure drives him toward criticism — and to an association of art with criminality and moral adventure."[18] On this issue mitnagdim as different as Lionel Trilling and Cynthia Ozick join the camp of the Puritans Cotton Mather and Nathaniel Hawthorne.

Trilling's writing became "representative" (in the sense that writing in the tradition from Augustine to Emerson is "representative") when "he turned self-questioning from a personal habit into a principle of criticism."[19] However, as in the cases of Hawthorne and Ozick, any personal introspection was banned from the works written for the public and confined to notebooks. Rationality and moral sensibility demanded such courtesy toward the public. As Hawthorne put it succinctly, "we must not always talk in the market-place of what happens to us in the forest."[20] Trilling's enormous control over himself transformed his constant introspection into "a source of an impersonal strength."[21]

Trilling's achievement was to accomplish the transition from his father's world to Morningside Heights without paying the price of complete intellectual assimilation. He retained his father's intellectual grammar, but expressed himself in the vocabulary of his consent culture. Trilling introduced the viewpoint of the Jewish rationalist into American literary criticism. Thus he managed to remain a Jew *and* to become one of the most celebrated figures in the American academy in his day.

Sociologically, Trilling's ascent in the academy was assisted by a new development in American culture at large. After his spectacular appointment at Columbia University in 1939, Trilling rose to fame in the forties, at a time when the world of the New York Intellectuals was falling apart and when Jews were beginning to move into the center of contemporary American fiction, as both authors and subjects. Here they came to be regarded as *the* representatives of the alienated sensibility in mass-culture America. Trilling's criticism was exactly in tune with the decade. With its "ubiquitous presumption of the editorial 'we,'" as one of his critics remarked, it "was always part homily and part confession, a research into the literature of the self and a meditation on the irreconcilable conflicts between, and within, the individual and society."[22] But one suspects that the celebrated Trilling not only expressed what many felt, but satisfied a general need among American intellectuals to *see* a post-Shoah Jew as representative of the fate of the American individual succumbing to the forces of progress and technology in the wealthy fifties.

OBSERVANCE OF THE ORDINARY

Lionel Trilling was born in New York on the Fourth of July, 1905, to Jewish parents of Eastern European origin. He was born in safety and comfort a year before a violent pogrom killed seventy Jews and injured ninety in his father's native city. Bialystok, then under Russian administration, was not a shtetl but a sizable town with a thriving, mostly Jewish-owned textile industry and a double intellectual elite.[23] Families such as Leo Wiener's cherished the spirit of the Haskalah and *Preussische Kultur* introduced during the brief time that Bialystok belonged to Prussia (1795–1807), whereas the Trillings belonged to the traditionally orthodox Bialystok Jewry.

As was the case with Lewisohn's father, the stigma of failure was attached to David Trilling's arrival in America. Destined for the rabbinate like so many Jewish boys who showed a certain nimbleness of mind, David protested in his own way: he broke down during the bar mitzvah ceremony. "In consequence, a thirteen-year-old had been shipped off to America, put out of sight."[24] There, along with thousands of others, he entered the garment business. Discontent with being a mere workman, he saved money to become a manufacturer of fancy fur coats. The coats sold well and David Trilling prospered as long as the market was stable. His manners and appearance were in keeping with his merchandise. By casual acquaintances he was referred to as "the perfect gentleman." But his daughter-in-law, Diana Trilling (née Rubin), a Radcliffe graduate, also knew his private side: "his family temper was violent. He was also an overbearing hypochondriac." Whether David Trilling was also given to fits of melancholy as was Jacques Lewisohn is not known. He certainly shared Lewisohn's inaptitude at business. His last and finally ruinous decision was to make raccoon coats for drivers of open cars, just when the cars were beginning to disappear.[25]

The stock market crash and the ensuing Depression finished the business. David Trilling and his family depended now on Lionel who, newly married in 1929, was making a meager salary—first at Hunter College, teaching evening and extension sessions and after 1932 as an instructor at Columbia. It is extraordinary how little the strenuous social circumstances described by Diana Trilling influenced Trilling's mind and literary thinking. They seem to manifest themselves primarily in the fact that it took him a decade to complete his dissertation and possibly in his eventual preference of an academic career over that of a fiction writer, a choice which he seems to have regretted slightly for the rest of his life.[26]

His mother knew what was good for her son. She "had early decided that Lionel was to have an Oxford Ph.D."[27] When she announced this ambitious goal to her son, he was four or five years old, and Oxford might very well have been on Mars as far as he was concerned. But Fanny Cohen knew what she was talking about. To her, just as to the choicest minds, Oxford "represented the highest idea of a university."[28] Her family had emigrated from Russia to England and settled comfortably into London's Jewish middle class. For Fanny Cohen, born and educated in the city's East End, the neighborhood of Israel Zangwill and the overpowering presence of Queen Victoria, whom she called her "little English mother,"[29] were as little mutually exclusive as were her passion for Victorian literature and the Yiddish theater. As a girl, Fanny wanted to become an actress. It is reasonable to assume that this plan met with opposition not only because of her parents' Orthodoxy, but also because a nice middle-class girl who studied the piano and read Tennyson and Browning simply did not become actress. When Fanny was sixteen the family decided to move to New York. Although Fanny was "literary to her fingertips"[30] she was not sent to college, possibly because the family could not afford it. For the rest of her life she would regret not having had the advantage of her younger sisters' elite Hunter College education. But she stubbornly cultivated her literary interests and took pride in her English accent. If her son, who played Lord Lionel to his sister's Lady Harriet, possessed for some time a "programmatic prejudice" (AL 227) in favor of the Victorian novel and on occasion sported a slight English accent it might very well be taken as a tribute to the splendid aspirations of his mother.[37] Trilling's British manners were the object of both admiration and contempt, but they were hardly a late development.[32] In his "Notebooks," Trilling remembers being taken by an uncle to a vaudeville theater in Rockaway Park in about 1912 to see Belle Baker: "I disliked her and thought her vulgar—the surprise at this at home and the great pleasure—the surprise was insincere, the pleasure sincere: I was innately 'refined'! . . . Remembering myself then, at 7, 8, 9?, I have the impression of someone enormously mature, much more mature than my uncle T., toward whom I must have felt some of my family's condescension —but I have the reminiscent sensation that I looked on this scene with a remote and censorious eye, the sense that there were better things!" (*NI* 504).

The Trillings' move from Far Rockaway to Manhattan's West 108th Street made it possible for Lionel to receive his bar mitzvah training at the Jewish Theological Seminary, a few blocks from Columbia University. He was instructed by Max Kadushin (born in 1895) who in turn was a student of Mordecai Kaplan, the founder of Reconstructionism. Kaplan's theory of Judaism as a civilization and his program for a Jewish life was attractive to Jewish intellectuals with stronger social and cultural than metaphysical ties to Judaism. Kadushin, however, although he attended services with his tutee at Kaplan's then-nascent Society for the Advancement of Judaism, remained within the traditional Conservative fold of the Jewish Theological Seminary.[33]

Despite Kadushin's tendency to "disappoint," the time spent with him seems not to have been entirely disagreeable, because thirty-eight years later Trilling remembers him quite affectionately in a footnote in his 1955 essay "Wordsworth and the Rabbis," as "one of the long-suffering men who tried to teach me Hebrew, with what success I have indicated; yet he did teach me—it was no small thing for a boy of twelve to be in relation with a serious scholar."[34] The footnote reenacts the student-pupil relationship of four decades earlier as Trilling acknowledges Kadushin's superb recent book, *The Rabbinic Mind* (1951), and his own simple-mindedness in Jewish matters in a wonderfully light sentence: "Dr. Kadushin has been kind enough to tell me that what I have said about the Rabbis is not wrong." But while Trilling gracefully admits his continuing ignorance of the intricacies of the Jewish intellectual tradition, he uses the occasion to display what he has done with his life instead of studying Talmud. As if to say, 'see, my gift did not lie fallow,' Trilling presents a well-informed, complex, nuanced interpretation of Wordsworth's poetry side by side with a simple, child-like reading of the most popular talmudic tractate, *Pirke Avot*. And as if to justify his worldly pursuit he formulates a hypothesis which he is ill-equipped to prove, "that the quality in Wordsworth that now makes him unacceptable [to the modern world] is a Judaic quality."[35] Hence, in bringing an "unacceptable" (Judaic) Wordsworth to the attention of the modern world, Trilling fulfills his obligation as bar mitzvah to stand up for his tradition in his own style. What amazes about this essay, "Wordsworth and the Rabbis," are not the readings, but the simple fact that Trilling should have thought of it *and* put it on paper.

Trilling's actual bar mitzvah took place at the Jewish Theological Seminary in 1918. Urged by his father, Trilling continued to lay tefillin while in high school and to study Hebrew for the sake of Jewish culture.[36] His mother kept a kosher kitchen and lit the shabbat candles on Friday nights.

A new phase in Trilling's life began when he graduated from DeWitt Clinton High School in 1921 and enrolled as a matter of course in Columbia College. The university was then about to overcome the crisis brought on by the loyalty craze of the World War I years. A few professors had been fired and the remaining faculty had been silenced into obedience by the firm government of the board of trustees and the president. Nicholas Murray Butler, who ruled Columbia between 1902 and 1945, "was one of the few university presidents who formally withdrew the privilege of academic freedom for the entire duration of the war."[37] Like the nation, the university was to stand "by the President declaring that it would volunteer as one man for the protection and defense of civil-liberty and self-government . . . ."[38] Patriotic fervor prevented Butler from perceiving the blatant contradiction between threat and goal: "This is the University's last and only warning to any among us, if there be, who are not with whole heart and mind and strength committed to fight with us to make the world safe for democracy."[39]

Hardly had the Teutonic foe been defeated and a semblance of trust between administration and faculty restored, when a new and even more immediate danger was spotted by the nation and the academic community: the host of immigrants, particularly of Eastern European Jewish immigrants. The specter of anti-Semitism rose and shone brightly. In January 1921, however, the year that would bring the first quota regulation restricting immigration from Eastern Europe, Butler was "one of the 119 signatories along with Presidents Woodrow Wilson, William Howard Taft, and Theodore Roosevelt of the . . . 'Christian Protest' against anti-Semitism." And in 1924, the year of the second quota regulation, when membership in the Ku Klux Klan exceeded four million, Butler complied graciously with the request for a Rosh Hashanah message on the issue of Christians and Jews by sending a statement to the Pittsburgh *Jewish Chronicle*. A bit lamely, he called the Klan "as un-American as hereditary monarchy" and dubbed its members "enemies of America, not its defenders."[40]

Yet despite Butler's public position against anti-Semitism and his "amicable social relations . . . with the Lewisohns, Klingensteins, Buttenwiesers, and Schiffs, who made large contributions to the university,"[41] and despite his warm friendship with the wealthy James Speyer and the influential Benjamin Cardozo, it was during Butler's presidency and certainly with his knowledge that Columbia developed the intricate selective admissions system already mentioned. The change in Columbia's admissions policies began in the tumultuous post–World War I climate. It was the continuation of the "loyalty craze" by other means.

Butler envisioned Columbia's mission as the education of the next generation of America's leaders; hence, the school was obligated to select from its applicant pool the most "desirable" types. Instead of implementing a straightforward quota system that would limit the enrollment of New York City Jews and make Columbia (again) the domain of the "good gentile out-of-state student,"[42] the administration introduced an intelligence test, the Thorndike Test for Mental Alertness. It was supposed to measure the "intelligence" and "quality of mind" of each applicant. There is nothing wrong with the desire to select the most intelligent applicants, but at that time the concept of intelligence was linked to theories of race and it was thought that the Nordic race (inhabiting northern and western Europe) was superior in intelligence to the Mediterranean and Alpine races, that is, to the inhabitants of southern and eastern Europe.[43]

A crash course with Columbia's leading anthropologist, Franz Boas, would have taught the administrators the absurdity of their reasoning. And had they persisted in their belief in the racial distribution of intelligence, even rudimentary knowledge of anthropology would have deflated their hope in obtaining an all-Gentile cream of the crop in an intelligence test, because the Jewish people boasted a good number of Nordic types in addition to its Alpines and Mediterraneans.[44] Yet there can be no doubt that the Thorndike test was introduced to reduce the Jewish enrollment.

Herbert Hawkes—who in 1918 succeeded Frederick Keppel as Dean of Columbia College—wrote in 1922, three years after Butler's announcement that "henceforth all applicants to Columbia College would be required to take either the Thorndike Test or the comprehensive entrance examinations devised by Harvard,"[45] about the pool of applicants that contained Lionel Trilling and Langston Hughes.

> What we have been trying to do is to eliminate the low grade boy. We had 1200 applications for admission last fall and could accommodate only 550. This meant that somebody had to lose out. We have not eliminated boys because they were Jews and do not propose to do so. We have honestly attempted to eliminate the lowest grade of applicant

and it turns out that a good many of the low grade men are New York City Jews. It is a fact that boys of foreign parentage who have no background in many cases attempt to educate themselves beyond their intelligence. Their accomplishment is over 100% of their ability on account of their tremendous energy and ambition. I do not believe however that a College would do well to admit too many men of low mentality who have ambition but not brains. At any rate this is the principle on which we are going.[46]

By 1921, then, when Trilling's class of 1925 matriculated, selective admissions was well under way. Although at all times through the twenties at least 40 percent of the freshmen came from immigrant families, Jews now made up only half of their number. Of Trilling's class only 22 percent were Jews.[47] Given the administration's efforts to reduce the number of Jews in the student body, it is difficult to believe the story that Trilling's mother went to see a Columbia officer "when Lionel was not accepted as a freshman in good standing because he had done badly in math."[48] If it is true, then it indeed testifies, as Diana Trilling suggests, to a complete lack of self-consciousness in Fanny Cohen's dealings with the Gentile world.

The year before Trilling enrolled, in September 1920, another future Columbia luminary entered the college. Meyer Schapiro, born in Shavly, Lithuania, in 1904, and not yet sixteen in September 1920, had worked full-time all summer like so many Brownsville teenagers. Schapiro had none of the "Bohemian attitude" and snobbish disregard for "scholastic pieties" Trilling seems to have sported in high school. Since the age of thirteen, Schapiro "had worked as a delivery boy for Western Union, a packer in a warehouse, an assembler in an electrical supply company on the Bowery and a clerk in Macy's adjustments office."[49] And now he was just as culture-hungry as Trilling. The difference between them was that Schapiro, who had won a Pulitzer scholarship and a Regents—both awards for intellectual merit—concealed neither his starvation nor his avidity, whereas Trilling had learned to disguise need as taste and eagerness as preference. A certain annoyed disdain for mere intellectuality and a nonchalant attitude toward dusty scholarship was part of the proper prep school education of the "desirable" Ivy League college student.

Students such as Schapiro (or in previous years Morris Cohen and Harry Wolfson), who in their ignorance of the genteel code of laissez-passer "took obvious pride in their academic success" and committed an even worse faux pas when they talked about it, changed the relaxed atmosphere in the prep schools and colleges when they began to be admitted in sizable numbers.[50] When Bernard Berenson attended Boston Latin School in 1881, and at the end of the academic year headed the class in English, history, geography, and zoology, he could still be considered an eccentric by his classmates; but in the 1920s there were so many Berensons that it was no longer funny. The newcomers obviously enjoyed intellectual challenges as well as the simple amassing of knowledge, and it was evident that they considered the university an educational rather than a social institution. They introduced an unknown spirit of competition and raised the standard of academic performance. This was certainly the case in most private and public high schools. Here, the race was for college scholarships and all the newcomers had was a "golden head."

Grinding was less relentless at the college level but still prevalent enough to alienate the natives. Academic excellence did not endear the Jews to their fellow students. Those raised in the genteel tradition resented the increased academic pressure as well as being outsmarted by a race that succeeded not by innate intelligence but by "underliving and overworking."[51] The half-adjusted Jewish students feared being associated with their starved and pushy coreligionists. Trilling's first story, "Impediments," which we will examine more fully soon, presents an excellent portrait of the Cohen-Wolfson-Schapiro type, from the snob perspective of the Berensons and Trillings. It sketches the loyalty conflict in which a Trilling type, suspended between a Jewish heart and Gentile manners, is caught when cornered by a Jewish fellow student of the other type and asked for friendship.

Meyer Schapiro, by contrast, did not experience a loyalty conflict in college. His full head-over-heels investment in Columbia's intellectual life and his academic pursuits as well as his studies with such enlightened professors as Franz Boas and John Dewey made him insensitive to the social pressures and blind to the academic power structure. Diana Trilling, however, who had gone through a Radcliffe education, supposed that "to all Jews and maybe to most non-Jews, too, certainly in New York, the university had an authority not unlike that of the state: remote, virtually absolute. And this view was fortified at Columbia by the public image of Nicholas Murray Butler who was known to associate with the great financiers and political leaders of the day and to want the Presidency of the United States."[52] But to Schapiro, it was completely irrelevant what Columbia represented and what it was in the world. "It consisted to me of a largely friendly faculty with some inspiring teachers. . . . I enjoyed the great libraries in which I loved to browse, the opportunities of learning in new fields, the gymnasium, the companionship of congenial, likeminded students with strong intellectual interests and readiness for conversation, whether serious or playful. We had little concern with authority, though we were aware of the conservatism of certain administrators and trustees."[53]

What Schapiro means by "readiness for conversation" is portrayed with a tinge of sarcasm in Trilling's story, "Impediments." But that the intensity of his protagonist Hettner is not altogether an invention or projection becomes obvious on perusal of Mark Van Doren's famed essay, "Jewish Students I Have Known." Student C, incidentally, is Meyer Schapiro.

> C's face was passionate, and it was positively beautiful. . . . C glowed—in his thick black curly hair, in his eager white cheeks, and in his darkly rolling eyes. He too knew everything, but what he best knew was the history of art. I never saw any of his own paintings, but I have sat hypnotized while he roamed my office and poured into my ears a bibliography of, say, Byzantine sculpture. I remember a very clear exposition he gave one day of certain modern theories concerning the spread of early cultures through the migration of symbols; he described the symbols, and he made as if to tell me all the places on the earth where they might still be seen. That I could not stay to hear was not because I was unwilling; I had another appointment—to which he conducted me, still talking. I heard now and then that his instructors often resented his knowledge, which they felt was intruded without cause during class discussions. I am sure, however, that his was the best of causes—a passion to know and make known. The passion of a pitcher to spill its contents, the passion of a river to flow and, if the sun shines, to sparkle.[54]

Van Doren's portrait of Trilling presents a type that is the exact opposite of these intense, endlessly talking, fiercely antagonistic Eastern European Jews, "drunk with literature," and paralyzing by their "perfect wit."[55] One is reminded of the early Theodor Herzl and Viennese (Jewish) dandies like the young Arthur Schnitzler.

> F, starting brightly as a freshman, grew more melancholy each year, and more beguiling. Something fastidious in his gentle nature kept him from irony and rendered him incapable of satire, though he was by no means unaware of absurdities; if he had been he would have been informed of them quickly enough by his friend A [Henry Rosenthal]. F spoke diffidently, with a hushed and harmless voice; and though he wrote exceedingly well he found it hard to decide what to write about. I thought I detected in him a particularly sensitive and at the same time healthy set of nerves, and said to myself that this was

equipment indeed for a story-teller or a poet. He became both—but was careful to maintain the amateur standing which his fastidiousness forced him to prefer. He took up this, he took up that, only to let both fall gracefully to his feet, which passed lightly on to other pleasant fields. He is a college instructor now in the Middle West, whence he writes back letters full of praise for a few persons and of blame for a few others. He still is feeling himself out—respectfully, with dignity, and with grace. What he will eventually do, if he does it at all, will be lovely, for it will be the fruit of a pure intelligence slowly ripened in not too fierce a sun.[56]

Although Trilling did not actually become a poet and did not begin publishing fiction until he was about to graduate from college, Van Doren was right to spot a writer's "equipment" in his student. In his "Notes for an Autobiographical Lecture," Trilling confessed to his continuing uneasiness with being called a critic. "It always startles me, takes me a little aback, if only momentarily, and raises an internal grin." His undergraduate ideas about his future career might have been elegantly vague, but the life of a "critic" was definitely not a goal in those days. "The plan that did please my thought was certainly literary, but what it envisaged was the career of a novelist." In his lecture Trilling does not speculate about "why [he] did not pursue, or not beyond a certain point, the career of a writer of prose fiction." But he makes it clear that his "conception of what is interesting and problematical in life, of what reality consists in and what makes for illusion, of what must be held to and what let go, was derived primarily from novelists and not from antecedent critics or from such philosophers as speculate systematically about the nature and function of literature" (AL 227–228).

The notion that Trilling's "criticism took its direction from the novel" (AL 228) is central to the understanding of his work. It explains why he "never limited his criticism by some idea of specialization or expertise but wrote on whatever books or authors engaged his interest."[57] The novel represented the fullness of life. It was the literary genre with the most immediate connection to the chaotic, unformed reality, the genre which was an account of "circumstances" and whose "practitioners" were least distanced from their subjects. Or, in Trilling's words, the novel was "the genre which was traditionally the least devoted to the ideals of *form* and to the consciousness of formal considerations; the genre which . . . was of all genres the most indifferent to manifest shapeliness and decorum, and the most devoted to substance, which it presumes to say is actuality itself;

the genre which is least disposed to say that it is self-sufficient and unconditioned" (*AL* 228).

What Trilling communicates here to the students of Purdue University is not simply the slightly antiquated opinion of a professional critic. His definition of the novel, given in an autobiographical lecture toward the end of his life, contains a secret of acculturation, a fundamental insight into the reading experience of Jewish immigrants. What Trilling says, simply put, is that the novel is not "art." Unlike poetry, the novel is not a hereditary idol revered by people from a certain tradition with a certain education which gives them all the rules that constitute art and which makes them appreciate poetry. The novel represents life; it tells of what one knows; it is literature of and for everybody. You do not have to *know* what makes it art, he says. Be modest. Use the novel as your entry ticket into the world of literary rules.

This is not to say that Jewish (and other) immigrants made it into American culture via the novel. Quite on the contrary, "the public school, free, democratic, open, urgent, [was] pressing on the young a program of reading not so much for its 'literary value,' though this counted too, as for the stamp of Heritage."[58] This led to absurd situations. During the first decade of the twentieth century little boys and girls, hardly out of Eastern Europe, were initiated by "the entirely ordinary daughters of the Irish immigration . . . into the astoundingly distant and incomprehensible premises of [English] poetry."[59] Around 1907, Sir Walter Scott's "The Lady of the Lake" was given as a school assignment to ten-year-old Shiphra Regelson. The little girl had stepped off the boat a year or so earlier.

Not thus, in ancient days of Caledon,
    Was thy voice mute amid the festal crowd,
When lay of hopeless love, or glory won,
    Aroused the fearful, or subdued the proud.
At each according pause was heard aloud
    Thine ardent symphony sublime and high!
Fair dames and crested chiefs attention bowed;
    For still the burden of thy minstrelsy
Was Knighthood's dauntless deed, and Beauty's matchless eye.

The assignment produced the desired effect. Shiphra's daughter, Cynthia Ozick, one of America's distinctive literary voices, describes that step off the boat into America's literary heritage:

She never forgot it. She spoke of it all her life. Mastering it was the triumph of her childhood, and though, like every little girl of her generation, she read *Pollyanna*, and in the last months of her eighty-third year every word of Willa Cather, it was "The Lady of the Lake" that enduringly typified achievement, education, culture. . . . What was accomplished was not merely that my mother "learned" this sort of poetry—i.e., could read and understand it. She learned what it represented . . . in the American social and tribal code. . . . What "The Lady of the Lake" stood for, in the robes and tapestries of its particular English, was the received tradition exemplified by Bryn Mawr in 1905, including [Henry] James's presence there as a commencement speaker.[60]

Two years after his commencement address, while little Shiphra was reciting "The Lady of the Lake," Henry James summarized his fears, after a visit to the Lower East Side, in the language of Sir Walter Scott.

The man of letters, in the United States, has his own difficulties to face and his own current to stem—for dealing with which his liveliest inspiration may be, I think, that they are still very much his own, even in an Americanized world, and that more than elsewhere they press him to intimate communion with his honour. For that honour, the honour that sits astride of the consecrated English tradition, to his mind, quite as old knighthood astride of its caparisoned charger, the dragon most rousing, over the land, the proper spirit of St. George, is just this immensity of the alien presence climbing higher and higher, climbing itself into the very light of publicity.

James concludes bleakly: "The accent of the very ultimate future, in the States, may be destined to become the most beautiful on the globe and the very music of humanity (here the 'ethnic' synthesis shrouds itself thicker than ever); but whatever we shall know it for, certainly, we shall not know it for English—in any sense for which there is an existing literary measure."[61]

Trilling, too, thought that there was "an existing literary measure."[62] But it was not to be imparted by thrusting Romantic poetry at immigrant children. That was an absurdity from which neither culture profited. The novel, with its apparent "artlessness"—and, hence, lack of prestige—but proximity to life, was a much more suitable means of acculturation. It seemed to demand a less exacting transition and could therefore be mastered with greater ease and greater cultural security. Read against the backdrop of what, in the 1920s, still counted as true mastery of Anglo-American culture, Trilling's appreciation of the novel not despite but because of its seeming artlessness made perfect "liberal" sense. It was democratic and "American"; that is, it was anti-elitist and anti-hereditary. In his preference of the novel over other literary genres, Trilling never wavered.

Trilling's later reading of Matthew Arnold exposed him to the view that all socioeconomic classes should contribute to the culture. This might have fortified his appreciation of the artless genre *sine nobilitate*. But the basis for this preference was formed by two complementary reading experiences at Columbia College: Trilling's arrival at Western literature from a different culture; and his participation in John Erskine's General Honors course. The line of development from young Trilling reading and listening at Columbia to the older Trilling lecturing about the novel is a straight one (with a short detour via moral obligation).

In his lecture at Purdue in 1971, Trilling links his view of himself as a teacher and the task he set for himself as a critic to his notion of the novel.

> In remarking that my work took its direction from the novel, I have in mind to point to its tendency to occupy itself not with aesthetic questions, except secondarily, but rather with moral questions, with the questions raised by the experience of quotidian life and by the experience of culture and history. Indeed, so far as the genre of the novel can be thought of as having, in some larger part of its sense of itself, a degree of bias against accepted literary forms and attitudes, to the extent that some part of its impulse might be called anti-literary, I would discover in this position the source, or the encouragement, of a tendency which I am aware of in my critical writing, which is to be a little skeptical of literature, impatient with it, or at least with the claims of literature to be an autonomous, self-justifying activity. (*AL* 228)

This understanding of the novel as the medium not of aesthetic but of moral concerns, its connection with the "experience of the quotidian," its observance of the ordinary, and Trilling's suspicion of the creation of "art for art's sake" are unsurprising views. Trilling had already formulated them most clearly in *The Opposing Self* (1955), his first collection of essays after he had given up writing fiction. Whatever other cultural or political reasons may have induced Trilling to emphasize in *The Opposing Self* "the essentially *conditioned* nature of existence," and to maintain that the relationship between art and the stuff of life "is most powerful and urgent when the work in question is most deeply planted in the soil of circumstantial reality and particularity,"[63] it seems more than reasonable to note first of all that these essays (published between 1950 and 1955) follow on the heel of a change in Trilling's intellectual universe. So far, he had thought of himself as a writer. But after his failure as a novelist—the reception of his only novel, *The Middle of the Journey* (1947), had been very cool[64]—and, more important, after the enthusiastic praise he had received as a critic for *The Liberal Imagination* (1950), Trilling's "career of a writer of prose fiction" (*AL* 227) was terminated. The critic now took over from the (failed) novelist as a moral agent to give an account of the social circumstances and the conditioned nature of existence.

Critics have been annoyed with Trilling's emphasis on the quotidian, the middle class, and the ordinary in *The Opposing Self*; they have interpreted this emphasis as Trilling's turn from liberalism to conservatism, if not political quietism. This rather common reproach has been most elegantly formulated by William Chace. "It would be easy to observe at this point how, in an age well-known for its political conformity and quietism, an age tranquilized by the American president of the time and by the satisfactions of widely shared consumer affluence, Lionel Trilling went about creating a sophisticated means by which he and his fellow intellectuals, all the readers of the little magazines, could surrender to the status quo."[65] Chace suspects that this is too simple an interpretation of Trilling's turn to the quotidian. I would argue that Trilling's appreciation of the ordinary does indeed reach deeper than and far beyond considerations of political opportunism or even the reasonable longing for "decency, seriousness, orderliness, and sense of responsibility that, in Trilling's view, needed to be rehabilitated in the postwar period."[66] Trilling's appreciation of the ordinary touched on the core of his being. On the one hand it was a legacy of the Enlightenment, to which he, like other Jews suspicious of Romanticism, wholeheartedly subscribed.[67] On the other hand, an appreciation of the ordinary, of the particular, and the quotidian was what connected the culture of his father to that of the English novel. It is important to understand the fundamental accord between the father's style and the British novel of manners, the congruence in weltanschauung (consisting in the observance of the ordinary) that took immanence, reality, and the quotidian seriously, because Trilling substituted for the style of his father the novel of manners during his move into the academy. This was a change in lexicon, not in intellectual grammar.

In the academy, the world of the British novel was what was known and mentionable, whereas his father's culture was neither. For Trilling, speaking of the novel became a manner of speaking the values of his descent culture. His notion of the novel could thus be called a cipher for his descent culture and its values. Trilling claimed that his work "took its direction from the novel," that his "conception of what is interesting and problematical in life, of what reality consists in and what makes for illusion . . . was derived primarily from novelists" and that, in brief, his work and weltanschauung spring from the novel. This claim loses some of its oddity when one recognizes in Trilling's notion of the novel the presence of his descent culture. A linkage between the two, with differing degrees of congruence, can be detected on three levels: the sociological, the familial, and the intellectual.

A sociological link between the novel and not so much Jewish but immigrant culture in general, has already been mentioned: the fact that the novel's seeming formlessness, and hence artlessness, provided a more dignified (because less uprooting) way for people unfamiliar with the rules of form and the laws of art to enter the world of English literature and culture. One was not expected to know anything *about* literature, because the novel with "its characteristic shaggy-bagginess" was "devoted to substance, which it presumes to say is actuality itself." And actuality, or life, could be assimilated by everybody. The novel, "indifferent to manifest shapeliness and decorum," was accessible to those in whose lives "shapeliness and decorum" had been (except on certain occasions) the least of worries. "The novel," Trilling would say in his essay "Manners, Morals, and the Novel," "is born in response to snobbery." Snobbery he defined as "pride in status without pride in function." Pride in status would begin to worry those students who, like the narrator in Trilling's "Impediments," had moved away from their descent into the consent culture. "[Snobbery] always asks: 'Do I belong—do I really belong? And does he belong? And if I am observed talking to him, will it make me seem to belong or not to belong?' "[68]

In *The Liberal Imagination*, where these questions appear, snobbery is exposed as the vice "of bourgeois democratic societies." The novel, itself without snobbery and truly democratic, was a stepping-stone in the ascendance to "status," because it familiarized the reader with manners, morals, and the speech of the culture aspired to. All one had to do as a newcomer was to observe. Hence, Trilling, reader of many British novels, found himself in the position "to particularize for [his modern American] students such matters as what it was that servants were needed for and how many were required for one or another kind of domestic establishment."[69] The novel functioned as cicerone into an unfamiliar world. This reading experience had its institutionalized counterpart in John Erskine's General Honors, or Great Books course (as we will see).

One of Erskine's essay titles had become a "kind of slogan" for the students of Trilling's generation: "The Moral Obligation to Be Intelligent." Trilling did not count himself "among those who were intelligent." But he had other qualities that were very close to what Erskine meant by intelligence and close to what guaranteed survival in the academy. "I would have been the first to say that I was observant, even perceptive, of certain things, that I was intuitive; and I rather prided myself on a quality that went by the name of subtlety. But intelligence I scarcely aspired to: it did not seem to me that this was a quality that a novelist needed to have, only a quick eye for behavior and motive and a feeling heart" (*AL* 231). Observance, subtlety, "a quick eye for behavior and motive and a feeling heart"; these were homebred qualities, developed as much in the Trilling household with its kosher kitchen and in arguments with Max Kadushin as through the reading of novels and planning of stories. What the novel —that is, Trilling's later perception of it as a genre—shared with the Trilling family was rootedness in reality, in the social world; it was the preoccupation with "moral questions, with the questions raised by the experience of quotidian life and by the experience of culture and history" (*AL* 228). Such a description conjures the hum of family discussions around the kitchen tables of thousands of New York Jewish households which had relatives left in pogrom-ridden Europe.

But the strongest link between Trilling's notion of the novel and his descent culture is forged beneath the sociological and familial, in the intellectual realm, which one might call the realm of "ideas" and which Trilling, faute de mieux, would refer to as "manners." He defines the latter in one of his essays in such a way that the definition may very well refer to the former. "They are the things that for good or bad draw the people of a culture together and that separate them from the people of another culture. They make the part of culture which is not art, or religion, or morals, or politics, and yet it relates to all these highly formulated departments of culture" (*JA* 207). What, then, are these "manners" or "ideas" in which the novel and Judaism (as inherited from his father) are so similar that it was possible for Trilling to use "manners" as a cipher for "ideas"? A mitnagdic mind can come up with a stunningly simple answer: the novel and Judaism are not only similar but identical in their observance of the ordinary.

Judaism's most fundamental assertion is the complete separation of transcendence and immanence (i.e., the positing of an absolute God). One of the consequences of this separation is the absence of theological speculation; positively put, it is the "this-worldliness" of Judaism. Taking immanence seriously does not equal materialism. It is an act of modesty, which forgoes speculation about that which transcends the human realm and instead turns to creation, which is revered (not worshiped) as a sign (not symbol) of the creator's power and benevolence. One way of showing this reverence, an act of courtesy as much as of gratitude, is the extraordinary number of blessings that are said by the observant Jew every day. There is "a blessing for every separate experience of the Ordinary," a "shower of Yeses that praise fragrant oils, and wine, and sex, and scholars, and thunder, and new clothes, and falling stars, and washing your hands before eating."[70] Translated into the literary realm, Trilling ascribes exactly this attitude to Sarah Yetta in Charles Reznikoff's *By the Waters of Manhattan.* "Her conception of the good life has all its spiritualities rooted in material things: for her the dignity of clean linen and fresh undergarments is important and the ultimate garment is the learning she is trying always to acquire."[71]

Such this-worldliness, or observance of the ordinary (in the double sense of to perceive and to revere), generates a certain moral seriousness because "what you are taught to praise you will not maim or exploit or destroy." But such observance also opens the sense for "the categories and impulses of Art" as the Jewish novelist Cynthia Ozick argues, "because it is all the handiwork of the Creator, everything Ordinary is seen to be Extraordinary. The world, and every moment in it, is seen to be sublime, and not merely 'seen to be,' but brought home to the intensest part of consciousness."[72]

To be Jewish, then, is to be observant: to be conscious at any moment of the world of phenomena and to respond to it with moral imagination. Hence, the following definition of Jewishness, which Trilling entered into his notebook, is more than a sociological statement (reflecting sensitivity to social slights); it reaches deeper: "Being a Jew is like walking in the wind or swimming: you are touched at all points and conscious everywhere" (*NI* 496).[73] The world of phenomena is to be taken seriously, dealt with, and not to be transcended. Or, in Cynthia Ozick's succinct formulation that links Henry James and Jewish observance: "The Jew has this in common with the artist: he means nothing to be lost on him, he brings all his mind and senses to bear on noticing the Ordinary, he is equally alert to Image and Experience, nothing that passes before him is taken for granted . . . ."[74]

The notion of the novel developed on the basis of this weltanschauung (the observance of the ordinary)—which is Trilling's as much as Ozick's—is a simple one: the novel's "classic intention . . . is the investigation of the problem of reality beginning in the social field" (*MM* 212).

Its task was, before Tolstoy, "to conceive the actuality of the life of common routine" (*OS* 146). "The novel, then, is a perpetual quest for reality, the field of its research being always the social world, the material of its analysis being always manners as the indication of the direction of man's soul" (*MM* 212).

"Ideally," the novel puts the reader into a "profound possession of reality."[75] Confined to immanence, devoted to the investigation of the ordinary, the novel eschews the transcendental impulse of art, that is, art for art's sake, and "redeems the individual from moral torpor." Its effect is "communal" (*JA* 212). The novel in its "classic intention" is the very opposite of "an autonomous, self-justifying activity" (*AL* 228). Of such idolatry, "making the ordinary into the Extraordinary,"[76] Trilling was "a little skeptical." He was in fact "impatient with it," just as he was exasperated at the effect of a literature that was "*blinding* people to reality, making them concerned only with themselves, creating such self-pity, such self-regard, that they can't respond to reality."[77] In the realm of the ordinary, "ego is not interesting."[78] This is the point where Lionel Trilling and Cynthia Ozick are farthest from Ludwig Lewisohn and Philip Roth. Trilling's notion of the novel can be summed up with the three main statements in Cynthia Ozick's essay "What Literature Means": "Literature is the recognition of the particular" (i.e., observance of the ordinary); "what Literature means is meaning" (i.e., it is not self-referential); "Literature *is* the moral life."[79] In Trilling's and Ozick's universe these statements are almost tautological.

Observance of the ordinary, as legacy either of the Enlightenment or of his fathers' world, was part of Trilling's intellectual grammar. It informed his view of literature as socially responsible, that is, moral activity, and determined his preference for the British nineteenth-century novel. It made him skeptical of the creation of literary and critical art for art's sake (as practiced by certain modernists and the New Critics) and impatient with those who used literature to inflate their egos. Hence he was ungracious toward Romantics of all sorts, who by declaring personal experience to be the sole basis of self-definition undermined the cohesion and thus the stability of society. What the mitnagdim feared in the hasidim, what Morris Cohen detested in Bergson and James, and what Ozick deplored in Harold Bloom, was precisely what Trilling criticized in the neoromantic culture of the sixties. It is nicely summed up by a younger Jewish rationalist: "It's foolish to make the self the measure of all events . . . ."[80] Observance of the ordinary was the rational (hence communicable, not experience-based) acknowledgment of the world of actuality; the novel was an account of the individual's difficulty with the given in space and time.[81]

When Trilling came to Columbia University as an undergraduate, he arrived as an observant Jew, that is, he came equipped with the tools of a novelist and intensely conscious of his Jewish descent. He noticed it as cultural difference. Jewishness manifested itself in the manners and behavior of his Jewish fellow students. For these differences he had a novelist's eye. They became the subject of his first fictions.

Keeping pace with the increasing secularization of American Jews on their way into Gentile culture, their observance of the ordinary changed, too, during the time of Trilling's maturation. The focus shifted from the rabbinic fixation on the world of the created to an acute awareness of social circumstances. The rabbinic mind of the fathers became the novelistic mind of the son, just as *talmud torah* was replaced by the study of secular literature. But observance and "text-centeredness"[82] remained intact as structures while their content changed. In Trilling's generation, this change in content did not yet affect the intellectual grammar. This structure would disintegrate in the next generation.

Trilling's oscillations and his dialectical mind have been described by many critics and connected to the social problems arising from his Jewish descent. Seen within the context of the present study, however, these oscillations between extremes, Trilling's "pendular shifts," and hard-won "dialectical poise,"[83] appear to link him to his immediate percursors, the immigrant academics, and their intellectual struggles. Yet Trilling's fear of the destructiveness of transcendental experience, his misgivings about sounding the abyss of the soul, and his aversion to the idol worship of those praising the "aesthetic mode of perception over the historical" (*JA* 219) show Trilling to be the son of much older fathers. These are concerns of a rationalist; they are shared by rabbinic minds.

While Trilling's oscillations and pendular shifts have attracted much attention, his remarkable intellectual consistency has gone almost unnoticed, and even when noticed has not been recognized as a consequence of a firmly established intellectual grammar. Its origins are buried in his descent culture, but its unfolding and operation can be observed in his fictions. These fictions explore alternative selves. Yet Trilling was not free to choose who he was to become.

THE TAMING OF THE JEW:
FICTIONAL SELF-REFLECTIONS

Trilling's parental equipment, a penchant for precise observation and an inkling of the intricacies of literature, proved exactly right for the type of education provided by Columbia College. What the school added was "the moral obligation to be intelligent" (AL 231). Intelligence was a sharpening of the capacity for observation.[84] It was an "awareness of difficulty and complexity" (AL 230). For Jewish youths moving into the Gentile world, such "intelligence" belonged to the survival kit. At Columbia, however, under the guidance of John Erskine, they were taught "to bring thought cogently to bear upon all subjects to which thought might be appropriate" (AL 230), that is, to shift the focus of their intelligence from social to cultural concerns. Trilling "was seduced into bucking to be intelligent by the assumption which was prepotent in Columbia College—that intelligence was connected with literature, that it was advanced by literature" (AL 231).

Given the great number of students from immigrant families (before Trilling's class of 1925, 40 percent of Columbia's undergraduates were Jewish), it is not surprising "that literature at Columbia College was taught on principles that were very different from those that prevailed in the Graduate School of the University," where the degree of acculturation was higher, or that these were "different principles than those that were in force even in undergraduate instruction at Harvard and Yale" (AL 231). But even at Harvard, the established principles of instruction were being transformed. The philology of Child and Kittredge, which had been so hospitable to a mind and character such as Leo Wiener's, had fulfilled its purpose, namely "to justify English studies without necessarily limiting them."[85]

Their philology, "the application of German positivism to letters, a laboratorial reduction of literature to its historical and mechanical parts," had first been scoffed at by Barrett Wendell as "alien tyranny," and then been radically assaulted by the generalist Irving Babbitt.[86] What the philistines were to Matthew Arnold, the philologists were to Babbitt. "He acknowledged that the philologist's use of historical method in tracing origins and influences in literature was legitimate, but he protested that too often such methods usurped the primary consideration of studying literature as a source of values and for 'the application of real standards of taste and judgment.'" Babbitt concurred with Matthew Arnold that high standards and trained leaders were needed in Anglo-American society, but he could not accept Arnold's suggestion in *Culture and Anarchy* that all socioeconomic classes should contribute qualitative leadership.[87] Babbitt's humanism remained decidedly elitist. In his essay collection *Literature and the American College* Babbitt writes: "The true humanist maintains a just balance between sympathy and selection. We moderns . . . tend to lay an undue stress on the element of sympathy. On the other hand, the ancients in general, both Greek and Roman, inclined to sacrifice sympathy to selection. . . . Ancient humanism is as a whole intensely aristocratic in temper; its sympathies run in what would seem to us narrow channels; it is naturally disdainful of the humble and lowly who have not been indoctrinated and disciplined."[88] Babbitt's essays were published in 1908, the year Kallen received his doctorate from Harvard and Wolfson arrived in Cambridge. By the 1920s, after Harvard's president had discovered his "Jewish problem" but failed in his attempt to implement a quota system, Babbitt's selective pagan humanism became untenable. But where Columbia's students would have exploded with vitriolic wit, Harvardians preferred gentle mockery; they simply said of Babbitt that his "fame was spreading around the world and had in fact already left Cambridge."[89]

It certainly found no hospitable home at Columbia, where another generalist, John Erskine, had pitched his tent and battled with the scholars. Erskine was a cultural aristocrat, a man with a distinguished academic pedigree. As Trilling wrote, "Erskine had been the pupil at Columbia of George Edward Woodberry [Spingarn's mentor], who at Harvard had been the pupil of Charles Eliot Norton, who had been the friend of Carlyle, Ruskin, and Matthew Arnold" (*AL* 233). Babbitt, by contrast, remained very much a man from the America that lay west of the Charles River, despite his education at Harvard (where Norton had been among his teachers). In their educational goals the cultural pedigrees of the two men are reflected in reverse: Babbitt, who had been exposed to the "rough egalitarianism of the great plains,"[90] insisted on intellectual elitism; Erskine, who was securely rooted in his tradition, could afford to share it.

The idea for Erskine's famed General Honors course, as Mark Krupnick suggests, might very well have derived from the Renaissance notion of "an education appropriate to an aristocratic ruling class."[91] Trilling himself indicated the similarities between the Elizabethan literature scholar's course and Sir Philip Sidney's *Defense of Poesie* (*AL* 233–234). But in the context of Columbia College, with its diverse student body, the idea "that men who were in any degree responsible for the welfare of the polity and for the quality of life that characterized it must be large-minded men, committed to great ends, devoted to virtue, assured of the dignity of the human estate and dedicated to enhancing and preserving it; and that the great works of the imagination could foster and even institute this large-mindedness, this magnanimity (AL 234)" became transformed from an aristocratic notion into a democratic practice. As Trilling describes it, Erskine's two-year course for selected juniors and seniors met for two hours a week "in groups of fifteen, under two teachers drawn from various departments, philosophers, historians, classicists, economists . . . . Its curriculum was the classics of the Western World, the Great Books, beginning with Homer and coming down through the 19th century . . . including not only works of literature but also philosophy and history, which were likely to be dealt with as if they were works of literature. We were assigned nothing else but the great books themselves, confronting them as best we could without the mediation of ancillary works" (AL 232). Intelligence, the capacity for observation, and intuition sufficed as analytic tools. Many Columbia students had an abundance of these tools.

Whatever Erskine's original intention may have been, his General Honors course became a superb instrument in the democratization of the genteel literary tradition and indispensable in the New York Intellectuals' process of acculturation. It dispensed with cultural prerequisites whose acquisition had thus far been a (gentle)man's entry ticket to the culture of America's ruling class. Babbitt, who emphasized as did Erskine "general critical intelligence,"[92] condemned his colleague as a dilettante and a popularizer. At Columbia, Erskine's course "met with the resistance and hostility of a considerable part of the faculty,"[93] ostensibly because to those "devoted to the ideals of exact scholarship" the course seemed "superficial" (AL 232). But the real fear was that with the easy availability of elite culture, the immigrant hordes, which had already stormed Morningside Heights, would first absorb and then usurp. They would replace the present defenders and bring about the downfall first of Columbia and then of America. That was precisely the reason that more than a decade later Trilling's appointment to a position in the English Department was opposed. Trilling's former dissertation adviser at Columbia, Emery Neff, articulated it perfectly when soon after Trilling's appointment he came to pay the Trillings a visit at home. Diana Trilling remembers, "what Emery Neff came to say was that now that Lionel was a member of the department, he hoped that he would not use it as a wedge to open the English department to more Jews."[94] In 1939, Neff was pleading a lost cause. But in the twenties Columbians were still under the impression that the tide could be stemmed. The administration implemented a quota system and the English Department did away with Erskine's course as soon as he retired. But it was too late. In 1934 the course was revived by the Frenchman Jacques Barzun, who invited Trilling to teach it with him.

In his memoir of Jacques Barzun, which Trilling wrote while already in the grip of his fatal illness and which he left unfinished, he recalls that during his freshman and sophomore years he had made "a series of rather half-hearted attempts to take part in college life." Eventually, he writes, "I took my stand with a group of young men who held themselves apart in skepticism and irony; they could not properly have been called Bohemians and the category intellectuals hadn't yet come to be freely used, but 'intelligentsia' was available and on the whole appropriate, for they had, it seemed to me, a strong tincture of the young men in Dostoievski and Chekhov; they suited my taste until I graduated."[95]

In the same memoir, Trilling emphasizes his own passivity and deference in contrast to Barzun's involvement and self-assurance, and claims that "Jacques's mental character had been pretty decisively shaped, as mine had not been . . . ."[96] What Trilling here calls a shaped "mental character" might simply have been an Arnoldian rootedness in culture. He observes that "the nature and extent of Jacques's acculturation" were remarkable, yet in his bearing "there doubtless was something that was not American in that it was touched with consciousness . . . . It was plain that this young man knew who he was . . . ."[97] Trilling, who in 1928 described "sense of self" in the same tactile words—"Being a Jew is like walking in the wind or swimming: you are touched and conscious everywhere"—was caught in a difficult situation during his college days. On the one hand, he was steadily losing ground and getting out of touch with his home base by succumbing to Erskine and the Columbia mystique, "directed to showing young men how they might escape from the limitations of their middle-class or lower-middle-class upbringings" (*AL* 234); he was acquiring "the characteristic American air of intending to have no consciousness of himself and no precision."[98] On the other hand, he was associating with exactly the people who reminded him constantly of his home base and kept him, literally, self-conscious. According to one critic, this "group of young men who held themselves apart in skepticism and irony" consisted of Clifton Fadiman (born in 1904), Herbert Solow (1903), Henry Rosenthal (1906) and Trilling.[99] It was a Jewish group devoted to intelligence and the vocation of writing.

There was hardly any continuity between Erskine's world, with its "great models of thought, feeling and imagination" (*AL* 234), the parental middle-class world of hard economic and cultural facts, and the intense world of the group of campus intellectuals to which Trilling belonged. What created a sense of unity and put Trilling at ease in this split world was his conviction of being a writer in the making. In his senior year he began to use his gift for observation to investigate his sense of self, his touchiness, which he concealed behind "a languid, sauntering elegance."[100]

Trilling commenced lightly. "Impediments," his debut in the *Menorah Journal* (June–July 1925), is a character sketch rather than a story. The Jewish narrator who is just settling in to do a night's work on a term paper is disturbed by a fellow student, a "scrubby little Jew with shrewd eyes and full, perfect lips that he twisted out of their crisply cut shape."[101] A battle ensues between gentleman and Jew, in which the two torture each other exquisitely. It ends with the physical victory and moral defeat of the gentleman narrator. The "Jew" named Hettner, who near midnight shows up at the narrator's doorstep to coerce him into friendship and acceptance, is both social and psychological threat incarnate: he is kinsman and alter ego. What makes the story interesting is that the combatants are equally strong and that the currents in this two-level battle run in opposite directions: while the narrator inflicts social suffering on his visitor, his visitor pains him psychologically.

Socially, Hettner is the nightmare of the Jewish snob at Columbia concerned with belonging. He is shabby, intense, serious, unappealing in dress, manners, and possibly character—in short, he is a family disgrace. "He was wearing a blue serge suit, very shiny and worn, and a grimy tie. The suit was the only one he had, I knew, for he was poor, yet I very much resented it. Blue serge suits are well enough, very handsome things, in fact, but when they are threadbare and lustrous they are detestable. A man may be as shabby as he pleases in a rough cloth, tweed or cheviot, and still look gay and interesting, but untidy blue serge gives him the look of a shop assistant" (*Im* 7).

The greenhorn's first crime is that he has not acquired the manners of genteel poverty. His second sin is his "crudeness and awkwardness," which are responsible for the faux pas that range from the wrong handling of a rice paper cigarette and his "showing off intellectually at a frightful rate" to his overlooking the subtle signals of being unwelcome. But Hettner's third and most distressing defect is his intensity and seriousness, which permit no play, no irony, no distance. He demands entry into the room of a man who has just sat down to write a paper on Browning, a paper indulging in distances, ironies, superficialities—"a few paragraphs of discreet eulogy, very graceful, a cursory re-reading of the important poems

with discreet comment, a discreet closing criticism with a discreet proph-
ecy that the poet will be read more and more . . ." (*Im* 5). Hettner breaks
into this chain of thoughts like one of Browning's "ruined questers, im-
perfect poets, self-sabotaged artists, failed lovers, inspired fanatics, char-
latans, monomaniacs, and self-deceiving confidence men,"[102] and begins
talking about—among other things—art, "a subject on which he had
done considerable reading" (*Im* 7). "He talked and scoffed because he did
not dare shut up, and his talk was an insistent and arrogant apology for
his existence" (*Im* 4). To the narrator, Hettner is what Meyer Schapiro
was to Mark van Doren or Mary McCarthy, "a mouth in search of an
ear."[103]

During their midnight battle, the narrator keeps on his guard, dodges
Hettner's intellectual attacks, shoots back flippant answers, parades his
social superiority "until it seemed that [Hettner's mouth] could no longer
refrain from screaming its misery" (*Im* 9). Finally, Hettner is "exhausted
as though after physical effort, but [the narrator is] fresh and tremen-
dously alive" (*Im* 10). The narrator's victory is near. He enjoys a moment
of decadent pleasure. "It was really rather funny, quite madly absurd, and
I shuddered with the same exquisite horror as when, a little boy, I held
captive a blunt gray toad" (*Im* 10). But then the visiting angel that has
fought with him denies the blessing and turns victory into defeat. "Hettner
rose and stood at the door, his hand on the knob. . . . He turned to me
and . . . said, "What a miserable dog you are'" (*Im* 10). Through his
refusal of empathy the narrator has lost his Jewish soul. In Jewish literature, comparison with a dog signals ultimate moral contempt.

Hettner, the shabby Jew, the gray toad, is the narrator's Jewish soul, or
alter ego, trying to slip into a polished but hollow shell. He appears at the
moment when the narrator sits down to work on Browning, whose "art
constantly explores the multiplicity of selves that inhabit apparently single, unitary personalities, some of them not at all unlike some of his
own."[104] But the narrator is on his guard and determined to keep the Jew
out. "I felt always defensive against some attempt Hettner might make to
break down the convenient barrier I was erecting against men who were
too much of my own race and against men who were not of my own race
and hated it" (*Im* 3–4). He has constructed for himself "a tower of con-
temptible ivory perhaps, but very useful" (*Im* 4), which allows him to
exist unperturbed in the college and to write discreet papers about the art
of multiple selves. What he fears above all is inner turmoil caused by the
indiscretion of another soul. "Hettner had come in for what he would call
an intelligent and serious conversation; that is he wanted to talk about

himself, to give me hints as to what he really was, to tell me things about his soul. I could see that easily. Now, I do not want to know about people's souls; I want people quite entirely dressed; I want no display of fruity scabs and luscious sores. I like people's outsides, not their insides; they would be, probably, too much like mine" (*Im* 6).

Apart from the last part of the final sentence, which in the story establishes Hettner as the narrator's psychic double, the paragraph contains a truth about Trilling. Jacques Barzun has described Trilling's lifelong great shyness, and others have noticed his sense of privacy and his need for it. In the early forties, when Trilling was visited by one of these intense Jews from Brownsville, a man a decade younger than himself, he did not tell him to leave but retreated behind his defenses. Alfred Kazin, his visitor, sees that "there was immense and even cavernous subtlety to the man, along with much timidity, a self-protectiveness as elegant as a fencer's." But where the story's narrator pretends to be all shell—reluctant to admit that he shares Hettner's intensity—and deceives Hettner, Kazin is not fooled by the mask. He sees Trilling's face as "furrowed, hooded, closed up with constant thought. The life was all within, despite his debonair practiced easiness of manners."[105]

To observation and intelligence Trilling would add a third perception-based virtue: discretion. Like intelligence, discretion connotes acute observation and the capacity to distinguish between phenomena, even between nuances. But unlike intelligence, discretion puts the emphasis on the judgment following the intelligent (i.e., analytic) observation. Discretion is the faculty to keep things separate. For Trilling, who began using the "we" of the British essayists in his early twenties,[106] this meant above all keeping the private self separate from the public "I." He was so successful in this separation that by the fifties his public appearance was taken for the whole man. Lack of critical intelligence on the part of the public would then elevate him into a representative man.

For Trilling, discretion—or the faculty to separate the private and the public—was the supreme cultural achievement. A self capable of discretion was a civilized self. What irritates the narrator about Hettner is that intense Jews like him are all soul, that they are at any moment completely invested in every action, every word, that they are all core, protected only by the thinnest of skins. Their vulnerability—disguised only by a stream of words pouring from a "mouth . . . kept in continual torture" (*Im* 9)—provokes cruelty, awakens the imp of the perverse in those capable of multiple selves. The narrator's exquisite aggression expresses his resentment at not having been spared knowledge of Hettner's soul. He punishes him for his lack of discretion, for not being civilized.

Very lightly, then, the story touches on a theme in Trilling's essays: "the high cost to the self of becoming civilized."[107] Freud's essay "Civilization and Its Discontents" and its importance for Trilling immediately come to mind, as does Trilling's peculiar use of Freud. In his application of Freud, Trilling was torn between criticial intelligence, that is the passion to know and to probe, and his sense of discretion. Mark Shechner formulated Trilling's ambivalence quite well when he wrote: "While many of Trilling's essays may be read as applied Freud, they are largely applications of his character and his outlook rather than his methodologies of interpretation. Trilling's relation to psychoanalysis was dominated by his shyness about its explanatory conventions and his penchant for leaving his insights with large helpings of rhetorical tact."[108] This rhetorical tact, which in a paradoxical move conceals from the reader's prying eye the naked facts that the critical intelligence has set out to discern and describe, was particularly noticeable when Trilling wrote about people, rather than literature. All his fictions, for instance, are exercises in character description. His most outstanding work in veiled analysis, however, is his memoir of Raymond Weaver, his one-time enemy in Columbia's English Department. In a single harmless anecdote after much pleasant rhetoric Trilling reveals Weaver's inner dynamics, "the virulence of the evil spirits."[109]

Trilling was fascinated less by the analytical possibilities Freud suggested than by his use of the imagination, by Freud's "significant affinity with the anti-rationalist element of the Romanticist tradition." Despite his rationalism, Freud seemed to possess a Romantic sensibility, "which makes poetry indigenous to the very constitution of the mind."[110] While the novel was an account of social circumstances, poetry for Trilling undertook the exploration of the self. It released the mind from its rationalist tether. Poetry's only constraints on the freewheeling self were the demands of form. It is the daring exploration of the self by imaginative means which for Trilling "puts Freud among the Romantics . . . . Together the Romantics and Freud do make use of strengths and freedoms arising from their nonrational conception of existence."[111] Trilling was intrigued by "the opposition between the hidden and the visible" perceived by Freud and the Romantics, but he himself refused to look too closely at the "hidden element of human nature," afraid to find crouching at the bottom of man's soul the imp of the perverse.[112] He knew that the glance into the pit—be it that of Hawthorne's physician/critic Chillingworth or that of Hawthorne's artist Ethan Brand or that of the scientist Freud—was essentially an act of the imagination, of self-reflection, and could be both creative and destructive. What Poe called the "Imp of the Perverse," who makes one look and jump, Trilling's fathers had called the *yetzer ha-ra*, the evil impulse.[113]

Trilling's peculiar uses of Freud (as cultural critic and not as psychoanalyst), his suspicion of poetry as "the imagination's more turbulent waters," his cautious "distance from patently troubled or demonic writers—from, in short, romantics"[114] are interrelated and present in a nutshell in the rather peculiar statement made by the narrator in "Impediments," quoted earlier in a different context: "Now, I do not want to know about people's souls; I want people quite entirely dressed; I want no display of fruity scabs and luscious sores. I like people's outsides, not their insides, and I was particularly reluctant to see this man's insides; they would be, probably, too much like mine" (*Im* 6).

Dress, like discretion, is what distinguishes civilized from uncivilized man; it is the means of self-restraint which, at the high cost Freud analyzed, makes culture possible. Dress, like discretion, is also a means of self-protection. In *The Scarlet Letter*, Chillingworth, in undressing Dimmesdale, commits the unpardonable sin. The physician destroys his patient by imagining who and what Dimmesdale must be. In his memoir of Trilling, Phillip Lopate remembers a classroom discussion of *Women in Love*:

> He came to D. H. Lawrence's idea about lovers plumbing the depths of each other's souls. He suddenly stopped and confessed, "I find something repellent about that notion." I raised my hand and asked him why, citing my hero Dostoevsky and his drive for honesty. "I don't know . . . Don't you find something destructive about all that delving into one another's depths?" he mused. "I should think lovers would want to keep some things mysterious. Hold a little bit off for a rainy day. What's left after it's all too known?"[115]

What worried Trilling was not so much the threat of boredom—that was rhetorical tact—but rather the destruction wrought by imaginative prying, the effect of the *yetzer ha-ra*. In his fathers' world speculations about the soul were taboo (as were speculations about God) so as to prevent the disintegration of the culture.[116]

It may seem somewhat out of proportion to develop the major themes in Trilling's writing from a little character sketch that William Chace has called "slight and now justly all-but-forgotten."[117] But it is part of the argument advanced here that Trilling's "mental character" was, despite his disclaimer in the Barzun memoir, "pretty decisively shaped" in his father's style when he went to Columbia. What Trilling developed later is derived from what was present then. Furthermore, the story is based on a real incident and announces Trilling's decision to turn away from Jewish culture and to terminate an association—his freelancing for the *Menorah Journal*—that this story had just initiated. Neither his heart nor his mind was invested in the *Menorah Journal*. His two dozen contributions between June 1925 and June 1931 were not exactly inauthentic or insincere. But the reviews (if not the stories) clearly indicate that Trilling was getting ready for bigger game. His frame of reference in the reviews is never Jewish culture, but always the world of Erskine's Great Books, from Homer's *Odyssey* to Joyce's *Ulysses*.

After Kaplan and Kadushin the next and last effort to claim Trilling for Jewish culture was made by his friend Henry Rosenthal. A student of Kaplan's at the Jewish Theological Seminary, Rosenthal was the only (religiously) observant Jew in Trilling's circle of friends. He is Van Doren's student A who would inform Trilling of his "absurdities." Van Doren presents him as a Hettner-Schapiro type.

> He presented his pale, ascetic features to my attention after one of the first meetings of the class and said without the flicker of a smile: "I have read Mencken. What are we going to talk about? Are we going to get past Mencken?" I had not mentioned Mencken in the class that day nor, I think, did I ever mention him, since he was not germane to the course. But if I did speak of him thereafter, I am sure I guarded my remarks with a glance at this face, the eyes in which were always dropped down in imminent disapproval, to see how truthful I must be. For I quickly learned to watch my step in the presence of—let us call him A. A developed the fiercest method of attack that I have ever known in my none too long experience with controversy. It was as if his mind lay in a coil—deadly, waiting, pale—from which at any moment it might rise and strike. . . . He wrote many brilliant essays for me, and during one period he was sole author of a little periodical whose issues he deposited weekly in manuscript upon my desk. Nothing that he ever wrote praised anybody or anything; he was inveterately satirical, and he did the job thoroughly with each new victim. . . . A graduated; and word came to me that he had gone into a seminary to make himself a rabbi. He had approved, then, of God! And I remembered that this was so. He still is in the seminary, and I hear that he has started something like a revolution against the teaching methods there. But I know that he still approves of God. I can see him in some future pulpit, pale as wrath itself, reminding his amazed hearers of all they never knew.[118]

In January 1928, Rosenthal published the companion piece to Trilling's "Impediments" in the *Menorah Journal*. While Trilling had chosen a line from Shakespeare as an epigraph—"Let me not to the marriage of true minds / Admit impediments . . ."—Rosenthal prefaced his "Inventions" with a line from Kohelet—"God made man upright; but they have sought out many inventions" (Eccles. 7:29). The slightness of Trilling's sketch (which he sent to the *Menorah Journal* at Rosenthal's suggestion)[119] is brought into sharp relief by the agonized intensity of Rosenthal's only half-satiric torrent describing the struggle from the perspective of "Hettner." Rosenthal's protagonist, Starobin (Hettner/Rosenthal), "who fancied himself a sort of animated earlock," finds himself provoked by Dolman, "an unhappy young swell, nursing under a mask of amused sensuality and geometrical courtesy a character he did not quite have and did not really want."[120] Dolman, "sedate and easy devil" who was "born spiritually blond" to a "heritage of suavity" and possessed "slow grace and ease," raises storms of aggression in Starobin (*In* 50–54). "He knew that fundamentally what all the Zionists wanted to do, and he certainly among them, was to twist those soft impassive lips of all the Dolmans with a little good coarse Yiddish—preferably a Yiddish salute to the flag of Zion, which he should repeat unwillingly, persuaded by the Maccabean fists of an experienced Chalutz [pioneer], a bronzed Palestinian bully of the second generation, heart-whole and astink with the soil" (*In* 49).

In Trilling's story, Hettner's aggression surfaces as verbal poking, biting, battering (*Im* 8), which the narrator wards off with brief sentences. Before Starobin enters into his duel with Dolman, he already knows that this will be the case. "The absurdity of hiring a Yerushalmi [Jerusalemite] to box Dolman's Western ears he now saw in a new light. Once it was to be taken for granted that Dolman, tenaciously genteel, would suffer the abuse only to slay the New Jerusalemite with an epigram. This was fairly trite, but it was a fairly trite operation to box a cultured person's ears. What could one do?" (*In* 53). Although Starobin discovers to his "blasting" astonishment "that Dolman was not at all ashamed" (*In* 52) to be a Jew, nor minded "a Jew so he had brains" (*In* 51), he decides to intensify his attacks and to enter on a "crusade in their senior year. Having resolved his attitude, as he thought, into simplicity, he had set out then, with a slightly hysterical earnestness, to find out what kind of Jew Dolman was anyhow. The way to do this was to try to convert Dolman" (*In* 55). This is just what Hettner plans to do when he shows up at the narrator's doorstep—to plead for the adoption of a Jewish soul. Starobin's "holy war" surfaces in Trilling's version, as "Hettner and I engaged in battle,

Hettner grave and purposeful, myself listening intently to what he had to say, polite and flippant" (*Im* 9).

Both Hettner and Starobin come to talk about their Jewish souls. Yet while in Trilling's story the narrator's defenses are impenetrable, Rosenthal's account at first leaves room for another outcome. But three torturous, witty pages later he, too, has to admit defeat. "Sick with the desperate humor of the thing Dolman sat on the couch, guarding himself against words with his legs bent up against him" (*In* 59). The stage is set for the final insult. In Rosenthal's story it comes from Dolman. He accuses Starobin of lack of discretion: "don't be a public Job, parading your boils" (*In* 60). The story ends with Dolman's Pyrrhic victory and Starobin's resignation to leave him alone.

The fictional Trilling of "Impediments" and "Inventions" declared his independence from the Jewish soul (which for students of Mordecai Kaplan was Jewish culture) long before the real Trilling could enact it. Between 1925 and 1931 Trilling remained affiliated with the *Menorah Journal*. Those were years of flux in Trilling's life, and he seems to have been reluctant to give up what provided at least the illusion of a home base before he was anchored somewhere else. Year after year, he contributed his share of stories and reviews. Unlike the critical pieces, which are shrewd, polemical, and well written, and which show independent literary judgment, the stories are not very intriguing. Not only do they lack the subterranean urgency of "Impediments," but their dutiful advocacy of the *Menorah Journal's* program of unashamed Jewishness is dull and unconvincing.

Three of Trilling's four stories are set at a university in the Midwest and depict a single male instructor in an ocean of Gentiles, trying to be decently Jewish. At no point does Jewishness seem to mean anything beside an accident of birth one is forced to accept gracefully. The fourth story, "Chapter for a Fashionable Jewish Novel," is different and slightly more interesting in its development of the double motif. An assimilated young woman and her impish sister vie for the attention of a young man who is torn between behaving like a respectable Jew (which is to say like a British gentleman) and wallowing in Jewishness. The latter gives him a sense of comfort similar to that Gregor Samsa feels when he finally accepts his transformation into a cockroach, stops walking upright, and drops to his feet. Amid his Anglicized dinner companions, the young man insists on talking about Jewish family behavior. When he detects boredom and dismay on the faces surrounding him, he is swamped by a sense of perverse exhilaration and indulges the fantasy of an orgiastic release from respectability. "He began to feel not like a prophet come howling from the wilderness to warn a people defiling holiness, but like a satyr leaped into a respectable home (passé theme of English drama), lustfully Hebraic, rowling gloriously, drunkenly, madly, in Jewishness, disgusting the inhabitants by the abandon and licentiousness of his Semitic existence. He smirked at himself: patriot by perversity."[121]

This theme of madness and restraint, marginality and assimilation, freedom and bondage would reappear seventeen years later in one of Trilling's best stories, "Of This Time, of That Place," published in *Partisan Review* in 1943. The thematic and structural resemblance of this late story to the fictional pieces of the 1920s is somewhat astonishing, as the doppelgänger and alter ego motifs are essentially related to Trilling's complex cultural situation, and by the 1940s these complexities seemed resolved. He was no longer oscillating between cultures. He had chosen his life-style. The late story, which positions a college professor between two students, one a madman (Hettner type, crazy Jew) and the other an opportunist (narrator, dinner companions), reflects on the choices Trilling had made and betrays some regret, if not even a slight sense of guilt. What had been Trilling's choices between 1925 and 1943?

In 1926, Trilling received his master's degree from Columbia and then left to teach for a year at an experimental college at the University of Wisconsin. On his return to New York, he was able to secure some teaching in the evening and extension sessions at Hunter College. In 1929 he married Diana Rubin and moved downtown from his parents' Upper West Side apartment to Greenwich Village. This change of residence was meant to signal his "solidarity with the intellectual life."[122] Also in 1929, and in slight contradiction to his move downtown, Trilling became part-time assistant editor of the *Menorah Journal*. In the Village, Trilling's affiliation with the *Journal* seems not to have been common knowledge, and according to Diana Trilling, her husband preferred not to discuss his work there.[123]

This does not mean that Trilling was ashamed of being Jewish or of working for a collegiate Jewish publication when *The Nation*, *The New Republic*, and *The Freeman* were all the rage. He might have preferred silence over discussion because affairs at the journal were enormously complicated. A number of articles vehemently critical of Zionism, submitted by Herbert Solow and printed by the journal's young daredevil editor, Eliot Cohen, were transforming this pleasantly simmering "literary stewpot" (in Cynthia Ozick's formulation) into a seething cauldron. For Trilling to discuss his work on the *Menorah Journal*, then, would have necessitated his taking a stand on matters vital to his "sense of identity"

(NT 11) and his clarifying "the general concept of Jewishness that had at first claimed [his] recognition and interest" (NT 12). Trilling was not capable of such clarification, not even in the fiction he was writing at the time. Nor did he desire to be, because clarification would have confronted him with clear-cut alternatives and demanded that he choose between descent and aspiration. Discussion of the crisis at the journal would have disrupted Trilling's smooth fadeout from Jewish culture.

But at the *Menorah Journal* itself, Solow's articles worked as catalysts. They increased the tension between the managing editor Cohen with "his clever young friends" (NT 12) and the board of directors, represented by the journal's founder and editor-in-chief, Henry Hurwitz—that is, between a group of leftist, culturally pluralist intellectuals in their mid-twenties and a group of well-established, middle-class Westchesterites mainly interested in getting "the kiddies into college" and repairing "the spiritual disintegration of their lives."[124] The ostensible subject of Solow's articles in 1929 and 1930 was a critique of Zionism and its politics. After the Arab riots of August 1929, the situation in Palestine was explosive. In the fall of that year Solow attended the Sixteenth Zionist Congress in Zürich and disliked most of what he saw there; in November 1929 he proceeded to Palestine, where his dislike of Zionist politics turned into anger. He accused the Palestinian Jews of "chauvinism of the most repulsive kind" and of unacceptable politics toward the Arabs.[125] Solow's viewpoint was not yet that of a Communist, but he was moving rapidly toward Marxist thinking. As Mark Krupnick points out, for Solow "Zionism ought to have been a movement of social protest, an alliance of Arab peasants and Jewish workers. Instead, Zionist policy was being made by European and American Jewish capitalists who relied on the support of English imperialists and Arab feudal landlords, the groups which in Solow's view were responsible for the problems of the Jewish settlers in the first place."[126]

Long on criticism and short on alternatives, Solow was not yet ready to give up the Jewish question for the social question. Eventually he sympathized with Judah L. Magnus's binational solution.[127] For the young Jewish intellectuals at the *Menorah Journal*, Zionism and its actualities were not a vital issue. What made Solow's articles explosive was the shift in thinking they indicated: in the terms of the time, it was a shift from questions of race to questions of class, from an ethnocentric, and hence particular, to an economic, and hence universalist analysis of society.

At first it seemed as if the two world views could be combined. But suitable topics, such as Zionism or the Jewish proletariat, were in limited supply. In his rhetorically tactful retrospective, Trilling attempts just such a combination.

> Suddenly it began to be possible—better than that, indeed: it began to be necessary—to think with categories that were charged with energy and that had the effect of assuring the actuality of the object thought about. One couldn't, for example, think for very long about Jews without perceiving that one was using the category of social class. It was necessary not merely in order to think about Jews in their relation to the general society but in order to think about Jews as Jews, the class differences among them being so considerable and having so complex a relationship to the general concept of Jewishness that had at first claimed one's recognition and interest. (NT 15)

Now, this is nonsense. It was not necessary "in order to think about Jews as Jews" to use the "category of social class." But if Jewishness "excluded religion [and] excluded Zionism" as social actuality as well as "ethnic aspiration" (NT 11) and was instead defined, as it is in Trilling's fictions, as a special kind of relationship to one's environment, then, of course, the issue of class becomes mixed up with "the general concept of Jewishness." But the "general concept of Jewishness" was nothing that engaged Trilling's mind very deeply. He had dutifully accepted the *Menorah* program because it seemed morally right "that the individual Jewish person recognizes naturally and easily that he *is* a Jew and 'accepts himself' as such, finding pleasure and taking pride in the identification, discovering in it one or another degree of significance. From which there might follow an impulse to kinship with others who make the same recognition, and perhaps the forming of associations on the basis of this kinship" (NT 11–12). But otherwise, Jewishness had no describable content for Trilling. Undetected, the particular thought-structure persisted, even though Trilling lost interest in the specifics of Jewish culture. In 1930, when matters concerning the Solow affair became even more complicated, Trilling left the *Menorah*. A year later Cohen resigned and most of his young crew left with him. Shortly afterward, Cohen "resurfaced as executive secretary of the NCDPP [National Committee for the Defense of Political Prisoners], with essentially the same team as before."[128] Trilling and his wife were drawn into the orbit of this auxiliary organization of the Communist Party, but Trilling's fellow traveling lasted only for a period of ten months in 1932 and 1933.[129]

In 1932 Trilling was appointed to an instructorship at Columbia College. He knew that this appointment "was pretty openly regarded as an experiment" (*NT* 13) because he was a Jew. Nevertheless, he had set his mind on a respectable career in the academy rather than on a glamorous life as journalist and fiction writer in the mad, anarchic freedom of the Village. Trilling's reasons for preferring the academy were partly economic. Academic salaries were dismal, but during the Depression any steady job was a blessing. However, there was also something about the academy that suited Trilling's temperament. It provided a protective shell for a man whose main interest was in ideas. Trilling was among the first, at a time when the university was not held in esteem by the intellectuals, to perceive its potential.

> It was at this time that the university began to play a decisive part in the cultural life of America. It was now, almost suddenly, that the academic disciplines seemed to many men to offer attractive professional careers and that literary men—poets and novelists—came to believe that the university offered a suitable base of operations. The English teaching profession became attractive not only because it was the profession that allowed one to escape from the established professions, to support oneself without taking part in the middle-class competitive life, but also because a large number of young literary men were drawn to conceive their life in letters as properly consisting not only of creative activity, but also of intellectual activity, of dealing with ideas, with theories—and could there be a more appropriate place for this enterprise than the university? (*AL* 234–235)

But it was in large measure due to Trilling and the pioneering work he did as cultural critic rooted in the academy that the university came to occupy this place in the minds of American intellectuals. The reception of *The Liberal Imagination* signals the turning point in this process of intellectual reevaluation.[130] But in the 1930s, when Trilling made his decision, this process had not yet set in. Trilling would transform himself into a critic in whose complicated observance of the ordinary the concerns of the uptown and the downtown intellectuals would meet.

Before Trilling could even dream of securing for himself a place in the university, two major obstacles had to be overcome—the genteel anti-Semitism of Columbia's English Department and the necessity of completing his dissertation on Matthew Arnold. To a certain extent the two obstacles were interlinked. It is safe to assume that Trilling had chosen his dissertation topic with an eye on the possibility of a career at Columbia, although Arnold's appropriateness in this respect was not his only attraction. The hardships of the Depression and the intellectual atmosphere in the Village, where Trilling had chosen to live across the street from Edmund Wilson, slowed down Trilling's writing to a snail's pace. He tried to bridge the gap between uptown aspiration and downtown residence by founding "his theory of Arnold's intellectual development on a philosophically rigorous conception of Marx's dialectic."[137] It did not work. Trilling wrote himself into a deadlock.

But to discard Marxist thought and to write a critical history of Arnold's ideas in the style of his dissertation adviser's studies on Carlyle and Mill was equally impossible. It would have made Trilling an intellectual outcast in the Village. His dissertation topic was embarrassing enough as it was. After much suffering Trilling encountered his savior in the men's room of the New School for Social Research. In this odd locale Trilling confessed his distress to Edmund Wilson and obtained relief.

> I was trying to write a book about Matthew Arnold and having a bitter time of it because it seemed to me that I was working in a lost world, that nobody wanted, or could possibly want, a book about Matthew Arnold. Nor was I being what in those days would have been called "subjective"—no one did want the book. They wanted it even the less because it was to be a doctoral dissertation: there was at that time a great deal of surveillance of the dwelling places of the mind, and ivory towers were very easily imputed; the university, it is true, was just then beginning to figure in people's minds more than ever before in America, but it did not enjoy the prestige, though ambiguous, which it now has, and I was much ashamed of what I had undertaken. But Wilson asked me how my book was getting on, and not merely out of politeness but, as was clear, because he actually thought that a book on Matthew Arnold might be interesting and useful. He wanted to read it. It is impossible to estimate the liberating effect which this had upon me, the sudden sense that I no longer had to suppose that I was doing a shameful academic drudgery, that I was not required to work with the crippling belief that I was "turning away" from the actual and miserable present to the unreal and comfortable past. The kindest and most intelligent of professors could not possibly have done this for me—it needed Wilson with his involvement in the life of the present which was so clearly not at odds with his natural and highly developed feeling for scholarship.[132]

It needed the quasi-official dispensation of the Village authority Wilson to set Trilling free. As Krupnick notes, in "successive revisions, Trilling found himself renouncing Marx's idea of the dialectic and interpreting Arnold positively in Arnold's own terms. But the concept of the dialectic remained."[133] Trilling was just about to get over his writer's block, when new trouble appeared on the horizon. "In 1936 the department chairman Ernest Hunter Wright called Trilling into his office and advised him to look elsewhere for a permanent appointment because there was no future for him at Columbia."[134] Trilling was thunderstruck. Cornered and threatened with losing what he most cared about, he burst into unusual activity and got ready to fight. His notebook becomes a battle diary.

On April 20, 1936, Trilling notes "Jacques B[arzun] called to report content of his dinner with [Harrison Ross] Steeves [chairman of the English Department] . . . . The reason for dismissal is that as a Jew, a Marxist, a Freudian I am uneasy. This hampers my work and makes me unhappy. E. E. Neff [Trilling's adviser] concurs in this opinion" (N1 498). On May 5, Trilling confronts Steeves. "Me cool and positive. Him friendly and 'realistic'. . . . Act motivated by concern for my welfare. I replied that if this is so I might well have been consulted . . ." (N1 498–499). The interview then centers on Trilling's pedagogical qualities as reason for his dismissal. Trilling stands up to Steeves and finally forces him to "delay positive action" (N1 499). One by one Trilling meets with members of the department: "called E. E. N. and made date to annihilate him on Thursday" (N1 500). He forces them to tell him to his face why he is being dismissed. Most faculty members give Trilling's teaching as the reason. Trilling is ready "to raise hell to say that the way I taught was the right way" (N1 501). Then the Thursday of Neff's annihilation arrives.

On the question of Trilling's quality as a teacher Neff retreats, claiming that he has only "the highest admiration." He sticks, however, to his complaints about Trilling's dissertation: "he felt that my sociological tendencies had hidden my literary gifts in the thesis as in the classroom" (N1 502). On the issue of Trilling's "Jewish-sensitivity" Neff goes into hiding behind Raymond Weaver's broad back: "had meant that I was too sensitive to Weaver's 'brutality.'" This brings Trilling to a boil. "I blew up." To which Neff replies "that the trouble had started with my appointment" because Trilling had been forced on the department. By the end of the interview Trilling concludes "that I was being fired for all the qualities I admired in myself" (N1 503); and Neff finishes with an all-too-obvious lie: "The whole business he had thought would be a warning not a dismissal: nonsense. There remains to see Steeves and tell him what I now know and to insult Weaver, publicly if possible (N1 503).

A month later Trilling has won the battle. Wilson's dispensation and the Columbia reappointment remove the writing block and change his life. The way into the academy is open:

Going through change of life and acquiring a new dimension. Principally a sense that I do not have to prove anything finally and everlastingly. A sense of life—of the past and present. Am no longer certain that the future will be a certain—Marxian—way. No longer measure all things by linear Marxian yardstick. But this is symbolic. A new emotional response to all things. New response to people, a new tolerance, a new interest. A sense of invulnerability. The result of my successful explosion at Columbia? The feeling that I can now write with a new illumination, getting rid of that rigid linear method that has irritated me in my reviewing for so long. . . . Sense of my own stature & less concern with it. (*N1* 503; June 13, 1936)

Two years later, in 1938, Trilling received his doctorate, and in 1939 he was appointed, as the first Jew in Columbia's English Department, to an assistant professorship, shortly after W. W. Norton published *Matthew Arnold*. The appointment was made by President Butler.

Liberated from the "Marxian yardstick," Trilling's dissertation could develop into his first "creative effort to know his present circumstances and to judge their defects, to know both current inadequacies and past achievements." Matthew Arnold became a "substantial representative" of the liberalism which Trilling would examine critically throughout his career. The true test that Trilling devised for Arnold involved an assessment of the Englishman's intelligence as Trilling understood it. He examined to what degree Arnold's mind was responsive to historical, cultural, and human complexity. Under Arnold's tutelage and with Wilson's dispensation, Trilling returned to the *Menorah* program, except that what the *Menorah* crew had called "Jewish" (and later, in the Village, called "class") would now be called "culture." As William Chace puts it, "along with Arnold, then, Trilling believed that the true life of the mind could be maintained only by those who rooted themselves in the cultural origins they inwardly knew they could not deny. Knowing oneself meant, for Arnold and Trilling . . . that one recognized . . . the 'conditioned,' the unavoidable, the circumstantial."[135]

In his next extended study, a book on E. M. Forster published four years later, in 1943, Trilling forces on his readers an even tougher recognition of man's "conditioned" nature, namely, the acknowledgment of the simultaneity of good and evil. The short book is designed as an argument against the "linear Marxian yardstick." Against the simplicity of the Marxian idea of man and the Marxist intellectuals' naive assumption of man's rationality, Trilling pits the "moral realist" Forster. Moral realism is the imaginative recognition of man's complexity. "The liberal mind is sure that the order of human affairs owes it a simple logic: good is good and bad is bad. . . . Before the idea of good-and-evil its imagination fails; it cannot accept this improbable paradox." In a related vein, Trilling argues with the help of Forster that man's historical conditioning is more complex than the liberals suppose it to be. In his novel *Howards End*, Forster points out "that on the one hand class is character, soul and destiny, and that on the other hand class is not finally determining."[136] The reduction of human affairs to matters of class shows a rigidity of mind that may easily lead to a zeal and ferociousness that makes intellect dangerous. It is in opposition to the excesses of the mind that Trilling, like Forster, praises "the life of simple instinct," or "the life of accepted calm."[137] These, then, had been Trilling's choices and decisions before he published his story, "Of This Time, of That Place" in the 1943 *Partisan Review*. The story assesses the costs of his decisions.

The character constellation and the theme are fundamentally the same as in "Impediments." The lexicon has changed and the introduction of a third character, torn between two irreconcilable positions, reduces the immediacy of the conflict and makes its solution a matter of "conscious choice."[138] Hettner has become the mad student Tertan. The narrator of "Impediments" is split into two: his assimilationist, i.e., opportunist tendencies and his urge to be successful within the system are acted out by the 'healthy' student Blackburn, whereas the struggle of conscience to join or oppose, to support an opportunist or to declare his solidarity with an outsider is located in the instructor Howe. The latter is also a poet and would like to rise to an assistant professorship. He resembles the narrator in "Impediments" in his civilized manners and "genteel poverty."[139] The story avoids the simplicity of putting Howe into a position in which he would have to choose directly between Tertan and Blackburn; but Howe is aware that the pressures, the expectations both students bring to bear on him, are antagonistic. They demand that he either undermine or perpetuate the social system in which they are all caught up. Again, the story is not so much a story as a study of the pressures on a civilized self.

The plot is simple. At the beginning of the semester Howe discovers an extraordinary student in his class, an exceptional, though not always lucid writer with a deep intuitive as well as analytic understanding of literature and a more than ironic distance from the academy. Tertan waves aside the devastating review Howe's latest volume of poetry has received from an established academic as a critic's admission "*prima facie* that he doesn't understand" (*O* 84). Halfway through the semester another student, Blackburn, shows up pleading to be admitted to Howe's class on

Romantic prose, "just for background" (O 86). He drops out again, but shows up for the Romantic poetry class in the following semester, and writes fantastically bad papers. Meanwhile Howe has discovered that Tertan is mad.

> It was a monstruous word and stood like a bestial thing in the room. Yet it so completely comprehended everything that had puzzled Howe, it so arranged and explained what for three months had been perplexing him that almost at once its horror became domesticated. With this word Howe was able to understand why he had never been able to communicate to Tertan the value of a single criticism or correction of his wild, verbose themes. Their conferences had been frequent and long but had done nothing to reduce to order the splendid confusion of the boy's ideas. (O 90–91)

He debates with himself whether the dean should be informed of Tertan's madness. It would liberate him from his responsibility. But is Tertan truly mad? " 'What is Tertan?' He alone could keep it still a question. Some sure instinct told him that he must not surrender the question to a clean official desk in a clear official light to be dealt with, settled and closed. He heard himself saying, 'Is the Dean busy at the moment? I'd like to see him' " (O 94).

Unthinking, Howe caves in. It turns out later that Tertan *is* clinically mad. Simultaneously, Howe is pressured by Blackburn to give him better grades on his papers and exams. The student tries foolish blackmail. He suggests that the bad review and Howe's recommendation of a mad student for a literary society indicate lack of academic judgment, of which lack the dean should be informed. Howe is flabbergasted and cries out, "Blackburn, you're mad." Although the direct attempts at blackmail are ineffectual, Howe gives in to Blackburn's madness. His is the madness of the system; it is ubiquitous and socially sanctioned. The boy can graduate. Howe is promoted and Tertan is committed to an institution.

Jewishness is apparently not an issue in this story. But that is just a matter of Trilling's not using the word *Jewish* for Tertan, so that the story would appeal to the diverse readership of *Partisan Review*. Trilling's description (via Howe) of Tertan is essentially that of a Hettner-type. "His face . . . was made up of florid curves, the nose arched in the bone and voluted in the nostrils, the mouth loose and soft and rather moist. Yet the face was so thin and narrow as to seem the very type of asceticism. . . . Howe noted that his suit was worn thin, his shirt almost unclean. He became aware, even, of a vague and musty odor of garments worn too long in unaired rooms" (*O* 82, 83).

His papers are "torrential rhetoric" (*O* 78) and in the classroom Tertan automatically stands up for his intellectual discharge. "He seemed unable to carry on the life of the intellect without this mark of respect for it. To Howe the boy's habit of rising seemed to accord with the formal shabbiness of his dress" (*O* 89). At one point Tertan's Hebrew flux is contrasted with the Greek stasis of one of his classmates by the German name Stettenhover. While Tertan, jumping from his chair, delivers one of his volleys, "Stettenhover slumped suddenly in his seat, his heels held out before him, making a loud dry disgusted sound. His body sank until his neck rested on the back of his chair. He folded his hands across his belly . . . . There was so much power in the big body, so much contempt in the Greek-athlete face under the crisp Greek-athlete curls, that Howe felt almost physical fear. . . . His eyebrows raised high in resignation, [Stettenhover] began to examine his hands" (*O* 89).

The contrast here is almost overdetermined. The emphasis on Stettenhover's hands during Tertan's speech epitomizes the mind-body contrast which the passage as a whole develops.[140] The negligent ascetic Tertan has certainly not much interest in his body. The physical positions of the two students—one jumping up and down, talking rapidly, the other slouching in his chair—indicate an opposition between intellectual agility/flux and stasis (despite the epithet "athlete" for Stettenhover); and the word *Greek* evokes its opposite, *Hebrew* or *Jew*. Henry Rosenthal had employed this pair in his story. Starobin, "a professional Jew" (*In* 54), in search of a companion at Columbia, on meeting Dolman "chanced upon one who was clean, a classic fellow. He was a Jew looking for another and had found a Greek" (*In* 52). Trilling had encountered in Arnold's *Culture and Anarchy* the Gentile view of this opposition. Because the moral evaluation Arnold attached to this opposition was biased in favor of his own culture,[141] Trilling was careful to preface the discussion of Arnold's text in his monograph with a Jewish summary of the Hebraism/Hellenism dichotomy.[142]

The Greeks, as people of the eye, nature, and static beauty (their athlete sculptures represent arrested motion as on Keats's Grecian Urn), stand over and against the Jews, as people of the ear (and mouth), history, and social ethics. For Arnold as for Babbitt, Hellenism is the culture of intelligence, imagination, and aesthetics; whereas "Hebraism is the root of anarchy."[143] From the Greek perspective, a people given to "flux, mutation, imminence, disorder"[144] produces madmen, who at other times are called prophets or poets. Tertan turns out to be all three. Just as Hettner had signaled Jewish (or Hebraic) thinking by his "timid scorn and mistrust" of the fine arts (in which he was well read), so Tertan holds Jewish views underneath an odd Greek cloak. He had written "a work of homiletics, which is a defense of the principles of religious optimism against the pessimism of Schopenhauer and the humanism of Nietzsche." *Humanism* is Tertan's "nomenclature for making a deity of man" (O 84). Tertan denies the possibility of man's transcendence and the knowability of God. But Howe hears Greek when Tertan speaks Hebrew.

> "Flux of existence," Tertan was saying, "produces all things, so that judgment wavers. Beyond the phenomena, what? But phenomena are adumbrated and to them we are limited."
> Howe saw it for a moment as perhaps it existed in the boy's mind —the world of shadows which are cast by a great light upon a hidden reality as in the old myth of the Cave. (O 89)

Because Howe is only half familiar with Tertan's world of radical immanence, his description of Tertan to the dean does not reflect Tertan's mind but Howe's understanding: "What he says is always on the edge of sense and doesn't quite make it" (O 97).

Nevertheless, the bond between Howe and Tertan is strong, subterranean, based on the kinship of "free souls and creative spirits" (O 76), based on the knowledge of the core, of the dynamics of the soul and the intoxicating power of the imagination that makes of the *tour d'ivoire* a *tour d'ivresse*.[145] Tertan had come to Howe as Hettner had to his fellow student or Starobin to Dolman, for a tête à tête of souls beyond manner. As were Hettner's, Tertan's needs are immense, a fact brought home to Howe when he reads the letter Tertan has written to the dean about him. In a three-part leap, he finds himself transformed in this letter into another Tertan.

First Howe is described as a Romantic temperament: "Of intellects not the first yet of true intellect and lambent instructions, given to that which is intuitive and irrational, not to what is logical in the strict word, what is judged by him is of the heart and not the head" (O 99–100). Then, he becomes a Greek, Tertan's Paraclete, "the one who comforts and assists" (O 99), a figure which in the second part of the letter, where the writer moves from the particular to the universal, is transformed into a Christ: "Here is one chosen, in that he chooses himself to stand in the place of another for comfort and consolation" (O 100). And finally, by turning the salvational energies on himself (the vehicle being his alter ego, Tertan), Howe becomes the ultimate Romantic, his own Christ: "for he must be the Paraclete to another aspect of himself, that which is driven and persecuted by the lack of understanding in the world at large, so that he in himself embodies the full history of man's tribulations and, overflowing upon others, notably the present writer, is the ultimate end" (O 100).

Howe immediately perceives what is at the root of Tertan's rapturously shifting comparisons. "This was love. There was no escape from it" (O 100). It was not, like Jewish *ḥesed* or Catholic *caritas*, a love anchored in social circumstance, but one freed from circumstance like the eucharistic *agape*, the love of Narkissos, or the rapture of Dionysos. It was a recognition of one's own kind beyond the world of phenomena, a supreme form of self-love, and hence inescapable. Yet, delving into the self too deeply was destructive (Narkissos) even though letting go of "social circumstance" might create community (agape) or a perfect poem (Dionysos). It was exactly such letting go—leading to "precious subjectivism," self-intoxication, obscurantism, and so forth—that the poet Howe had found himself accused of by the academic critic who had called him "almost dangerous" (O 81). Two decades later Trilling would accuse modern literature, which he regarded as the "canonization of the primal, non-ethical energies"[146] of exactly such "precious subjectivism." Tertan's letter to the dean outlines the intellectual grammar of "modern literature," which Trilling would spell out in greater detail in his essay "On the Teaching of Modern Literature" (1961).

On his first reading of the academic's review, Howe had been amused by the critic's "multiplication of himself into 'the Howes'." But when he recognizes the pagan and Christian roots for his multiple selves, which are all tied into one representative man, he becomes uneasy. "This becoming the multiform political symbol by whose creation Frederic Woolley [the critic] gave the sign of a sudden new life, this use of him as a sacrifice whose blood was necessary for the rites of rejuvenation, made him feel oddly unclean" (O 81). As a man of Jewish sensibility malgré lui, he considers participation in the "rites of spring" unclean, treyf, although he might have made a perfect paschal lamb. In the end, however, he decides to sacrifice Tertan, the "other aspect of himself" before he enters "the rites of rejuvenation," the commencement exercises of his college, and begins his new life as assistant professor.

Howe has decided against the life of soul-probing, of narcissistic psychoanalysis, of "precious subjectivism," and in favor of "the real lives of real people" (O 81), a life that acknowledges social circumstances and is spent in an effort to tame the irrational energies of the self. He decides in favor of civilization, or culture. The life of the Romantic poet gives way to the life of the professor of Romanticism. And yet he feels "oddly unclean" when he sacrifices the emotional, subversive Tertan aspect in order to preserve the established social structures. While there is something wholesome about the world of the ordinary, the price of the entry ticket is high. Too much has to be sacrificed; and the world Howe enters is more than unappealing. It is deadening and dead to the life of imaginative excitement. But it promises emotional stability, social acceptance, and security. Trilling's deep regret about Howe's decision is obvious.

To say, then, that Trilling's story is about the "psychic costs of assimilation"[147] is to be aware of a curious inversion. For Trilling, the world of his fathers was not downtown—neither in the bohemian Village nor on the proletarian Lower East Side—in the worlds of (Jewish) utopians and idealists. What he knew of Jewish life (outside his father's home) took place uptown, at the Jewish Theological Seminary or at Columbia. What he knew of Judaism, the observance of the ordinary, happened in the world of the middle class struggling with the hard facts of life. It was the middle class which willy-nilly had to be aware of the social circumstances. For Trilling, to join their ranks was to remain true to himself. It was, to use a set of terms Trilling developed in the early 1970s, an act of "sincerity," an act that attempted a concord of self and social environment; not an act of "authenticity," that plunging into the self whose frame of reference for self-realization is "the universe and man's place in it."[148] Coming out in defense of the middle class was to preserve what little there was in Trilling of a Jewish self.

In 1939, Trilling joined the academy but did not submit to its genteel pressure. His mission was to make the academy a place that would acknowledge the complexity of the ordinary, of the social circumstance. But the Tertan in him was not yet dead; he continued to oppose the Columbia professor. In 1948, after Trilling had published his last piece of fiction, his novel *The Middle of the Journey*, he wrote in his "Notebook": "Suppose I were to dare to believe that one could be a professor and a man! and a writer!—what arrogance and defiance of convention. Yet deeply I dare to believe that—and must learn to believe it on the surface" (*N1* 511). A dozen years after Wilson's magnanimous dispensation, a sense of guilt and even more of regret crept into Trilling at having relinquished the life of personal freedom for the life of social bondage. When he received his promotion from associate professor to George Edward Woodberry Professor, he wrote in his "Notebook": "My being a professor and a much respected and even admired one is a great hoax. But sometimes I feel that I pay for the position not with learning but with my talent—that I draw off from my own work what should remain with it. Yet this is really only a conventional notion, picked up from my downtown friends" (*N1* 511).

Regrets at having sacrificed "another aspect of himself" certainly played a role in Trilling's troubled friendship with his former student Allen Ginsberg and with Norman Mailer. The poet and the novelist were two romantically rebellious figures of the Tertan type. In public, Trilling disapproved of their actions and pronouncements. But privately he was divided between concern and affection. As Mark Krupnick observed: "Ginsberg and Mailer, in their different ways, lived out a part of Trilling, the anti-social part, which he himself sacrificed but which, at various times in his career he sought, somewhat wistfully, to reclaim."[149]

The anti-social parts that Ginsberg and Mailer acted out were quite different, but to a Jewish mind they were both offshoots of the same evil root, or *yetzer ha-ra*. Ginsberg and Mailer plunged into the ocean of experience. But whereas the poet disappeared with a howl sounding the depth of his soul, the cautious novelist, having inhaled before plunging, popped to the surface with a moan suffering from an inflated self. Both Ginsberg and Mailer tried to transform the exploration of the ego into art. Trilling, however, despite his undeniable fascination with the Romantic (authentic) self, remained critical of the enterprise and feared the effects of the imagination cut loose from its rationalist tether.

Ginsberg is usually considered the model for Tertan. When Ginsberg, on leave from Columbia's Psychiatric Institute, came to see Trilling (in the late 1940s), the latter experienced a "sense of fatigue and indifference —the absence of some grain, some resistant element." But he is aroused when he and Ginsberg discuss Jack Kerouac's book. "I predicted that it would not be good & insisted. But later I saw with what bitterness I had made the prediction—not wanting K's book to be good because if the book of an accessory to a murder is good, how can one of mine be? —The continuing sense that wickedness—or is it my notion of courage—is essential for creation" (*N1* 513).

On the basis of the thought processes at work in "Impediments" and "Of This Time, of That Place," which one might call mitnagdic thinking, this odd "Notebook" entry is easy to decode. At the heart of the imagination, Trilling suspects an impulse which is both creative (book) and destructive (murder). The "wickedness . . . essential for creation" had been given the name *yetzer ha-ra* in the world of Trilling's father; Trilling will call this "generative force" *authenticity*, "which implies the downward movement through all the cultural superstructures to some place where all movement ends, and begins."[150]

The yetzer ha-ra, the wicked impulse of creativity, grows out of the authentic self, out of what Cynthia Ozick calls a "whirlpool, abyss, chaos, whatever name you want to give it. Everyone who writes, and has even a small amount of gift for it," she claims, "has chosen to speak out of the whirlpool or whirlwind."[151] The courage, of which Trilling speaks, is to look into the abyss of the self and not to stop there, but to transform the seen, the secret, into fiction, to bring it into the daylight and anchor it in the world of social circumstances. This is an act of taming, of civilizing, which is achieved at the cost Freud suggested; nonetheless it requires "courage (for the act)."[152] Fiction, then, contains (in a double sense) the yetzer ha-ra, the anarchic (simultaneously destructive and creative) forces of the authentic self.

> The secret sharer who writes the fiction climbs aboard only when the captain allows [him] to—i.e., in fiction only. I have often thought —what if I released the fiction writing secret sharer to go free in the Real World? What would I become? . . . The chaos within me must *not* become incarnate in the "world of phenomena." The chaos within is the yetzer ha-ra—the *terrifying* secret sharer, embodiment of the abyss, demonic Doppelgänger, trickster, gamester, Loki or Mercury.
> The yetzer ha-ra *makes up* stories. That is why the yetzer ha-ra belongs inside stories. . . . the fire of the yetzer ha-ra [is] extremely dangerous. . . .[153]

When what Trilling called the "primal stuff"[154] is set free in the Real World or is howled out untamed by circumstance in poetry, when the forces of the authentic self become "howls" or "precious subjectivity" or letters "on the edge of sense" (like Tertan's to the dean), then murder, the physical assertion of one self over another, is indeed a possibility.[155] Its harmless version is self-celebration. About two decades after the Tertan story (1943) and the Ginsberg-Kerouac "Notebook" entry, Trilling wrote about Tertan/Ginsberg's harmlessly inflated counterparts.

> Whether or not the artist derives his powers from neurosis, he certainly derives them from a species of insanity, from megalomania, from his absurd belief in his own myth. This is what accounts for the achievement of Mailer and Bellow and even Malamud. They believe they are great men, they insist on being the center of their universes: all revolves around them. To impose, to impose: this is their single aim; it acts as a real thing, although it arises out of the absurdity. I

defeated myself long ago when I rejected the way of chutzpah and mishagass in favor of reason and diffidence. (N2 13)

Trilling's "Notebook" entry is curious in its envious resentment. The clear-minded Trilling's argument would be that "unsureness . . . vulnerability . . . absolute *not*-full-of-oneselfness [are] signs of the real writer,"[156] because they signal openness toward the world of circumstance. But the civilized critic here gives way to the discontented and even resentful writer turned educator who has had his mind set on the taming of the Jews. After years of civilizing labor, who should pop out of Pandora's American literature box? Hettner and Tertan, turned fiction writers embarked on an ego-trip around the Jewish Self—not unlike that undertaken by Ludwig Lewisohn. Half in earnest, half in jest, Trilling admits defeat. There is no taming of the Jews. His last sentence permits two different readings.

The obvious meaning is Trilling's disapproval of "chutzpah" (boldness, impertinence) and "mishagass" (craziness) and the implicit attribution of his failure ("defeat") to a culture turned crazy or "adversarial" in the age of unreason. The second, subterranean meaning mirrors the remorse of a writer who once believed in the *Menorah* program of self-acceptance as Jew and in Arnold's insistence on cultural rootedness. What defeated Trilling as a writer was that he abandoned "chutzpah" and "mishagass," signifying here the world of Jewish culture, so that he could join—shy, reasonable and civilized—the ranks of the Gentiles at Columbia. He gave up his home base, his rootedness; but the intellectual imprint he retained prohibited the descent into the self freed from social circumstance. Is not the artist "the man who goes down into that hell which is the historical beginning of the human soul, a beginning not outgrown but established in humanity as we know it . . .?"[157]

Trilling's last two good works of fiction, "The Other Margaret" (1945) and *The Middle of the Journey* (1947), retain the double and alter ego structures, in order to argue their moral points. Not much is left of the dazzling mitnagdic argumentation of the earlier stories, which contrasted in a sweep the self-centered cultures of Hellenism, Christianity, and Romanticism with a collectivity-oriented ideal of moral seriousness, observance of the ordinary, and rootedness in circumstance. For reasons of his own Trilling preferred to call the latter "middle class" rather than "Jewish." Although little is left of the flamboyant structural and intellectual contrasts set up by the earlier stories, the essence of Trilling's moral argument is preserved in the two late works of fiction.

Both focus on maturation after an insight into the hard fact of death. Maturation here is equated with a growing moral realism. In "The Other Margaret," maturity means the ability to acknowledge that action is not determined by class or by one's allegiance to any group but by individual choice, "that under the shadow of death, social melioration is no more than a fancy and personal responsibility is everything."[158]

In *The Middle of the Journey* the "self in crisis," John Laskell, is confronted with a variety of alternative selves and their extreme ideas about life. Having emerged from severe illness, Laskell finds the theoretical, virtuous "yardsticks" of his friends—ranging from Communism to ascetic Christianity—unattractive and untrue. He advocates modulation, personal responsibility, acceptance of the given without giving up ideals or individuality, which is the center of resistance against the vulgarity of "all conscious virtues."[159]

In 1947 Trilling's choice, made over a decade earlier, had become acceptable to a majority of intellectuals; thus it is indeed possible to read *The Middle of the Journey*, as Mark Shechner suggests we do, as the "testament of a generation's disillusionment and conversion, which brought forth the chastened position and subdued aesthetics of the postwar era."[160] After World War II American intellectuals needed Trilling as a cultural spokesman, and Trilling performed to the end the task for which he had civilized himself, even though the culture that crowned him representative man turned against him in the sixties. He remained sincere in a culture indulging itself in authenticity. He remained true to his mitnagdic mind; yet it was hardly suspected, let alone understood, that what he was saying in the Columbian tongue was structured by the grammar of a much older culture.

A MIND IN REPOSE ABOVE THE BATTLEGROUND OF THE HEART

Instead of "intellectual grammar," Trilling would have preferred to say "mental character" or "mode of thought." But neither of these terms conveys as clearly as "grammar" the idea that the signified is an intellectual *structure*, and not a mentality. It determines not being, but thinking—that is, the perception of the world, and the reflection about the self's relation to it. Intellectual grammar is acquired, not inherited. But it is acquired at an early age, formed by those who first teach the decoding of the world. Hence, it is a cultural product. The first decodings are usually just a dichotomous distinguishing, a separation of one thing from another: self from mother, mother from father, family from nonfamily, cultural kinsmen from others, etc. The move from binary to pluralist thinking is a late development, demanding a rather secure sense of self, perhaps even cultural rootedness.

The foundations of one's intellectual grammar, a sort of dichotomous grid imposed on an amorphous mass of phenomena, are laid by those who first speak to the child, usually the parents or close relatives. Therefore it may seem as if intellectual grammar were inherited. It is the intellectual imprint of one's descent culture. This first imprint had a particularly good chance to develop into a complex intellectual grammar in Jewish culture, because the weltanschauung of the Jews was not only significantly different from that of their neighbors, but it also induced them to prefer social separation. Group cohesion used to be strong, and the group control over the child almost exclusive. This was certainly true for the Jews of Eastern Europe; but it was also true for a large number of Jewish communities in America, particularly in such cities as New York and Chicago. Jewish children of Trilling's generation still had a good chance of growing up completely within their descent culture. But even when the parents moved out of what they considered the narrow confines of Jewish culture, basic distinctions were often preserved.[161]

Although Trilling spent his childhood "in a world predominantly non-Jewish" his family was culturally Jewish and his first intellectual educators at the Jewish Theological Seminary were "professional Jews," to use Henry Rosenthal's phrase. There is no doubt that Trilling was sufficiently exposed to his descent culture to develop an intellectual grammar based on a Jewish perception of the world.

But Trilling also grew up in America; hence his thinking was flexible. He grew up speaking as an American while perceiving the world as a Jew. From the beginning, his intellectual grammar was applied to more than the specifics of Jewish culture; therefore, the substitution of universal ("American") for particular ("Jewish") meanings, undertaken most significantly during his passage into the academy, did not shake his sense of identity to the degree to which it had upset those of some of his precursors. Trilling had practice in making transitions; yet few of these led to radically new insights, because the preestablished grid of possible dichotomies remained unchanged.

In Trilling's case these dichotomies can be reduced, as has been suggested by his critics, to the opposition of self and culture, which within the Jewish world is a rather recent dichotomy.[162] Trilling differs significantly in his intellectual grammar from such precursors as Morris Cohen and

Harry Wolfson, because for Trilling having an individual self was a matter of course whereas for his precursors the positing of such a self was already a revolutionary, bondage-breaking act. However, Trilling never explored this self very deeply. He remained suspicious of its force when it was freed from communal (i.e., cultural) ties; he needed to see the self in relation to culture, to social circumstance. Trilling believed that "literature is dedicated to the conception of the self."[163] But the literature he cherished, and tried himself to write, was precisely literature that examined the self in relation to culture (as does the *Bildungsroman*, or the novel of manners). His personal literary preference was classical (that is to say anti-Romantic in the manner of the Goethe of *Elective Affinities*) rather than Victorian. He detested pieties. And his own literary thinking, though gracefully expressed, was tough-minded, anti-sentimental.

Trilling's focus on culture rather than the self (even when writing about such ego-centered issues as Freud's psychoanalysis) derived from his deep rootedness in his time and his place,[164] which in turn was derived from his descent culture's observance of the ordinary. This focus on the ordinary, on the world of phenomena, on the given, is central to Trilling's thinking. However, the eyes of the rabbinic sages became in Trilling's secular world the eyes of a novelist and later the eyes of a critic.

In the transition from the religious to the secular world, observance became observation. Trilling elaborated the meaning of "observation" to include "intelligence" and "discretion." Intelligence adds to observation the element of analysis, which makes it possible to read "manners as the indication of the direction of man's soul" (*JA* 212). Discretion adds to observation and analysis the capacity to distinguish and separate. Foremost among the separations Trilling considered constitutive of the civilized self were that of private and public sphere, inside and outside, soul and role ("dress," manners), authentic and sincere. Trilling liked "people quite entirely dressed" (*Im* 6). Then it was safe to look at them. Concerning manners, his perceptions were acute, his cultural criticism incisive. But other forms of vision—utopian, aesthetic, or psychological—were foreign to him. They focused on matters beyond the realm of the ordinary, beyond the realm of "the real lives of real people" (*O* 81). So did the utopias of religion or Marxism, and so did art, "the image of perfection" which transmuted "that which is alive into that which has the moveless-ness and permanence of things past, assimilating it in some part to death" (*JA* 220–221). And so did the dark "hidden element of human nature" which necessitated psychological vision.[165]

This is not to say that Trilling was not interested in and fascinated by what lay beyond culture. Utopias, however, never held his attention for very long. But the "hidden element of human nature," its subversiveness, its antagonism to culture captivated him. Yet he was not free to explore the dynamics of the soul; he was never on comfortable terms with the literature exploring the "Abyss."[166] Dutifully, but with great ambivalence, he taught Dostoevsky, Conrad, Lawrence, Mann, and Kafka.

Over the years, the aspect of the dark "hidden element" presented itself to Trilling in a variety of aspects. He was fascinated by the intense Jewish souls (the Hettners, Tertans, Rosenthals, Ginsbergs), by his Romantic alter egos on the brink of sense, by the hellish soul-probing of Romantic poetry, by the "discovery and canonization of the primal non-ethical energies" in neo-Romantic, that is, "modern" literature, by the "Howls" of the counterculture, by the self-destruction of the white middle-class elite, and last but not least, by "biological fact" and the "death instinct." Of these forces, adversarial to culture, only the hard fact of death and the reality of the death instinct were given his un-ironic attention.

But the omnipresence of death in Trilling's work, minutely analyzed in Daniel O'Hara's monograph, is perhaps less surprising when death is considered without Christian rescue in mind. Death is final; as its border, death defines life. It creates historic time. Trilling's speculations and imaginings did not attempt to go beyond death. He was rather impatient with those who either disputed its finality by coupling it with rebirth or aestheticized it and thus gave immortality to what was mortal.[167] Exactly such transcendence constituted the intellectual link between paganism, Christianity, and Romanticism. Art was essentially a representation of death, of arrested time, with a claim to life everlasting. Trilling's last unfinished essay contains a great critique of art from the perspective of one puzzled by its paradox. Trilling's view of art is that of one staring at the dead man on the cross without belief in the body's promise of eternal life, that is, of one incapable of the all-transcending leap of faith.

> It is not alone the art and thought of Yeats's Byzantium that has in it the element of fixity, of movelessness, or what I am calling death—all thought and art, all conceptual possession of the processes of life, even that form which we call love, has inherent in its celebration and sanctification of life some element of this negation of life. . . . Nowadays it is not often observed as a paradox of human spirit in the West that, for all its devotion to will in action, it finds pleasure and the image of perfection in what is realized and brought to its end—in the perception that art, even when it is at pains to create the appearance of intense and vigorous action, has the effect of transmuting that which

is alive into that which has the movelessness and permanence of things past, assimilating it in some part to death. (*JA* 220–221)

For Trilling, death was final. His was not a culture of second chances, nor one of transcending leaps, be they religious or artistic. He opted for the world of phenomena, the given, the ordinary, of which the boundary was death. Yet this did not free him from moral obligation. On the contrary, this choice, as Cynthia Ozick points out, first creates moral seriousness. "The secret is in intrinsicness, in caring above all for the Ding an sich: which is what carries everyone anyhow. To look beyond it is by definition frivolous. Death-the-Leveler leaves no choice to Ambition but to turn to the striving for getting things as right as possible."[168] The hard fact of death, the impossibility of transcendence, does more than define the self; it also places all responsibility on the self. Not class, race, or gender, but the individual is responsible for actions, as Trilling spelled out in "The Other Margaret." Therefore, Trilling preferred a literature that depicted the self in struggle with social circumstance.

Trilling was hard-pressed, however, to say what exactly this "self" was. For that reason he appreciated the attempts of the "moderns" to get at this self. He was less pleased, however, with their discoveries, which became part of the moderns' "sense of being." "I spoke of the modern self as characterized by its intense and adversarial imagination of the culture in which it had its being, and by certain powers of indignant perception which, turned upon the unconscious portions of culture, have made them accessible to conscious thought."[169] The "research into the self" was a necessary though dangerous undertaking.[170] Trilling's reluctance to embark on such thinking, his more than ambivalent relationship to the "hidden element in human nature," and his peculiar perception of it become obvious in his essays on Freud.

Freud held a double fascination for Trilling. First, Freud's research material "is exactly the stuff upon which the poet has always exercised his art" (*FL* 34). With some qualifications it may be said that "the working of the unconscious mind [is] equivalent to poetry itself" (*FL* 52). Its material and findings make "psychoanalysis . . . one of the culminations of the Romanticist literature of the nineteenth century" (*FL* 35). Second, what prevented Freud from falling into the abyss and writing Howls was the rationalist tether that constrained his imaginative mind. "Freud believes that positivistic rationalism, in its golden-age pre-Revolutionary purity, is the very form and pattern of intellectual virtue" (*FW* 40). Trilling concurred; he agreed also with Freud's goal. As Trilling wrote of Freud, "The aim of psychoanalysis, he says, is the control of the night side of life. It is 'to strengthen the ego, to make it more independent of the super-ego, to widen its field of vision, and so to extend the organization of the id.' 'Where id was,'—that is, where all the irrational, non-logical, pleasure-seeking dark forces were 'there shall ego be,'—that is, intelligence and control" (FL 40–41). Like Trilling, Freud saw, but did not believe. "If Freud discovered the darkness for science he never endorsed it. On the contrary, his rationalism supports all the ideas of the Enlightenment that deny validity to myth or religion" (FL 41). That was very much Trilling's own position.

One of the more disquieting experiences for readers of Trilling's work is to see him succumb to what might be a myth. In his 1955 address, "Freud: Within and Beyond Culture," the emphasis is shifted from Freud the researcher into the self to Freud the cultural analyst, who sees "the self as formed by its culture," but who "also sees the self as set against the culture, struggling against it, having been from the first reluctant to enter it."[171] But in order to struggle against culture and, eventually, "to stand beyond the reach of culture" (FW 93), the self needs an unshakable foundation. Trilling, claiming to follow Freud, sees this foundation in "biological fact" (FW 97). Almost immediately Trilling defends "this emphasis on biology" as a "liberating idea" (FW 98). "It proposes to us that culture is not all-powerful. It suggests that there is a residue of human quality beyond the reach of cultural control, and that this residue of human quality, elemental as it may be, serves to bring culture itself under criticism and keeps it from being absolute" (FW 98).

He then reveals the contemporary reason behind the need for this center of resistance. American culture of the fifties was seductive. It co-opted its intellectuals. The old centers of resistance, the Yiddishist, Unionist, and Marxist cultures of downtown New York, Chicago, and Boston closed shop. Their former agitators became part of the economic establishment, and their intellectuals now professed their belief in the academy: "the individual's old defenses against the domination of the culture become weaker and weaker" (FW 98). What happened was simple enough: postwar America had unexpectedly caught up with Trilling's ideals—it had become (to a large extent) a contented middle-class culture living "the life of accepted calm." This development engulfed Trilling. From being an intellectual opponent, he had developed into a cultural representative, a captive of America's educated middle class. Trilling looked for a way out of this unwanted bondage. What there had been in him of "religious or ethnic difference" (FW 98) that might have set him apart had been smoothed

out in favor of middle-class values, a process which, as Trilling now recognized, had been repeated on a grand scale in America. He believed
himself "controlled . . . destined and fated and foreordained." Because we
are, as he thought, inescapably doomed by the surrounding culture, "there
must come to us a certain sense of liberation when we remember our
biological selves" (FW 99).

Trilling found himself reduced to the tiniest center of resistance, and
to one that was not even accessible to reason. "We reflect that somewhere
in the child, somewhere in the adult, there is a hard, irreducible, stubborn
core of biological urgency, and biological necessity and biological *reason*,
that culture cannot reach and that reserves the right, which sooner or later
it will exercise, to judge the culture and resist and revise" (FW 99). A few
years earlier, the enlightened Trilling would have opposed this Lawrentian
view as indeed "reactionary" (FW 98). And what the sentence means
exactly is far from clear. In Nazism "biological *reason*" revised culture.
Trilling gets into even more dangerous waters when he tries to make "biological fact" the basis of group cohesion. However, the example he chooses
has the merit to clarify what the point is of this biology business.

> But then too, it sometimes happens that a people living under im-
> posed conditions of a very bad kind, the opposite of the conditions of
> that free and democratic society which the ego and the superego are
> said to need for health and maturity, living, indeed, under persecu-
> tion, will develop egos and superegos of an amazing health and
> strength. . . . They have their psychic casualties, their psychic scars
> are manifest, but they survive in sufficient dignity. And if we ask why
> they thus survived, the answer may be that they conceived of their
> egos and superegos as not being culturally conditioned and dependent
> but as being virtually biological facts, and immutable. And often they
> put this conception of their psyches to the ultimate biological test
> —they died for the immutability of their egos and superegos. (FW
> 100–101)

It is a safe guess that the people Trilling has in mind are the Jews.[172] On
a first reading Trilling sounds disturbingly like the older Lewisohn and
advocates of an ethnic (that is, merely descent-based) definition of the
Jewish people. But it would be surprising if Trilling, like Kallen and
Lewisohn, fell back on a Romantic definition of the Jews. A more careful
reading of his essay discloses that at the heart of Trilling's argument dis-
cussing "the interaction of biology and culture" (FW 100) lies in fact the
difficult question of at what point historical experience, that is previous
cultural conditioning, becomes a heritage shaping the ego and superego.

"It is clear to me," Trilling had said about himself ten years earlier, "that my existence as a Jew is one of the shaping conditions of my temperament, and therefore I suppose it must have its effect on my intellect."[173]

Having neither intellectual, nor political, nor religious platform on which to stand while opposing the quietist Moloch of American middle-class culture, Trilling fell back on himself as biological fact, hoping to find there a center of resistance shaped by heritage. But it was precisely his "heritage," his rationalism, which made him drop the idea of a biological basis for and hence biological determination of the self. To be Jewish (and to have a self) was a matter of mind, not of biology. Trilling would have to look elsewhere for a "principle of permanence [that] can be conceived as a protest against the genre of cultural criticism itself."[174] It was Trilling's deep-rooted observance of the ordinary (which Krupnick calls "patrician rationality") that kept him from giving in to the seduction of Schopenhauer, whose name replaces that of Hegel in Trilling's late essays. And it was Trilling's "allergy to closure" (Krupnick) that prevented him from taking refuge in art, because art was in some sense a celebration of death.

Yet the idea of death as a means to go "beyond culture," as a means to transcend history in an ultimate celebration of self, to transform the self into a work of art, was enticing, and Trilling looked at it with fascination. Critics have taken this fascination for admiration and acceptance, while it was only another version of Trilling's confronting an alternative Romantic self that was not for him. At no point, to say it bluntly, did Trilling want to become a Christ or make his own self into a work of art. Of such violence he was not capable. Yet he watched his alter egos do it and knew of the price they paid; they either howled in pain or became masters "of the genre of silence."[175]

One such alter ego who chose death in life, who preferred body over mind, who killed himself as a Jew so that he might live as an artist, was Isaac Babel. Though Babel (in Trilling's representation) has aspects of Trilling/Howe, he was a Tertan-figure who pretended to accept the ethos of his worst enemy, the Stettenhovers. Babel joined the Cossacks in 1920, when they participated on the side of the revolutionary forces in the Russian civil war, and wrote stories about his experiences in their midst. Babel's desperate act was a madness that gave birth to an art focused on killing. For art to rest on death was nothing new: Christianity and its culture had popularized the idea. But atheist modernity gave the screw another turn by extolling the moment of *translatio*, the committing of the murder. Trilling was disturbed when he first encountered the stories of

Babel in 1929, and almost a quarter of a century later, in 1955, when he composed his introduction to Babel's collected stories, Trilling still felt unnerved by the effect the Russian-Jewish writer had on him. As a rationalist Trilling fears the Tertan-Babels and their intensity of soul just as much as the Stettenhover-Cossacks and their intensity of body. But as a Jewish intellectual he feels a kinship with the vulnerable Tertan-Babels. This sense of kinship, the recognition of something familiar in this strange writer, allows the "willing suspension of disbelief in the selfhood of someone else" (*FW* 81–82). Trilling guesses Babel's "secret" (the fear of a Jew surrounded by an alien culture). And he is familiar with the battleground of Babel's heart, above which the mind is suspended in repose. He recognizes the subversive irony in Babel's art, which seemingly celebrates the art of the Cossacks but at the same time slew them with words. The Cossacks of the Revolution knew that too. They feared Babel's "intensity, irony, and ambiguousness" (*IB* 107), the secret at the center of his art, and eventually silenced this mouth in search of an ear.

Trilling's essay, "Isaac Babel," is an homage to Babel, but it is also a grand polemic against art as the idolization of death (as in paganism and Christianity) and its intensified version in modernity, the idolization of murder. Its counterforce must be the power of mind that counteracts myth and subverts cult through irony.

In Trilling's view, Isaac Babel, an acculturated Jew from Odessa, joins the Cossacks because "his relation with his father defined his Jewishness." Like Trilling Babel had almost no Jewish learning; Jewishness was defined for him when he saw "his father on his knees before a Cossack captain on a horse, who said, 'At your service,' and touched his fur cap with his yellow-gloved hand and politely paid no heed to the mob looting the Babel store" (*IB* 114). The mind seemed powerless in a world of physical violence. It was this image of his father which (for Trilling) informed Babel's notion of the Jew "as a man not in the actual world, a man of no body, a man of intellect, or wits, passive before his secular fate" (*IB* 113). Babel's father "thought about large and serious things, among them respectability and fame. He was a shopkeeper, not well to do, a serious man, a failure. The sons of such men have much to prove, much to test themselves for, and if they are Jewish, their Jewishness is ineluctably involved in the test" (*IB* 114). Trilling's father, too, was a serious man, a failed shopkeeper.

Thus, to escape his fate of being a Jewish intellectual (it proved to be inescapable), Babel joined the Cossacks, whose principle of existence "stood in total antithesis to the principle of the Jew's existence." They were "physical, violent, without mind or manners. . . . the natural and appropriate instrument of oppression" (*IB* 110). And they were admired by many Russian intellectuals. "Tolstoi had represented the Cossacks as having a primitive energy, passion, and virtue." All that was taboo in Babel's Jewish world came to life in the world of the Cossacks and was idolized by the Russian intellectuals. Babel could not resist. When Maxim Gorky told him that he thought "that Babel's first work was successful only by accident" (*IB* 116) and that he should "go among the people," Babel "released the fiction-writing secret sharer to go free in the Real World."[176]

But his attempt to join was not entirely successful. His "mode of thought" (*IB* 107) was different. His release was not complete. One of Babel's stories "ends with the narrator imploring fate to 'grant me the simplest of proficiencies—the ability to kill my fellow man'" (*IB* 116). Babel cannot disappear into the Cossack crowd; his face sticks out from among them. "The face is very long and thin, charged with emotion and internality; bitter, intense, very sensitive, touched with humor, full of consciousness and contradiction. It is 'typically' an intellectual's face, a scholar's face, and it has great charm. I should not want to speak of it as a Jewish face, but it is a kind of face which many Jews used to aspire to have, or hoped their sons would have" (*IB* 111).

His face was expressive of the "autumn in his heart" (*IB* 112). Babel tried hard to ride with the Cossacks. He "carries as far as he can his sympathy with the fantasy that an ultimate psychic freedom is to be won through cruelty conceived of as a spiritual exercise" (*IB* 119). The Cossacks' violence becomes the vehicle of epiphany, "the power of levitation" in his work; it becomes art. And yet Babel knows all the time—this is the secret, the secret that creates the all-important distance and subverts the seeming idolatry of his art—that his art is based on the murder of a Jew. He indicts himself, as well as the Christian Russian intellectuals, in his description of the clergyman Pan Apolek's art. "Pan Apolek's 'heretical and intoxicating brush' had achieved its masterpiece in his Christ of the Berestechko church, 'the most extraordinary image of God I had ever seen in my life,' a curly-headed Jew, a bearded figure in a Polish greatcoat of orange, barefoot, with torn and bleeding mouth, running from an angry mob with a hand raised to ward off a blow" (*IB* 124). When the Cossacks of the Revolution, "the reactionary elements of Soviet culture were established in full ascendancy" (*IB* 105), Babel fell silent, "a torn and bleeding mouth." He wrote nothing after 1932. But that was not enough. "In 1937 he was arrested. He died in a concentration camp in 1939 or 1940" (*IB* 107).

Trilling's empathy for Babel was deep, and his sorrow about the sacrifice of the artistic self was real. But even in America it is impossible to forget the reality of Pan Apolek's picture. In Bialystok, seventy were slain and ninety left with torn and bleeding mouths, a year after Trilling's birth. Babel recognized, in the Jew in Pan Apolek's picture, his own alter ego. And Trilling recognized in both the Cossack Babel and the running Jew the dialectical image of himself. Faced with the question of self-realization, Trilling decided that the answer was not to be found in the self-indulgence of pagans, Christians, and Romantics of all sorts, but—if at all—in the thoughtful recollection of the "conflicting tendencies of culture" (*IB* 107) in his heart. Self-realization was a matter of the mind, the gaining of distance in the act of writing. At that moment his own mind was in repose above the battleground of his heart.

Lionel Trilling was a pioneer of sorts for the Jewish critics who came after him, not only by virtue of his being the first Jew in Columbia's English Department, but perhaps even more so through his successful attempts to reduce the distance between Bialystok and Far Rockaway; between the Jewish Theological Seminary and Columbia College; between creative and analytic writing; between cultural and academic analysis. He came to be regarded as a Columbia man and as a spokesman for literary academe. It pleased him to be thought of as a true inhabitant of Morningside Heights, because his professorship was a victory. It marked the happy ending of a painful conquest, the fall of the WASP Bastille. Now the way into (what was then considered) the innermost heart of American culture was open and clear for the Jews. It would be up to Trilling's successors to consolidate that victory and to transform a narrow path for a few into an open road for all.

6   Released into America

While Lionel Trilling was struggling for acceptance at Columbia University, gifted students were preparing for similar battles at Harvard and Yale. Despite veiled quotas that continued to regulate the admission of students from less desirable social groups to elite universities, Jews entered major universities in sizable numbers during the thirties and were decreasingly deterred from choosing an academic career in English and American literature by the well-known threat that the profession might not welcome them.

Harvard's student body during the first decade of the twentieth century contained some of the first Jewish philosophy professors in America. Thirty years later a new Jewish generation was studying at the best schools in the country. That generation would produce the first Jewish professors to be fully integrated into American English departments. Unlike their philosophical predecessors, these students were not immigrants speaking with accents and somewhat embarrassed about their un-American ways. Rather, they tended to be sons of immigrants, whose first language was English (even though they might still be able to understand their parents' German, Yiddish, or Russian). They regarded the United States unequivocally as their country.

There was nothing self-conscious then about these students' desire to study the intellectual tradition of America. They were interested in exploring the soil in which they were taking root; they were equally propelled by a tremendous intellectual drive that encompassed delight in sharp analysis as well as pleasure in reading and writing.

Among the Jewish students who emerged as the first Jewish critics to teach English and American literature in the American academy were the Yale students Charles Feidelson, his roommate Richard Ellmann (who later taught at Oxford), and Charles Muscatine, as well as the Harvard students Daniel Aaron, Meyer Abrams, Harry Levin, and Leo Marx. Their contemporary Leslie Fiedler was educated in the West and came to Harvard only briefly on a Rockefeller fellowship in 1946–1947.

These men (there were no Jewish women professors in this generation) became fully integrated into the academy; one should note, however, that they all became pioneers in their respective academic disciplines: Harry Levin, for instance, introduced modernism into literary studies at Harvard and later built up the comparative literature department. Daniel Aaron was Harvard's guinea pig in the American Civilization program and its first graduate (in 1938). He would remain committed to studies at the crossroads of history, politics, and literature. Leo Marx joined the new program in American Studies at the University of Minnesota (1949), and Meyer Abrams, the first Jewish professor in Cornell University's English department, established a completely new intellectual basis for the study of English Romanticism.

That these academics opened up new fields rather than settling into already established and respectable academic niches is perhaps comparable to the pioneering of Jews in such disciplines as anthropology a generation earlier. Anthropology, particularly at Columbia under Franz Boas's direction (from 1899), was crowded with Jewish students on their way into other academic disciplines. This field was relatively new and therefore free of genteel prejudice; moreover, Boas's work (which focused on physical anthropology, American Indian languages, and comparative ethnology) deconstructs the basis for the claim to superiority of any ethnic group.[1] Unlike the Jewish students at Columbia, their colleagues at Harvard and Yale could not look to role models. But there were enlightened mentors in Cambridge and New Haven impressed by the intellectual fire of these students; they directed their research and pointed out to them that for the time being it might not be a bad idea if they poured their energy into new (and unprejudiced) areas.

The situation at Harvard in the second half of the thirties, when Aaron, Abrams, and Levin (all born in 1912) were preparing their careers there, invites comparison to the situation in the teens, which saw Cohen, Kallen, and Wolfson assembled in Harvard Yard. Of course, times had changed and America's political radicalization had made Jews acceptable in progressive and avant garde circles. But much of Cambridge's social snobbery had survived intact and presented the same old challenges to newcomers. As in the case of their precursors in philosophy, the weltanschauungen developed by the literature students and the careers they cut out for themselves were shaped as much by their descent culture as by their personal ability to deal with the tension between their origins and an (imaginary or real) American hostility toward it. Incidentally, the academic fates of the younger group mirror those of the older: one of the literature students made Harvard his permanent home (Levin), one had access to its distinguished academic circles but departed (Aaron), and one, unfazed by Cantabrigian exclusiveness, pursued his ideas and left when a job opportunity presented itself (Abrams).

But unlike their predecessors, Aaron, Abrams, and Levin did not develop a dichotomous mode of thought, both because the social difference between their descent and consent culture was much less pronounced than in the generation of their fathers; and because their exposure to Jewish thought was minimal, so that their minds were not shaped by their fathers' intellectual grammar. This does not mean, however, that from then on everything went smoothly. A brief outline of three lives in Cambridge must suffice here to indicate the future problems of Jews in the American academy.

Harry Levin arrived at Harvard in 1929, seven years after the remarkable year that saw the publication of *The Waste Land* and *Ulysses*, but also the assassination of Germany's Jewish Secretary of State, Walther Rathenau, and the attempt to implement Jewish quotas at Harvard. In 1929 Harvard's Jewish student body was still trying to keep a low profile. Harry Levin did not mind such invisibility. He came from Minneapolis, a city rabid with anti-Semitism during the twenties, where his father had managed to occupy a respectable position against all odds.

At Harvard, Levin was determined not to take too much notice of the odds, and to stake everything on the life of the mind and the excitement of literature. Intellectual brilliance and enormously hard work as well as a certain graciousness toward those who could not otherwise be won enabled Levin to achieve his goal. At first the presence of Irving Babbitt, the unconventional and yet elitist midwesterner, helped Levin to settle in. But in 1932, a year after Levin had won the Bowdoin Prize and Harvard had published his essay, *The Broken Column: A Study in Romantic Hellenism*, a demi-god arrived in Cambridge:

The pedagogical event of my senior year at Harvard was the presence of T. S. Eliot as Charles Eliot Norton Professor of Poetry. For my generation, which had read him early enough to experience the tensions of novelty, he was still the poetic revolutionary as well as the critical arbiter. And there was a legend become a reality before our very eyes—the legendary reality of a middlewestern boy who, by way of New England, had somehow managed to enter the mainstream of English literature. It was quite improbable and, obviously, inimitable.[2]

Of course, Eliot was inimitable, but it was not quite improbable for midwestern boys to attempt, by way of New England, to enter the mainstream of English literature. Levin was introduced to Eliot, who was then preparing his notorious, anti-Semitic University of Virginia lectures, collected in *After Strange Gods*; Eliot befriended him. Levin graduated in 1933 and went abroad for a year. He visited Eliot in London and planned to call on Joyce in Paris. But the latter was too ill to receive him. In 1934, when Eliot published Levin's first article in the October issue of *Criterion*, Levin returned to Harvard to join the newly established Society of Fellows. During his five years as Junior Fellow, Levin published what he refers to as "occasional writings": seventeen reviews, mostly for *The Nation*; five essays for *Sewanee Review* and other publications; four miscellaneous pieces as varied as his own satiric poetry and an edition of Ben Jonson's *Selected Works*.[3] Most significant, Levin had begun to write and publish work on James Joyce (not least of all on *Finnegans Wake*) and other moderns, which induced the poet and critic Allen Tate to call him a "young Turk."

In 1939, when Levin's fellowship at the society concluded, Harvard's English department could not afford to turn down a man of such independence and ability without being openly anti-Semitic. A few years earlier Theodore Silverstein, the assistant to Professor John Livingston Lowe, had not been promoted, quite possibly because he was Jewish. In 1939, Harvard's Committee of Eight, appointed to investigate the recent dismissal of two radical professors, pointed out that it was informed "that certain members of the faculty object to the appointment of Jews to the tutorial staff in the belief that they are unacceptable to undergraduates."[4] In Levin's case the appointment was approved. He joined the English department in 1939, and was tenured in 1944, a year before Trilling became associate professor at Columbia.

Daniel Aaron, born as was Levin in the Midwest in 1912 to immigrant parents in comfortable financial circumstances, floated into Harvard in

1933. He attended the University of Michigan, enjoyed his *jeunesse dorée*, indulged his taste for European literature and history, fell in with a "group of Bohemian types" who were "contemptuous of middle class respectability of the kind Michigan students had,"[5] and finally graduated in 1933 at the age of twenty. He had only the vaguest notion of what he was going to do. Depression-era Chicago, with its thousands of people out of work, soon dashed his hopes of becoming a newspaperman. He decided to go to graduate school, because he had done well in Michigan's English honors program and had been advised — as he remembers — to continue his studies, despite his "Jewish extraction."

When he arrived at Harvard in the fall of 1933, the school — like the political world surrounding it — was in a state of flux. New people rose to power everywhere. At Harvard two sovereigns were retired: Lawrence Lowell was succeeded by James Bryant Conant as president, and Irving Babbitt became professor emeritus and died the same year. But the changes did not make themselves felt immediately. The English department was disappointingly detached from the excitement of the world: "I was just being there," recalls Daniel Aaron, "watching things going on around me; and finally being rather disenchanted with the distance of the courses that I was taking from anything that was going on. You studied Anglo-Saxon and Chaucer and Beowulf. It isn't that I didn't like these courses. But I felt very much on the fringe."

Although Aaron found kindred spirits in his roommates Charles Olson and John Finch, he continued to feel dissatisfied and depressed. When he received an offer from his former mentor at the University of Michigan to come back to teach in the fall of 1935, Aaron jumped at the chance. In Michigan he began to read American literature and history for the first time. He happened to take a course with Howard Mumford Jones, who immediately became a major influence on Aaron. In 1936, Jones accepted an offer from Harvard to build up its American Civilization program and Aaron went with him back east.

During the three years from 1936 to 1939, which Aaron spent in Cambridge, he taught for Kenneth Murdock, Perry Miller, and F. O. Matthiessen, and was integrated into the college in a singular way. Casting around for new talents and minds, President Conant offered Aaron a counselorship in American Civilization. Initially, the program was directed at Harvard youths who would be spending time abroad. They would be exposed to the political arguments of fascists and communists and would best be able to resist and gainsay them as Americans well informed about their country's history, politics, and culture.

Needless to say, the Old Boston crowd had nothing but disdain for things American. Aaron remembers that his office "turned out to be the place where all the misfits came; only very few Harvard people. My brother-in-law, for example, and his crowd, who belonged to the clubs and all the rest of it, would not be caught dead there. They made a great distinction between greasy people, who did that sort of thing, and themselves." But Aaron did not mind. He attracted people such as Granville Hicks and Henry Nash Smith and even some of his own freshmen who were "very Harvard." But on the whole, he says, those who came "were the lost, the people who didn't fit in and just found it a place to go." The seriousness with which Aaron went about his task as American Civilization counselor was interlinked with his growing political awareness.

In 1935, he had already been "very pro-Roosevelt and generally sympathetic with liberals." But the radical scene that he had explored in Chicago out of curiosity and for his amusement was too "strange and outlandish" to captivate him. At Harvard, his political awareness became acute, in unison with his increasing knowledge of and interest in America. The Marxist study group meeting at Aaron's house, however, was not politically activist. It was "simply an assembly of interesting, lively, likeminded people," some of whom were members of Harvard's communist cell. This did not disturb Aaron. The Marxist study group put him in touch on a rather informal basis with people such as Hicks and Matthiessen, Daniel Boorstin, and Robert Gorham Davis. And sometimes even Harry Levin appeared at Aaron's doorstep to participate in the discussion. Simultaneously, Aaron began to participate actively in academic life. He wrote articles and befriended people such as Stewart Mitchell, the editor of *The New England Quarterly*, who was "very Old Boston." Perry Miller and Kenneth Murdock, too, would invite Aaron to their homes.

In 1938 Aaron passed his general exam in American Civilization and in 1939 he received an offer from Smith College in Northampton, Massachusetts. "It was then very international and at the height of its eminence," Aaron remembers. "William Allen Neilson, who had been at Harvard and was considered one of the outstanding college presidents of his time, had made it into a fantastic school. It was the center for antifascist movements among the Italians, and among the Germans." It was the perfect school for Daniel Aaron: independent, intellectual, progressive; smart without being smug. He remained there for some thirty-five years during which he wrote three ground-breaking studies on the Progressives (*Men of Good Hope*, 1951), on radical writers (*Writers on the Left*,

1961), and on the reaction of classic American writers to the Civil War (*The Unwritten War*, 1973). In 1975 Aaron returned to Harvard, finally ready to move from the margin—indispensable perch in the quintessentially American tradition of dissent—into that center, where dissent had first been transformed into a politics of consent.

Unlike Harry Levin and Daniel Aaron, their contemporary Meyer Abrams grew up on the East coast, in Long Branch, New Jersey, in a household whose language remained exclusively Yiddish until the boy made acquaintances outside the family. His father was engaged in the affairs of his shul and was orthodox in a social rather than an intellectual way. That Meyer Abrams went to Harvard and not to City College of New York or Columbia was the work of his high school principal. He was the descendant of an old American family and had gone to Harvard himself. Being secure in his heritage, he did not mind sharing it. He recommended Jewish students to his alma mater when he thought they were bright and should be sent there.

When Abrams arrived at Harvard in the fall of 1930, he was awed by its antiquity and prestige. But his awe disappeared quickly in the surprises and routines of daily life in the college. Abrams acclimated well. As President Lowell had foreseen, the Houses accommodating all undergraduates on campus were a major factor in the integration of Harvard's increasingly diverse student body. "We lived very well," Abrams remembers. "We had lots of space. We ate our meals in the Houses, on white table cloths with waitress service. . . . It was a very plush time, in which we were carefully insulated from the Depression outside, not by intention but in fact. We were aware that there was this awful world out there where you couldn't get jobs. But we were leading a good life."[6] Because in Depression-era America all careers seemed equally doomed to end in unemployment, Abrams was not very particular about his professional decisions. Until his senior year he thought he would go to law school. He majored in English because he enjoyed reading and did not know what else he wanted to do. His senior thesis, on the effects of opium on four British writers, was published as number 7 of the Harvard Honors Theses in English in 1934 (when Levin was publishing in *Criterion* and Aaron and his roommates were ridiculing the "dry-as-dust scholars.")

Abrams' attitude toward literature changed during the year he spent at the University of Cambridge, after his graduation from Harvard. In England he worked with I. A. Richards, read Arthur Lovejoy and R. S. Crane, and, most important, Ludwig Wittgenstein. The latter became a major influence on Abrams' thinking. But Abrams' lifelong interest in metaphor was awakened by Richards. Two years after his return to Harvard, Abrams received his master's degree (1937) and in 1938 he was appointed instructor in the English department; he completed his doctorate in 1940, and from 1942 to 1945 worked as research associate in Harvard's psycho-acoustic laboratory. From this post he was liberated by a job offer from Cornell University. Although Abrams suspects that only the decimation of the faculty at Cornell due to World War II had made the appointment of a Jew to an assistant professorship in English acceptable, he maintains that he was received openly in Ithaca. "I never felt that I was discriminted against when it came to promotion, salary, social life, and so forth. That does not mean that there was no anti-Semitism. But it never reached me directly."

During the forties Abrams published little. But in 1953, the year he was tenured at Cornell, he published his seminal study, *The Mirror and the Lamp*, in which he traced the shift from mimetic (and pragmatic) to expressive theory. The book established Abrams immediately as a luminary in the field of English literature. Abrams' second major work, *Natural Supernaturalism* (1971) confirmed his stature. Here Abrams demonstrated the continuity of Christian concepts, schemes, and values in Romantic literature, and argued that they were simply displaced from a supernatural into a natural frame of reference. With this work Abrams propelled himself by an act of imaginative consent into the sacred heart of Anglo-American high culture.

Is there anything specifically Jewish in the criticism of the comparatist Levin, the history-minded Aaron, and the critical pluralist Abrams? Not overtly. There are still certain intellectual preferences, cultural concerns, and moral positions (such as Abrams' staunchly rationalist stand vis-à-vis the deconstructionists, for instance) which link this generation to that of the immigrant academics. But they might very well be traced to other influences than these critics' Jewish descent. The thinking in binary terms, developed by their precursors in the academy to negotiate between descent and consent culture, has disappeared.

Sociologically, the careers of Levin, Aaron, and Abrams are part of the American Jewish success story. While one-third of Europe's Jewry was being reduced to ash, the sons of those fortunate enough to have been forced to emigrate long before the conflagration enjoyed life, liberty, and the pursuit of happiness. They found America generous, receptive, and accommodating at last. While European Jews were being exiled from humanity—driven into ghettos, box cars, fake showers—American Jews finally achieved the release into the ordinary freedom of equality.

Yet even if these sons born to freedom now thought the tablets of the Law to be broken, some in the next generation of academics recognized that the fine white ash covering most of Europe replaced on their shoulders the burden which their fathers had been enticed to lay down for a brief moment of respite.

Notes

Preface

1. Alfred Kazin called attention to an essay written in 1919 in which Thorstein Veblen "expressed the hope that the Jews would never form a nationalistic movement of their own, since that would be a loss to world culture." Kazin quotes from Veblen's essay: "It appears to be only when the gifted Jew escapes from the cultural environment created and fed by the particular genius of his own people, only when he falls into the alien lines of gentile inquiry and becomes a naturalized, though hyphenate, citizen in the gentile republic of learning, that he comes into his own as a creative leader in the world's intellectual enterprise. It is by loss of allegiance, or at the best by force of a divided allegiance to the people of his origin, that he finds himself in the vanguard of modern inquiry. . . . He becomes a disturber of the intellectual peace, but only at the cost of becoming an intellectual wayfaring man, a wanderer in the intellectual no-man's-land, seeking another place to rest, farther along the road, somewhere over the horizon." Alfred Kazin, *On Native Grounds: An Interpretation of Modern American Prose Literature* (1942; Garden City: Anchor-Doubleday, 1956), 103.

2. Carl E. Schorske, "A Life of Learning." Charles Homer Haskins Lecture delivered at the American Council of Learned Societies, Washington, D.C., 23 April 1987 (ACLS Occasional Paper No. 1): 2.

Chapter 1. Beginnings

1. Harry A. Wolfson, "Monis, Judah," in *Dictionary of American Biography* (New York: Charles Scribner's Sons, 1934), 13: 86–87; Albert Ehrenfried, *A Chronicle of Boston Jewry: From the Colonial Settlement to 1900*, ed. and pub. Frederika Ehrenfried Bernstein and Irving Bernstein (1963), 84–105; Samuel Eliot Morison, *Three Centuries of Harvard, 1636–1936*, 7th ed. (Cambridge: Belknap-Harvard University Press, 1965), 30–31; David Levin, *Cotton Mather: The Young Life of the Lord's Remembrancer, 1663–1703* (Cambridge: Harvard University Press, 1978),

209

83; Nitza Rosovsky, *The Jewish Experience at Harvard and Radcliffe*, an introduction to an exhibition by the Harvard Semitic Museum on the occasion of Harvard's 350th anniversary, September 1986 (Distributed by Harvard University Press, 1986), 4–5.

2. John Higham, "Social Discrimination Against Jews in America, 1830–1930," *Publications of the American Jewish Historical Society* 47 (September 1957): 3. Cf. Nathan Glazer, "Social Characteristics of American Jews, 1654–1954," *American Jewish Yearbook* 55(1955): 3–41.

3. Higham, "Social Discrimination," 11.

4. Ibid. For the argument in this passage I am indebted to John Higham's article.

5. Dan Oren, *Joining the Club: A History of Jews and Yale* (New Haven: Yale University Press, 1985), 263. Hendel concludes, however, that "Yale is too great an institution to be deterred by slight things from acquiring the services of a really great scholar. . . . It is always possible that when a man finds a great environment he shows *only* his own greatness and power. This is what I hope. So I welcome more than I can say the experiment with Weiss."

6. Higham, "Social Discrimination," 11. See also Henry Feingold, *Zion in America: The Jewish Experience from Colonial Times to the Present* (New York: Hippocrene Books, 1974), 143.

7. Rosovsky, *The Jewish Experience*, 9. Cf. Marcia Graham Synnott, *The Half-Opened Door: Discrimination and Admissions at Harvard, Yale, and Princeton, 1900–1970* (Westport, Conn.: Greenwood Press, 1979), 181; Dan Oren, *Joining the Club*, 317; 11.

8. *Die Deborah* 26 (1881): 268; quoted in Rudolf Glanz, *Jews in Relation to the Cultural Milieu of the Germans in America up to the Eighteen Eighties* (New York: Marstin Press, 1947), 43–44.

9. Cf. Ronald Sanders, *Shores of Refuge: A Hundred Years of Jewish Emigration* (New York: Henry Holt, 1988). On pages 343–346 Sanders describes a pogrom in the Ukraine in 1919. In Proskurov more than a thousand Jews were killed in a single day, on 15 February 1919.

10. Oren, *Joining the Club*, 315; Glazer, "Social Characteristics," 11. Absolute figures for New York in Moses Rischin, *The Promised City: New York's Jews, 1870–1914*, 3rd ed. (Cambridge: Harvard University Press, 1977), 270.

11. "The relationship between traditional Jewish attitudes toward learning and the existence in the United States of free public schools is perhaps the central factor in the accommodation of East European Jewry with American culture." David A. Hollinger, *Morris R. Cohen and the Scientific Ideal* (Cambridge: MIT Press, 1975), 19.

12. Glazer, "Social Characteristics," 15. The figures for the Big Three are: Yale, 4%; Harvard, 4.3% (that is, 95 of 2,196 students were Jewish); Princeton, eleven Jews matriculated in 1908. Cf. Oren, *Joining the Club*, 320; Synnott, *The Half-Opened Door*, 38–40; 181.

13. "Professional Tendencies Among Jewish Students in Colleges, Universities, and Professional Schools," Memoir of the Bureau of Jewish Social Research, *American Jewish Year Book 5681*, vol. 22 (13 September 1920 to 2 October 1921): 381–393.

14. These figures are taken from a table excerpted by Synnott (*The Half-Opened Door*, 16) from the material provided by the Bureau of Jewish Social Research. Synnott's table includes schools as diverse as the College of Dental and Oral Surgery (80.9% of the students are Jewish); City College of New York

(78.7%); New York University (47.5%); Hunter College (38.7); Columbia University (21.2%); University of Chicago (18.5%); Harvard (10%); Cornell (9.1%); Dartmouth (2.8%); Princeton (2.6%); West Point (2.2%); Amherst College (1.9%); Bowdoin (1.9%); Williams College (1.4%). Six schools together comprise 50% of the Jewish student enrollment in the United States (CCNY, NYU, Columbia, U. of Pennsylvania, U. of Chicago, Hunter College). Alexander Bloom, in *Prodigal Sons: The New York Intellectuals and Their World* (New York: Oxford University Press, 1986), 29, prefers the high figures (Columbia 40%; CCNY and Hunter "between 80 and 90 percent") which he takes from Stephen Steinberg, *The Academic Melting Pot: Catholics and Jews in American Higher Education* (New York: McGraw-Hill, 1974) because this study is "more recent." He mentions, however, that Heywood Broun and George Britt, in *Christians Only: A Study in Prejudice* (New York: Vanguard Press, 1931), give the figures as "22.5 percent for Columbia and 36.53 percent for NYU" (Bloom, 393). They come closer to the figures given in the *American Jewish Year Book 5681*, which Synnott and I prefer.

15. *The Menorah Journal* 2 (October 1916): 260–262.

16. Synnott, *The Half-Opened Door*, 17. On Columbia University specifically, see Harold S. Wechsler, "Columbia and the Selective Function," in *The Qualified Student: A History of Selective College Admission in America* (New York: John Wiley, 1977), 65–211.

17. Morison, *Three Centuries of Harvard*, 374.

18. The first Jew appointed by Eliot was the historian Charles Gross, a graduate of Williams College with a Ph.D. from Göttingen. He spent years doing research in England while applying "for a teaching position to one college after another, without success, and was on the point of returning to his father's clothing business in Troy, New York," when Eliot appointed him to an instructorship in medieval history in 1888. He was promoted to the rank of full professor in 1901. Morison, *Three Centuries of Harvard*, 375. For other early Jewish professors (none in non-Semitic language or literature departments) see Oren, *Joining the Club*, chap. 6; Lewis S. Feuer, "Stages in the Social History of Jewish Professors in American Colleges and Universities," *American Jewish History* 71 (June 1982): 432–465.

Chapter 2. A Philologist

1. Gershom Scholem, *From Berlin to Jerusalem: Memories of My Youth*, trans. Harry Zohn (New York: Schocken, 1980), 46.

2. Norbert Wiener, *Ex-Prodigy: My Childhood and Youth* (New York: Simon and Schuster, 1953), 11, 42, 144. This attempt was probably confined to the children, because when Solomon Wiener's wife, "Grossmutter Wiener," came to America years later, she would still read Yiddish newspapers. A large part of the biographical information on Leo Wiener is taken from his son's autobiography. This is a problematic source for other than factual information (dates and places), because Norbert's relationship to his father was deeply troubled.

3. See also Leo Wiener, "Stray Leaves From My Life," *Boston Evening Transcript*, 19 March 1910: 2.

4. Ibid. "Indeed, one of the most reputed Jew-baiters of the time, Dr. Nagel, was one of the stanchest adherents of vegetarianism." And so was Hitler. Richard Wagner thought that "the Jewish practice" of eating meat was "the bane of modern civilization." Cf. Jonathan Lieberson, "Bombing in Bayreuth," *The New York Review of Books* 35 (10 November 1988): 30.

5. "Minute on the Life and Services of Professor Leo Wiener," *Harvard Ga-*

zette, 9 March 1940: 123 (dates Wiener's arrival in New Orleans to 1882). Wiener published his memoirs under the title "Stray Leaves From My Life," in the *Boston Evening Transcript,* 19 March, 26 March, 2 April, and 9 April 1910.

6. For Münsterberg's trapping of the medium Palladino, see "Muensterberg on Palladino," *Boston Evening Transcript,* 21 January 1910: 7.

7. Norbert Wiener considered this a consequence of nepotism. The *Harvard Gazette* of 9 March 1940 stated diplomatically: "One of the seasonal overturns which mark the history of our state universities caused him to lose his position . . ." (123).

8. So reads Wiener's official Harvard obituary (ibid.).

9. Gerald Graff, *Professing Literature: An Institutional History* (Chicago: University of Chicago Press, 1987), 70.

10. Quoted in Graff, *Professing Literature,* 71.

11. Norbert Wiener (1894–1964), the "father of cybernetics," graduated from high school in September 1906 and from Tufts College in June 1909. He entered Harvard the same year, as one of five prodigies, and received his doctorate in philosophy in 1913. After further studies in Europe, he began teaching mathematics at the Massachusetts Institute of Technology in 1919. His autobiography is a balanced account of the psychological and emotional difficulties encountered by a wunderkind, which in Wiener's case were exacerbated by his parents' psychological problems. When he was eleven years old (and attending high school) he had the "wild idea . . . of forming some sort of organization among children of my age to resist the authority of their elders" (*EP* 98).

12. *Harvard Gazette,* 9 March 1940: 123.

13. Cf. such titles as "English Lexicography" (1896); "Spanish Studies in England in the Sixteenth and Seventeenth Century" (1898); *Contributions Toward a History of Arabic-Gothic Culture* (4 vols.; 1917–1921); "The Philological History of 'Tobacco' in America" (1924); *Mayan and Mexican Origins* (1926); "The Sumerian Origin of the Egyptian Hieroglyphs" (n.d.). All titles are found in Harvard's Widener Library.

14. A. A. Roback in an obituary for Leo Wiener for the *Jewish Telegraphic Agency,* 29 December 1939. Harvard University Archives, HUG 300. On anti-German attacks on Münsterberg, see Morison, *Three Centuries of Harvard,* 377, 453. On Münsterberg's German chauvinism and his philosophy, see Bruce Kuklick, *The Rise of American Philosophy, Cambridge, Massachusetts, 1860–1930* (New Haven: Yale University Press, 1977), 196–214. On Münsterberg's cultural alienation, see Phyllis Keller, *States of Belonging: German-American Intellectuals and the First World War* (Cambridge: Harvard University Press, 1979), 5–118.

15. "Says Russians Are Turning to America," *The Boston Globe,* 11 November 1915. Harvard University Archives, HUG 300. In the same year, Leo Wiener published *Interpretation of the Russian People* (New York: McBride, Nast, 1915) in which he predicted the 1917 Revolution.

16. But it came to the fore in private. "Of our few meetings or rather encounters, I have not the most pleasant recollections. Professor Wiener would stop to deliver himself of a tirade against the Jews for one grievance or another. All his trials and tribulations seemed to come 'from my own people,' to use his words." A. A. Roback, obituary for Leo Wiener.

17. Leo Wiener, *The History of Yiddish Literature in the Nineteenth Century* (New York: Charles Scribner's Sons, 1899), 24. The Harvard "Minute on the Life and Services of Professor Wiener" attributes his interest in Yiddish to a rebellion against his elders: "Both father and grandfather had been strong proponents of the view

that the Jews should adopt literary German rather than their own mixed Yiddish dialect; and this insistence led the young idealist, surcharged with the hazy and idealistic Russian liberalism of the seventies, to revolt in favor of Yiddish as the tongue of the folk." *Harvard Gazette*, 9 March 1940: 123.

18. Leo Wiener, *History of Yiddish Literature*, 14, 13. The villains in the slandering of Yiddish were, of course, the German Jews, "its most violent opponents . . . who, since the day of Mendelssohn, have come to look upon it as an arbitrary and vicious corruption of the language of their country" (13).

19. Ibid., 10–11.

20. Irving Howe and Eliezer Greenberg, eds., *A Treasury of Yiddish Stories* (New York: Viking, 1954), 56.

21. Cynthia Ozick, "Toward a New Yiddish," in *Art and Ardor* (New York: E. P. Dutton, 1984), 177.

22. Leo Wiener, *History of Yiddish Literature*, 202–203. The plural *criterions* instead of *criteria* is a hypercorrection on Wiener's part. By adopting an English plural ending in place of the Greek, Wiener meant to signal his mastery of English and his willingness to privilege English word forms. Such hypercorrection can be a measure of linguistic and cultural insecurity.

23. *Heymishkayt*, a sense of at-homeness, is really impossible to translate. All of Proust's *A la recherche du temps perdu* is a huge translation of this one word.

Chapter 3. Three Professors of Philosophy

1. Quoted in Leo W. Schwarz, *Wolfson of Harvard: Portrait of a Scholar* (Philadelphia: Jewish Publication Society of America, 1978), 37.

2. Nitza Rosovsky, *The Jewish Experience*, 28.

3. Lewis S. Feuer, "Recollections of Harry Austryn Wolfson," *American Jewish Archives* 28 (April 1976): 27.

4. Feuer, "Recollections," 28.

5. For the significance of these terms, see Preface.

6. Sarah Schmidt, "Horace M. Kallen and the 'Americanization' of Zionism," *American Jewish Archives* 28 (April 1976): 62.

7. For an analysis of Wolfson's talmudic hypothetico-deductive method of textual interpretation and its relation to the method taught by Rabbi Epstein, see Hillel Goldberg, *Between Berlin and Slobodka: Jewish Transition Figures from Eastern Europe* (Hoboken, N.J.: Ktav Publishing House, 1989), 37–62.

8. Harold Stearns, a neighbor of Wolfson's in Divinity Hall in 1912, writes in his autobiography: "A brilliant Jewish scholar, named Wolfson, lived next to me, and I found him quiet and interesting—and devastatingly well informed on almost any subject I brought up, except the subject of girls, or, indeed, of sex life in general, about which he appeared to be as innocent as a babe unborn." Harold Stearns, *The Street I Know* (New York: Lee Furman, 1935), 79. In "The Confessions of a Harvard Man," in which Stearns calls Wolfson "a clean Emersonian soul," he remembers an evening discussion during which Wolfson (whom he calls "Wilder"), "when caught in the statement 'the Greeks had the right "dope" on women—they kept them in the kitchen,' advocated in a lengthy and a highly logical and ingenious speech a return to the class system, kingship and slavery, to prove his point. Remarkable as his argument was—he tried to show how the feeling of security more than compensated for social inequality—we all felt that he was showing how sharp his wits were rather than attempting to voice his real convictions." *The Forum* 51 (January

1914): 71, 73–74. On that issue see also Hillel Goldberg, *Between Berlin and Slobodka*, 42–43.

9. Feuer, "Recollections," 39, 40, 47. Nathan Glazer and Daniel Bell, for example, came to Harvard University in 1969. See Goldberg, *Between Berlin and Slobodka*, p. 47.

10. Abraham Mapu, the creator of the modern Hebrew novel, was born in Slobodka, a poverty-stricken suburb of Kovno, in 1808.

11. Robert Alter, *The Invention of Hebrew Prose: Modern Fiction and the Language of Realism* (Seattle: University of Washington Press, 1988), 8–9.

12. The Rabbi Isaac Elchanan Theological Seminary, America's first official yeshivah, was founded in 1897 for the advanced study of Talmud and the training of Orthodox rabbis who were to help "civilize" the Eastern European immigrants without estranging them from their tradition. Its director, Rabbi Lichtenberg, eventually found it necessary to tell his outstanding student: "Wolfson, you will never be a good rabbi, you don't mix with people. You're a yeshiva bachur." Feuer, "Recollections," 26.

13. Harry A. Wolfson, *Crescas' Critique of Aristotle: Problems of Aristotle's "Physics" in Jewish and Arabic Philosophy* (Cambridge: Harvard University Press, 1957), xi.

14. Aryeh L. Motzkin, "Harry A. Wolfson as Interpreter of Medieval Thought," *Interpretation* 9 (August 1980): 138.

15. Graff, *Professing Literature*, 94.

16. "The expository part of his work is a variegated texture into which are woven many different strands. Mosaic in its structure, it is studded with garbled phrases and expressions torn out of their context and strung together in what would seem to be a haphazard fashion." Wolfson, *Crescas*, 24.

17. "In this method the starting point is the principle that any text that is deemed worthy of serious study must be assumed to have been written with such care and precision that every term, expression, generalization or exception is significant not so much for what it states as for what it implies. The contents of ideas as well as the diction and phraseology in which they are clothed are to enter into the reasoning. . . . Serious students themselves, accustomed to a rigid form of logical reasoning and to the usage of precise forms of expression, the Talmudic trained scholars attributed the same quality of precision and exactness to any authoritative work, be it of divine origin or the product of the human mind. Their attitude toward the written word of any kind is like that of the jurist toward the external phrasing of statutes and laws, and perhaps also, in some respect, like that of the latest kind of historical and literary criticism which applies the method of psychoanalysis to the study of texts." Wolfson, *Crescas*, 24–25.

18. Wolfson, *Crescas*, 25–27.

19. Wolfson, *Crescas*, 29.

20. Harry A. Wolfson, *The Philosophy of Spinoza: Unfolding the Latent Processes of His Reasoning*, 2 vols. (Cambridge: Harvard University Press, 1934), 1: 22.

21. Wolfson, *Spinoza*, 1: 5.

22. Wolfson, *Spinoza*, 1: 10.

23. Harry A. Wolfson, *Philo: Foundations of Religious Philosophy in Judaism, Christianity, and Islam*, 2 vols. (Cambridge: Harvard University Press, 2nd rev. ed., 1948), 2: 457.

24. Wolfson, *Philo*, 1: 4.

25. Wolfson's *Philo* book evolved from a complete manuscript on Greek philosophy. In 1941, Wolfson took the six chapters on Philo that were already in

galley proofs and began to work on them. By 1947, they had become a two-volume publication.

26. "The harmonization of apparent contradictions and the inter-linking of apparent irrelevancies are two characteristic features of the Talmudic method of study." Wolfson, *Crescas*, 26.

27. "He is one of those philosophers who does his thinking in private and presents to the public only the maturity of this thought. . . . If almost without any exception he adopts philosophic views without telling us that he adopts them only according to a new version of his own, it is perhaps because at his time philosophic views and concepts had not yet become rigidly fixed by the constant hammering of commentators and one could still freely reshape them for some particular uses without having to offer an apology or explanation. Perhaps, also, at his time he could envisage a class of readers who were so well acquainted with the original meaning of the views and concepts with which he dealt that he felt no need of constantly reminding them of the revisions he had introduced." Wolfson, *Philo*, 1: 105. Philo's "misprisions" here find a commonsensical explanation. A Bloomian "anxiety of influence" seems not to have been at work in antiquity.

28. Wolfson, *Philo*, 1: 82–83.

29. He ate at Harvard's non-kosher cafeterias and did not attend shabbat services. He did, however, attend the High Holiday services led by Harvard's Conservative rabbi, Ben-Zion Gold, a close friend of his since 1958 (interview with Ben-Zion Gold, 7 June 1988).

30. About Philo's nephew, Wolfson writes: "He forsook Judaism and henceforth found no difficulty in rising to high office . . . ." Wolfson, *Philo*, 2: 406. And about Philo's messianism Wolfson writes: "The solution found by Philo for the Jewish problem of his time was the revival of the old prophetic promises of the ultimate disappearance of the diaspora. Without mentioning the term Messiah, he deals in great detail with what is known in Jewish tradition as the Messiah and the Messianic age" (Wolfson, *Philo*, 2: 407). The three traditional features of the Messianic age are the reunion of the exiled, the establishment of national prosperity in the homeland, and the reign of peace between men and men and between men and beasts (cf. Wolfson, *Philo*, 2: 408–409).

31. Wolfson talked about his serious intention of becoming a Hebrew poet and novelist to Lewis Feuer (cf. "Recollections," 29) and to Rabbi Gold. But he gave up this plan after meeting the celebrated Hebrew writer Reuben Brainin. While Feuer claims that Wolfson changed his mind when he learned of Brainin's poverty, Gold suspects a different reason: "It was not the poverty. There was something in the appearance and manner of Brainin that made Wolfson say: 'That can't be my idea, I suppose.' . . . There was something unappealing about Brainin . . . and Wolfson had impeccable taste" (interview with the author, 7 June 1988).

32. Wolfson had just been promoted from instructor to assistant professor. "The understanding was that he would not be permanent and that he would receive only such salary as 'interested persons could contribute'" (Kuklick, *The Rise of American Philosophy*, 457). For years, Wolfson's salary was paid by Boston's Jews, solicited by such notaries as Julius Mack and Felix Frankfurter. Harvard did not spend a penny on the scholar who would become known as its "sage." Despite the misery this situation created, Wolfson was deeply loyal to Harvard (Lewis Weinstein, interview with the author, Boston, 24 June 1988). When he was "[a]ssigned to the faculty committee investigating Lowell's formal quota proposal [in 1921], he trod softly and refused, he later recalled, to do anything to embarrass the university" (Kuklick, 457). Wolfson first knew some financial security in 1925

when the glove manufacturer Lucius N. Littauer was persuaded to endow a chair for him in Hebrew Literature and Philosophy.

33. Harry A. Wolfson, "Escaping Judaism," *Menorah Journal* 7 (June 1921): 71.

34. Wolfson's shorter publications, such as "Double Faith Theory in Clement, Saadia, Averroes and St. Thomas, and Its Origin in Aristotle and the Stoics," *Jewish Quarterly Review* 33 (October 1942–January 1943): 213–264, as well as the sequence of his major works (Crescas, Spinoza, Philo, Church Fathers, philosophy of the Kalam), show him to belong firmly to this ideal interfaith, international philosophic community.

35. Wolfson, "Escaping Judaism," 76–77.

36. Wolfson, "Escaping Judaism," 77–78.

37. Rabbi Ben-Zion Gold, interview with the author, 7 June 1988.

38. Alter, *The Invention of Hebrew Prose*, 10.

39. Wolfson, "Escaping Judaism," 78. See also El. Lycidas (alias for Harry Wolfson), "Pomegranates," *Menorah Journal* 4 (February 1918): 16–26; and 4 (June 1918): 162–170.

40. Rabbi Ben-Zion Gold, interview with the author, 8 June 1988.

41. Wolfson, "Escaping Judaism," 71.

42. After pointing out the general significance of "science" in turn-of-the-century America, David Hollinger continues to describe its special importance for Eastern European Jewish immigrants. "Science was unquestionably a central element in the Western tradition these newly emancipated immigrants were seeking to absorb, but it also had one significant distinction that made it especially attractive. Science aimed, by definition, to enter a dialogue with the most universal and timeless segments of experience. Science sought truth of a sort that would command assent from persons of any national, religious, or ethnic background; it was concerned with propositions that were in no way culture-bound. As such, science differed from literature, which, while often containing insights that seemed to apply to the entire human species, was nonetheless shot through with cultural particularity. . . . Science was potentially the basis for a fully secular ideology that would exclude no one from full participation in modern life." David A. Hollinger, *Morris R. Cohen and the Scientific Ideal* (Cambridge: MIT Press, 1975), 58–59.

43. Horace M. Kallen, *Cultural Pluralism and the American Idea: An Essay in Social Philosophy* (Philadelphia: University of Pennsylvania Press, 1956), 47.

44. Ira Eisenstein, "Dialogue with Dr. Horace M. Kallen," in Horace M. Kallen, *What I Believe and Why—Maybe: Essays for the Modern World*, ed. Alfred J. Marrow (New York: Horizon Press, 1971), 183.

45. Kallen, *Cultural Pluralism*, 98.

46. Horace M. Kallen, "Democracy Versus the Melting Pot," *The Nation* 100 (25 February 1915): 220.

47. Horace M. Kallen, *Zionism and World Politics: A Study in History and Social Psychology* (Garden City: Doubleday, Page, 1921), 280.

48. Horace M. Kallen, "What I Have Learned Betting My Life," in Kallen, *What I Believe*, 172. (The copy of this book in Harvard's Widener Library belonged to Harry Wolfson and has the following dedication on the front page: "For Harry Wolfson, whose spirit has also a share in this book of essays chosen by Drs. Marrow and Everett. With shalom b'simchah [greetings, with happiness] from his oldest friend, Horace M. Kallen.")

49. Morris R. Cohen, in particular, would take issue with Kallen's (and Louis

D. Brandeis's) position that Zionism and Americanism were compatible. "This 'profoundly mistaken' belief ignored the fact that 'liberal America has traditionally stood for separation of church and state, for the free mixture of races,' and for an 'ideal of freedom' that Zionists actually feared. Zionism partook of 'tribalism,' a doctrine that may eventually triumph in history, but which is 'none the less evil.'" Hollinger, *Morris R. Cohen*, 210. A "review [of] significant criticisms of the concept of cultural pluralism" is given in Werner Sollors, "A Critique of Pure Pluralism," in Sacvan Bercovitch, *Reconstructing American Literary History* (Cambridge: Harvard University Press, 1986), 250–279. In a thought-provoking essay Sollors pits Kallen's theory against some problematic private letters to Barrett Wendell. More criticism is mentioned briefly in William Toll, "Ethnicity and Freedom in the Philosophy of Horace M. Kallen," in Moses Rischin, ed., *The Jews of North America* (Detroit: Wayne State University Press, 1987) 153–154. Toll's own objection to Kallen is that "he legitimated American Jewry's multiple loyalties only by leaving the content of Jewish ethnicity an enigma" (164).

50. John Higham, "The Pot That Didn't Melt," *The New York Review of Books* 37 (12 April 1990): 13.

51. Toll, "Ethnicity and Freedom," 153.

52. Eisenstein, "Dialogue," 182.

53. Kallen, "What I Have Learned," 167.

54. Milton Konvitz, "Horace Meyer Kallen (1882–1974): Philosopher of the Hebraic-American Idea," *American Jewish Year Book* 75 (1974–1975): 56. This essay was recently collected in Milton R. Konvitz, ed., *The Legacy of Horace M. Kallen* (London: Associated University Presses, 1987), 15–35. All references to this essay will be to the *American Jewish Year Book* version.

55. All autobiographical quotes are from Eisenstein, "Dialogue," 179–180. Konvitz, "Horace Meyer Kallen," 57.

56. Kallen, "What I Have Learned," 167–168.

57. Kallen, "What I Have Learned," 168. Spinoza, who had been excommunicated in 1656, formulated in his *Tractatus Theologico-Politicus* (1670) "a devastating critique of the Bible as a source of philosophical truth. Spinoza read the Bible not as a book of timeless truths but as a historical source relevant only to the period of the ancient Hebrews." David Biale, *Power and Powerlessness in Jewish History* (New York: Schocken, 1986), 113. "The laws revealed to Moses by God," Spinoza claimed, "were nothing more than a code appropriate to the peculiar state or empire of the Hebrews; consequently . . . no nation but themselves need be held bound to receive this code, nor even the Jews themselves to observe its precepts, save whilst their empire endured." Benedict de Spinoza, *Tractatus Theologico-Politicus*, ed. Robert Willis (London: Trübner, 1862), 26. In particular, Spinoza attacked the Jews' belief in their chosenness: "Arguing in the Theologico-Political Tractate [*sic*] for the equality of all peoples before God, [he] insists that whatever election the Jews were beneficiaries of was national and social, that it 'had no regard to aught but dominion and physical advantages, for by such alone could one nation be distinguished from another.'" Kallen, *Zionism and World Politics*, 31.

58. Kallen, "What I Have Learned," 170–171. All quotes in the paragraph are from this source.

59. Kallen, "What I Have Learned," 171.

60. Eisenstein, "Dialogue," 182. Sarah Schmidt, "Horace M. Kallen and the 'Americanization' of Zionism," *American Jewish Archives* 28 (April 1976): 61. A slightly different version of this essay appeared as "Horace M. Kallen: The Zionist

Chapter," in Milton R. Konvitz, ed., *The Legacy of Horace M. Kallen*, 76–89.

61. Eisenstein, "Dialogue," 181. Toll, "Ethnicity and Freedom," 155.

62. Eisenstein, "Dialogue," 182.

63. Kallen, *Cultural Pluralism*, 99.

64. Konvitz, "Horace Meyer Kallen," 58.

65. Feuer, "Stages in the Social History," 454. Eisenstein, "Dialogue," 178.

66. Toll, "Ethnicity and Freedom," 157. On the influence of Josiah Royce on Kallen's concept of cultural pluralism and on his Zionism, see Werner Sollors, *Beyond Ethnicity: Consent and Descent in American Culture* (New York: Oxford University Press, 1986), 179–186.

67. Sarah Schmidt, "Horace Kallen and the Americanization of Zionism" (Ph.D. diss., University of Maryland, 1973), 38.

68. Fritz Fleischmann, "Barrett Wendell," *American Literary Critics and Scholars, 1880–1900*, vol. 71 of *Dictionary of Literary Biography* (Detroit: Gale Research Company, 1988), 286.

69. Schmidt, "Horace Kallen" (diss.), 40; Sarah Schmidt, "Horace M. Kallen" (article), 63.

70. Schmidt, "Horace Kallen" (diss.), 34. Milton Konvitz quotes Kallen as saying: "It is upon the foundation and against the background of my Jewish cultural milieu that my vision of America was grown." Konvitz, "Horace Meyer Kallen," 77.

71. Konvitz, "Horace Meyer Kallen," 56.

72. The best analysis of Kallen's Zionism, its development as a reinterpretation of Judaism in light of the "American idea," is given in Sarah Schmidt's dissertation, "Horace Kallen and the Americanization of Zionism."

73. Sollors, "A Critique of Pure Pluralism," 265.

74. Schmidt, "Horace Kallen" (diss), 40.

75. Cf., for instance, Kallen's essay "The Ethics of Zionism," *The Maccabean* 11 (August 1906): 61–71.

76. Kallen, Foreword to *Judaism at Bay: Essays Toward the Adjustment of Judaism to Modernity* (New York: Bloch, 1932), 4–5.

77. Robert Alter, "Epitaph for a Jewish Magazine: Notes on the 'Menorah Journal,'" *Commentary* 39 (May 1965): 52.

78. Elinor Grumet, "The Apprenticeship of Lionel Trilling," *Prooftexts* 4 (May 1984): 154.

79. Mark Krupnick, "The Menorah Journal Group and the Origins of Modern Jewish-American Radicalism," *Studies in American Jewish Literature* 5 (Winter 1979): 58.

80. Grumet, "The Apprenticeship," 154; 160.

81. Alter, "Epitaph," 53. For a discussion of the uneasiness of some contributors see 52 ff.

82. Krupnick, "The Menorah Journal Group," 58. Alter, "Epitaph," 52.

83. Alan Wald, *The New York Intellectuals: The Rise and Decline of the Anti-Stalinist Left From the 1930s to the 1980s* (Chapel Hill: University of North Carolina Press, 1987) 29, 30.

84. Kallen, "Hebraism and Current Tendencies in Philosophy," in *Judaism at Bay*, 7; Matthew Arnold, *Culture and Anarchy*, 19th ed., ed. J. Dover Wilson (Cambridge: Cambridge University Press, 1981), 131.

85. Kallen, "Hebraism and Current Tendencies in Philosophy," 8.

86. Ibid., 9.

87. For a discussion of this polarity, see also Susan Handelman, *The Slayers of*

Moses: The Emergence of Rabbinic Interpretation in Modern Literary Theory (Albany: State University of New York Press, 1982), 29–37; and Lionel Trilling, *Matthew Arnold* (1939; New York: Harcourt Brace Jovanovich, 1979), 256n.

88. Kallen, "Hebraism and Current Tendencies in Philosophy," 9.

89. An example would be the teachings of Leo Baeck; see, for example, Leonard Baker's account of Baeck's inaugural lecture at the Hochschule on 4 May 1913, entitled "Greek and Jewish Preaching." Leonard Baker, *Days of Sorrow and Pain: Leo Baeck and the Berlin Jews* (New York: Oxford University Press, 1978), 59–61.

90. Kallen, "Hebraism and Current Tendencies in Philosophy," 7, 10.

91. Ibid., 8, 11, 12, 15.

92. *Pirke Avot* 1.1.

93. Kallen, "Judaism, Hebraism and Zionism," in *Judaism at Bay*, 28–41, at 38–39. In a previous, amusingly polemical article, "On the Import of 'Universal Judaism'" (reprinted in *Judaism at Bay*, 16–27) Kallen had ridiculed the "universal Judaism" proclaimed by Reform Jews and exposed it as a contradiction in terms, designed to please but devoid of meaning. Kallen's attack gave rise to sharp protest in the Reform press, to which Kallen responded in his article, "Judaism, Hebraism and Zionism."

94. Toll, "Ethnicity and Freedom," 160.

95. Sollors, *Beyond Ethnicity*, 182.

96. Philip Gleason, "American Identity and Americanization," in *Concepts of Ethnicity*, ed. William Peterson, Michael Novak, and Philip Gleason (Cambridge, Mass.: Harvard University Press), 107. The term "hyphenated American" is Kallen's. He used it in his essay, "Nationality and the Hyphenated American," published in the *Menorah Journal* 1 (April 1915): 779–86, two months after his first formulation of cultural pluralism had appeared in *The Nation* (February 1915). Kallen's article in *The Nation* had been designed in part as a reply to the Anglo-Saxon nativist Edward A. Ross.

97. Horace M. Kallen, "Democracy Versus the Melting Pot, Part Two," *The Nation* 100 (25 February 1915): 220.

98. Kallen, *Cultural Pluralism*, 69.

99. Kallen, "Nationality and the Hyphenated American," *Menorah Journal* 1 (April 1915): 82.

100. Kallen, *Cultural Pluralism*, 50.

101. "Democracy is anti-assimilationist. It stands for the acknowledgment, the harmony and organization of group diversities in cooperative expansion of the common life, not for the assimilation of diversities into sameness." Kallen, "Zionism: Democracy or Prussianism," *The New Republic* 18 (5 April 1919): 311. In his critique of cultural pluralism, Stephen Steinberg points out that "democracy and pluralism are not as compatible as the ethnic pluralists would like to think, primarily because pluralist structures tend to reinforce existing class inequalities. In the final analysis, Kallen's model of a 'democracy of nationalities' is workable only in a society where there is basic parity among constituent ethnic groups. Only then would ethnic boundaries be secure from encroachment, and only then would pluralism be innocent of class bias and consistent with democratic principles." Stephen Steinberg, *The Ethnic Myth: Race, Ethnicity, and Class in America* (New York: Atheneum, 1981), 260–261.

102. Kallen, *Cultural Pluralism*, 97.

103. Sollors, "A Critique of Pure Pluralism," 259.

104. Ibid., 270–271.

105. Quoted from Horace Kallen's *A Free Society* (1934) in Elmer N. Lear,

"On the Unity of the Kallenian Perspective—Or Contra the Diplopia of Certain Critics," *Jewish Social Studies* 44 (Summer/Fall 1982): 217. This article was recently reprinted in Konvitz, ed., *The Legacy of Horace M. Kallen*, 108–130.

106. Gleason, "American Identity," 99.

107. Kallen, *Cultural Pluralism*, 91.

108. Kallen, "Zionism," 311.

109. "The group culture will seem to have a nature independent of them all [the individuals]; to be a whole different from its parts, with ways and works evincing its own different laws of persistence, struggle and growth, and capable of determination without reference to the dynamic specificity of the parts. If the individuals of the culture are psychosomatic organisms, the culture is a super-organic psychosoma . . . . It is their overruling providence, the shaper of their fates and fortunes, with a cyclical life history peculiar to itself . . . ." Kallen, *Cultural Pluralism*, 45.

110. Kallen, "Zionism," 311.

111. Schmidt, "Horace M. Kallen" (article), 65.

112. Ibid., 68.

113. Ibid., 62.

114. Kallen, "Judaism," 32.

115. Morris R. Cohen, "Zionism: Tribalism or Liberalism?" *The New Republic* 18 (8 March 1919): 183.

116. Ibid.

117. Sidney Hook, "Morris Cohen—Fifty Years Later," *American Scholar* (Summer 1976): 435; 429.

118. Cohen, "Zionism: Tribalism or Liberalism?" 183, 182.

119. Ibid., 182.

120. Ibid. Philip Gleason pointed out that Kallen, whose theory of cultural pluralism encouraged the advocacy of Zionism, "was also a romantic in his racism. Because cultural pluralism came to be understood as liberal, anti-Anglo-Saxon, and antiracialist, it comes as a surprise to discover that Kallen shared the kind of romantic racialism represented by Anglo-Saxonism before it was absorbed into biological racism. Kallen's racialism was romantic in that he valued diversity as such and did not attempt to rank human groups as superior or inferior according to any absolute scale of merit. But he also resembled the romantics in attributing the distinctive characteristics of peoples to inborn racial qualities whose origin and nature were obscure. He did not discuss them in clear-cut biological or physical-anthropological terms, but 'ancestry' played a crucial role, and even more central was a *Volksgeist*-like element of 'inwardness.'" Gleason, "American Identity," 99–100.

121. Cohen, "Zionism: Tribalism or Liberalism?" 183.

122. Cynthia Ozick, letter to the author, 20 July 1988.

123. Hollinger, *Morris R. Cohen*, 31.

124. "A fair number of his students have become professional philosophers, but they have not built on Cohen's work or even referred to it. Instead, they have developed on their own after initially transferring their allegiance to [John] Dewey, [Alfred North] Whitehead, G. F. Moore, and others. Herbert Schneider, Joseph Ratner, Morton White, Lewis Feuer, Paul Weiss, and most distinguished of all, Ernest Nagel have been properly respectful but have not continued Cohen's work in any noticeable way." Sidney Hook, "Morris Cohen," 430. The same is true for other students of Cohen's mentioned by David Hollinger: William Barrett, Hook himself, Louis Finkelstein, Paul Goodman, Joseph Lash, Richard Morris, Benja-

min Nelson, Samuel Thorne, Philip Wiener, and Bertram Wolfe. See Hollinger, *Morris R. Cohen*, x.

125. For the most complete account, interpretation, and criticism of Cohen's "principle of polarity," see Arturo Deregibus, "Logico e metafisica: il Principio di Polarità," chap. 2 of *Il razionalismo di Morris R. Cohen nella filosofia americana d'oggi* (Torino: G. Giappichelli, 1960), 95–164.

126. Hollinger, *Morris R. Cohen*, x. Cohen calculated that he taught about fifteen thousand students. Cf. Morris R. Cohen, *A Dreamer's Journey* (New York: Arno, 1975), 148.

127. The tradition to which Cohen refers here is based on a midrash: "It happened that a man was ploughing, when one of his oxen lowed. An Arab passed by and asked, 'What are you?' He answered, ' I am a Jew.' He said to him, 'Unharness your ox and untie your plough' [as a mark of mourning]. 'Why?' he asked. 'Because the Temple of the Jews is destroyed.' He inquired, 'From where do you know this?' He answered. 'I know it from the lowing of your ox.' While he was conversing with him, the ox lowed again. The Arab said to him, 'Harness your ox and tie up your plough, because the deliverer of the Jews is born.' 'What is his name?' he asked; and he answered, 'His name is "Comforter." . . .'" *Midrash Rabbah*, 3rd ed. (London: Soncino, 1961) Lamentations 1:16, §151, p. 136.

128. Alter, *Invention of Hebrew Prose*, 7.

129. *Shomers mishpot: oder der sud prisyazhnikh of ale romanen fun Shomer: stenografirt vort as vort fun Sholem Aleichem* (Berditshov: Yakov Sheftil, 1888). The verdict reached in the trial of all of Shomer's novels is devastating. Among other things Shomer is asked "as er sol sakh derbaremen of'n aremen zhargon un sol, lekhol hapohot, di alte shmatess sayne nisht iberdruken nokh amol, un sayne "hekhst interessante" romanen solen avek ahin, vu hin der liber shabess-koidesh get avek" (102). In short, Shomer is asked to show a little mercy toward the poor Yiddish language; he should not reprint his old rags and his "highly interesting" novels should disappear without a trace like the holy sabbath.

130. "Shomer," *Encyclopaedia Judaica* (Jerusalem: Keter, 1972), 14: 1454.

131. This was true until the Russian Revolution. Cf. Morris Dickstein's memoir, "Origins," in *Partisan Review* 51 (1984): 839–846.

132. Cynthia Ozick, "Passage to the New World," *Ms* 6 (2 August 1977): 70–74; 87. Here Ozick reprints her mother's memoirs of the journey from the province of Minsk to New York. Cf. Morris Cohen, *A Dreamer's Journey*, 51–62; Sidney Stahl Weinberg, "Leaving Home," chap. 4 of *The World of Our Mothers: The Lives of Jewish Immigrant Women* (Chapel Hill: University of North Carolina Press, 1988), 65–81; Charlotte Baum, Paula Hyman, Sonya Michel, "They Made a Life: East European Jewish Women in America," chap. 4 of *The Jewish Woman in America* (New York: New American Library, 1977), 91–120.

133. Interview with Jeffrey S. Gurock in *The Jewish Advocate* (Boston), 28 July 1988: 6. Gurock examines the achievements of some Orthodox women in *The Men and Women of Yeshiva: Higher Education, Orthodoxy, and American Judaism* (New York: Columbia University Press, 1988). See, e.g., the life of David Kepesh's mother in Philip Roth's novel *The Professor of Desire* (1977).

134. Cf. Marshall Sklare, "Jewish Education and Identity," chap. 5 of *America's Jews* (New York: Random House, 1971). Sklare points out that "in the process of acculturation secular learning came to be substituted for the old sacred learning. Thus for some the American college became a kind of secular yeshivah. The institution most perfectly exemplifying this trend is the City College of New York, which has afforded the opportunity for higher education to the largest num-

ber of immigrant children" (158–159).

135. "[Cohen] once told me that Dewey, if he had really wanted to, could have arranged for Cohen to join the department of philosophy at Columbia. I asked Dewey about this, and it turned out that by the time Dewey had gotten to know Cohen well, he had dropped the reins of control in the department. The person who really barred Cohen from a post at Columbia was F. J. E. Woodbridge, Cohen's first graduate teacher in philosophy—perhaps more for social reasons than for any others." Hook, "Morris Cohen," 430–431.

136. Leonora Cohen Rosenfield, *Portrait of a Philosopher: Morris R. Cohen in Life and Letters* (New York: Harcourt, Brace & World, 1962), 9. In this work (5–24), a fraction of Cohen's diary has been reprinted. On the importance of Franklin, see also *DJ* 85–86.

137. Cf. Hollinger, "Ethnic Diversity," 139.

138. Hollinger, *Morris R. Cohen*, 79.

139. Ibid. "Opposites such as immediacy and mediation, unity and plurality, the fixed and the flux, substance and function, ideal and real, actual and possible, etc., like the north (positive) and the south (negative) poles of a magnet, all involve each other when applied to any significant entity." Morris R. Cohen, *Reason and Nature: An Essay on the Meaning of Scientific Method* (New York: Harcourt Brace, 1931), 165.

140. Hollinger, *Morris R. Cohen*, 6, 7.

141. "This domain [of pure reason] is an island, enclosed by nature itself within unalterable limits. It is the land of truth—enchanting name!—surrounded by a wide and stormy ocean, the native home of illusion, where many a fog bank and many a swiftly melting iceberg give the deceptive appearance of farther shores, deluding the adventurous seafarer ever anew with empty hopes, and engaging him in enterprises which he can never abandon and yet is unable to carry to completion." Immanuel Kant, *Critique of Pure Reason*, trans. Norman Kemp Smith (London: Macmillan, 1929), 257.

142. The *Jewish Encyclopedia* mentions 1893 as the year in which the Educational Alliance emerged. Nathan Glazer, in *American Judaism* (90), gives the year as 1891. "New York," vol. 9 of *The Jewish Encyclopedia* (New York: Funk and Wagnalls, 1906), 280. This encyclopedia was a creation of German American Jews; it was designed, among other reasons, to flaunt Jewish learning and culture, and thus to counteract increasing ethnic prejudice. The numerous educational and philanthropic institutions founded by these Jews in the late 1880s (and which are described in the encyclopedia) were set up to provide relief, of course, but also to "edit" the living version of their culture arriving en masse from the Old Country, i.e., to transform the Eastern European immigrants into Jews better suited to the taste of modern Americans. "But it is also true that out of the Educational Alliance and the University Settlement came the first Eastern European Jews to establish themselves within the American academic community—Morris R. Cohen, J. Salwyn Schapiro, Paul Klapper, and Louis Dublin." Feuer, "Stages in the Social History," 458.

143. Hollinger, *Morris R. Cohen*, 27.

144. Quoted in Hollinger, *Morris R. Cohen*, 28.

145. Glazer, *American Judaism*, 32–33.

146. Horace L. Friess, *Felix Adler and Ethical Culture: Memories and Studies*, ed. Fannia Weingarten (New York: Columbia University Press, 1981), 29. Friess was a student and later son-in-law of Adler's. Although his monograph is remarkably free of flattery, it is nevertheless protective of Adler. For an account of Adler's

German studies, see 26–35. A different view is presented by Benny Kraut, *From Reform Judaism to Ethical Culture: The Religious Evolution of Felix Adler* (Cincinnati: Hebrew Union College Press, 1979); on Adler's German studies, particularly his reception of Kant and of Matthew Arnold's concept of God as moral power, see 44–75.

147. Friess, *Felix Adler*, 39.

148. Ibid., 40.

149. Ibid., 40–41.

150. Ibid., 45.

151. Kraut, *From Reform Judaism to Ethical Culture*, 104. This claim is supported by Richard Hofstadter and Walter P. Metzger in *The Development of Academic Freedom in the United States* (New York: Columbia University Press, 1955), 340.

152. Kraut, *From Reform Judaism to Ethical Culture*, 100–101.

153. Friess, *Felix Adler*, 55. For Adler's reception of Emerson, see Friess, 41–42; Kraut, 106.

154. Friess, *Felix Adler*, 55.

155. Ibid., 49.

156. All quotations are taken from Urbach, "The Struggle Between Learning and Practice in the Creation of the Image of the Sage," chap. 16, sec. 7, of *The Sages: Their Concepts and Beliefs* (Cambridge, Mass.: Harvard University Press, 1987), 603–620.

157. Although teaching was encouraged—"Raise up many disciples" (*Pirke Avot* 1.1)—it was clear that teaching had to be done without recompense: "Make not of the words of the Torah a crown wherewith to aggrandize yourself, nor a spade wherewith to dig . . . whoever makes profit out of the words of the Torah destroys his own life" (*Pirke Avot* 4.5); Urbach, *The Sages*, 609.

158. Cf. Hollinger, *Morris R. Cohen*, 49. The chapter entitled "Philosophy at Harvard" takes up only four pages in Cohen's 208-page autobiography.

159. Hollinger, *Morris R. Cohen*, 53.

160. Ibid. Cf. also Morris Cohen, "The Insurgence of Reason," chap. 1 of *Reason and Nature*.

161. Morris R. Cohen, "The Conception of Philosophy in Recent Discussion," *The Journal of Philosophy, Psychology, and Scientific Method* 7 (21 July 1910): 403.

162. Cohen, "The Conception of Philosophy," 408.

163. Hollinger, *Morris R. Cohen*, 51–52.

164. Ibid. Even Cohen's most important philosophical contribution, the "principle of polarity," is basically a summing up of the work of his precursors, with which Cohen was quite familiar. Cf. also Deregibus, *Il razionalismo di Morris R. Cohen*, 118–119.

165. Morris R. Cohen, "On American Philosophy: 1. The Idealistic Tradition and Josiah Royce," *The New Republic* 20 (3 September 1919): 150.

166. Morris R. Cohen, "On American Philosophy: 2. William James," *The New Republic* 20 (1 October 1919): 256; 257. On Cohen's opposition to James and Bergson, and his related desire to develop a method that would justify his belief that "the laws of logic and mathematics do hold of nature" (later the "scientific method"), see Hollinger, "The Method of Reason," chap. 6 of *Morris R. Cohen*, 139–163.

167. Diary note dated 22 October 1936, quoted in *DJ* 266. Cohen's statement, "Tenacity is the key to my life," is true in more than one sense.

168. Hook, "Morris Cohen," 432.
169. Ibid., 431.
170. Lewis Feuer, "Talmud to Mill," review of *A Dreamer's Journey* and *Studies in Philosophy and Science*, by Morris Cohen, *The New Republic* 120 (28 March 1949): 21.
171. Hook, "Morris Cohen," 428.
172. Cf. Hook, "Morris Cohen," 428; Hollinger, *Morris R. Cohen*, 75.
173. Hook, "Morris Cohen," 426–427.
174. Ibid.
175. Irving Howe, *A Margin of Hope: An Intellectual Autobiography* (New York: Harcourt Brace Jovanovich, 1982), 62.
176. Sklare, *America's Jews*, 159. "True to traditional norms he achieved his position by strength of mind rather than body, by mental rather than physical courage, by manipulating the abstract rather than the concrete."
177. Quoted in Hook, "Morris Cohen," 436.
178. Morris R. Cohen, *Reflections of a Wondering Jew* (Glencoe: The Free Press, 1950), 18. The copy in Harvard's Widener Library bears the inscription: "To the author's old friend Harry Wolfson." See also Leonora Cohen Rosenfield, "The Judaic Values of a Philosopher: Morris Raphael Cohen, 1880–1947," *Jewish Social Studies* 42 (Summer/Fall 1980): 191.
179. Hollinger, *Morris R. Cohen*, 212.
180. Cohen, *Reflections*, 119.
181. Ibid., 120.
182. Ibid., 122.
183. Ibid., 122, 119, 123, 139, 123.

Chapter 4. Men of Letters

1. Cohen in 1939 co-founded and subsequently co-edited the journal *Jewish Social Studies*; Lewisohn had been on the original editorial board of *Opinion: A Journal of Jewish Life and Letters* in 1931, joined the staff of the *New Palestine* in 1943, and served as contributing editor of *Judaism* from its founding in 1952 until his death in 1955.
2. Ludwig Lewisohn, *Israel* (New York: Boni and Liveright, 1925), 157. Further references to this work will be indicated by *I*.
3. Sacvan Bercovitch, interview with the author, Cambridge, Mass., 10 February 1988.
4. The term here designates the Jewish people, as in the title of Lewisohn's book.
5. See his analysis of Lewisohn's *Expression in America* (New York: Harper & Brothers, 1932) in Granville Hicks, "The Sunset Glow of Individualism," *The New Republic* 70 (13 April 1932): 240–241.
6. Alfred Kazin, *On Native Grounds: An Interpretation of Modern American Prose Literature* (New York: Doubleday, 1956: 1st ed. 1942), 207.
7. Gordon Hutner, "The Dynamics of Erasure: Anti-Semitism and the Example of Ludwig Lewisohn," *Prospects* 16.
8. Kazin, *On Native Grounds*, 203–204. For an analysis of Kazin's response to Lewisohn, see Gordon Hutner, "The Dynamics of Erasure."
9. Almost from the beginning, Lewisohn was viewed as a case of psychic disturbance; see, e.g., Jacob Zeitlin, "The Case of Mr. Lewisohn," *Menorah Journal* 8 (June 1922): 187–191; David Eckerling, "The Case of Ludwig Lewisohn," *Reflex*

5 (September 1929): 14–20; Louis J. Bragman, "The Case of Ludwig Lewisohn: A Contribution to the Psychology of Creative Genius," *American Journal of Psychiatry* 11 (September 1931): 319–331. James Wise ends the introductory paragraph in his laudatory portrait with: "His intellectual growth, his sex experience, his emotional development, his spiritual adventures, are alike set down for all men to read and know. One might even, with the exception of his essays in the field of literary criticism, gather his writings under one comprehensive title: The Case of Ludwig Lewisohn." James Waterman Wise [Analyticus, pseud.], *Jews Are Like That* (New York: Brentano, 1928), 109. A more recent study emphasizes the influence of Lewisohn's mother on her son's work: Ralph Melnick, "Oedipus in Charleston: Ludwig Lewisohn's Search for the Muse," *Studies in American Jewish Literature* 3 (1983): 68–84. Daniel Walden concludes that Lewisohn represents "what used to be called a classic case of unresolved Oedipal conflict in which his tight-knit, German-Jewish, Victorian family clashed with the loneliness, libidinal drives, and needs and errors of a freedom-seeking young man in New York." Daniel Walden, "Ludwig Lewisohn: Up the Literary Stream from Charleston and Beyond," in: Samuel Proctor and Louis Schmier with Malcolm Stern, eds., *Jews of the South: Selected Essays from the Southern Jewish Historical Society* (Macon, Ga.: Mercer University Press, 1984), 121–130.

10. Ludwig Lewisohn, *Up Stream: An American Chronicle* (New York: Boni & Liveright, 1922), 15.

11. Georg Hirschfeld, *The Mothers*, trans. and with an introduction by Ludwig Lewisohn (Garden City: Doubleday, Page, 1916), xiii.

12. Meaning, they did not convert — a strong temptation in times of rising German anti-Semitism. The rate of conversion was closely watched by those who remained "loyal." "Around 1910 the monthly newsletter of the Berlin Jewish Community Council, which was sent to all members free of charge, began to print on the last page the names of those who had left the Jewish fold. . . . This column was widely and carefully read even when nothing else in the whole issue was." Gershom Scholem, *From Berlin to Jerusalem: Memories of My Youth* (New York: Schocken, 1980), 11.

13. Scholem, *From Berlin to Jerusalem*, 9–10, 23.

14. Lewisohn, *Up Stream*, 18; Scholem, *From Berlin to Jerusalem*, 10, 28–29; Walter Benjamin, "Berliner Kindheit um Neunzehnhundert," in Walter Benjamin, *Gesammelte Schriften*, vol. 4, pt. 1, Tillman Rexroth, ed. (Frankfurt am Main: Suhrkamp, 1972), 259–260; 278; 282–283; 285.

15. The degree to which Christmas was a nonreligious holiday for the Scholems is illustrated by a 1911 incident. "Under the Christmas tree there was the Herzl picture in a black frame, and my mother said: 'We selected this picture for you because you are so interested in Zionism.' From then on I left the house at Christmas-time." Scholem, *From Berlin to Jerusalem*, 28.

16. Ibid., 42. Gerhard emigrated to Palestine in 1923; Reinhold emigrated to Australia in 1938; Werner was murdered at Buchenwald in 1940.

17. Helge Normann Nilsen suggests as recurring themes in Lewisohn's work "the quest for security and love in a family setting and the love of an esthetic perfection that contains the seeds of metaphysical revelation." But she does not call attention to the fact that the psychological need underlying both themes, the restoration of Oneness, is identical. Helge N. Nilsen, "The Road to Judaism: Spiritual Development in Ludwig Lewisohn's Autobiography," *MELUS* [Multi-Ethnic Literature of the United States] 14 (Spring 1987): 59–70. In his portrait of Lewisohn, "*Up Stream* Revisited," (*Mid-stream* 35 [February/March 1989]: 46–50),

George M. Saiger concentrates on the Jewish theme; as one of the people best informed about Lewisohn's life, he offers a valuable summary of the facts. It is a bit unfortunate that the psychiatrist Saiger does not investigate as a professional the connection between historical facts and Lewisohn's psychic suffering, which surfaced clearly later in his life.

18. Louis Schmier, ed., *Reflections of Southern Jewry: The Letters of Charles Wessolowsky, 1878–1879* (Macon: Mercer University Press, 1982), 160. Schmier's work also contains an extensive bibliography of Southern Jewry. See also Charles Reznikoff and Uriah Engelman, *The Jews of Charleston: A History of an American Jewish Community* (Philadelphia: Jewish Publication Society of America, 1950).

19. Sollors, *Beyond Ethnicity*, 201.

20. Ludwig Lewisohn, "A Study of Matthew Arnold: 1. His Poetry," *The Sewanee Review* 9 (October 1901): 442–456; "A Study of Matthew Arnold: 2. Formative Influences: The Influence of Goethe," *The Sewanee Review* 10 (April 1902): 143–159; "A Study of Matthew Arnold: 3. Arnold's Critical Method," *The Sewanee Review* 10 (July 1902): 302–319.

21. Lewisohn, "Matthew Arnold: 1. His Poetry," 445–446.

22. Ludwig Lewisohn, *Expression in America*, 182; 141.

23. In his monograph, Seymour Lainoff claims that "Brewer" is the pseudonym for George Rice Carpenter. Seymour Lainoff, *Ludwig Lewisohn* (Boston: Twayne, 1982), 7. This seems unlikely because Lewisohn usually used very obvious pseudonyms in his autobiography ("St. Marks" = St. Matthew's; "Ferris" = L. M. Harris; "Brent" = Trent; etc.). It is more likely that "Brewer" stands for Professor *Brander* Matthews, whose role in Columbia's English department matches Lewisohn's portrait much better than that of the rather inoffensive Professor Rice. Matthews, a Columbia man by education and a professor there from 1891 to 1924, belonged, with Henry van Dyke and Perry Bliss, to those "who kept alive until World War I the nationalist idiom" and who insisted on teaching American literature as an exemplification "of the march of the 'English speaking race . . . as this race is steadily spreading abroad.'" Graff, *Professing Literature*, 72; 231.

24. Harold Wechsler, *The Qualified Student: A History of Selective College Admission in America* (New York: John Wiley, 1977), 131–132. I am much indebted to Wechsler's excellent presentation of the admissions policy at Columbia.

25. Heywood Broun and George Britt, *Christians Only: A Study in Prejudice* (New York: Vanguard, 1931), 102. Wechsler, in *The Qualified Student*, details the slow evolution of this screening process for the college. He does not comment on the selection of graduate students.

26. Wechsler, *The Qualified Student*, 164.

27. Horace Coon, *Columbia: Colossus on the Hudson* (New York: E. P. Dutton, 1947), 55; 51. Frederick P. Keppel, *Columbia* (New York: Oxford University Press, 1914), 2.

28. Quoted in Coon, *Columbia*, 62.

29. Wechsler, *The Qualified Student*, 137.

30. Ibid.

31. Ibid.

32. Ibid., 136.

33. Ibid.

34. Concerning the highest university office, the presidency, it took another thirty years for the situation to relax completely. The first Jewish president was Paul Klapper, who became head of Queen's College in 1937; Brandeis University chose a Jewish President, Abram Sachar, in 1948; and in 1967, the University of

Chicago appointed Edward H. Levi; by 1971 Jews had also served as presidents of Dartmouth and the University of Pennsylvania. Saul Cohen (born in 1925) headed Queen's College from 1977 to 1978. It was not until 1977, when first Chicago and then Yale offered their highest positions to Harvard's noted dean, Henry Rosovsky (born in Gdansk in 1927), that the choice of a Jewish president was no longer unusual. Rosovsky declined both offers, in order to complete his task at Harvard (see Oren, *Joining the Club*, 274–278). When the Harvard presidency became vacant in 1990, Rosovsky was a desirable candidate. But he preferred "to work with my colleagues on the search commitee . . . to find a new leader for our University" (*Harvard Magazine* 93 [September-October 1990]: 86). Harold T. Shapiro (born in Montreal in 1935) was appointed president of Princeton in 1987.

35. Wechsler, *The Qualified Student*, 141–142.

36. Quoted in Wechsler, *The Qualified Student*, 142.

37. Ibid., 142, 143.

38. Joel E. Spingarn summarized the power of the board of trustees (and hence of its Committee on Education) in his pamphlet, *A Question of Academic Freedom, Being the Official Correspondence Between Nicholas Murray Butler . . . and J. E. Spingarn . . . During the Academic Year 1910–1911, with Other Documents* (New York: Printed for distribution among the alumni, 1911), 2–3.

39. Quoted in Wechsler, *The Qualified Student*, 143.

40. Marshall van Deusen, *J. E. Spingarn* (New York: Twayne, 1971). Although Spingarn's "'influence' has remained problematical at best" (van Deusen, Preface), it is nevertheless surprising that he is not mentioned at all in Kazin's *On Native Grounds*. He is dealt with briefly in Gerald Graff's *Professing Literature* (126–128).

41. Lewisohn, *Expression in America*, 422.

42. Unpublished memoir by Spingarn, quoted in van Deusen, *J. E. Spingarn*, 15. For almost all biographical information on Spingarn I am indebted to van Deusen's monograph.

43. Quoted by van Deusen (18) from the first of the (unpublished) lectures that Spingarn delivered at the New School for Social Research in New York in the spring of 1931. Woodberry's sparkling personality flattened in his writings. Stuart P. Sherman, in a letter to Spingarn (1 July 1922) declining the invitation to contribute an essay on Woodberry to a commemorative volume, writes: "But my real feeling for his personality all comes to me second hand from the tales of Columbia men to whom he was obviously so very much more of a spirit and kindling torch than one can divine from his books.—Isn't it a commendable thing, in a way, that he did to youths of the older generation, what a man like Dean Briggs remembers of his bright youth in the classroom, a fire and radiance that cool somehow and lose their quickening immediacy on the printed page." Jacob Zeitlin and Homer Woodbridge, eds., *Life and Letters of Stuart P. Sherman* (New York: Farrar & Rinehart, 1929), 2:581–582.

44. The title for Lewisohn's history of American literature, *Expression in America*, seems to have been inspired by Spingarn, with whose works Lewisohn was familiar. He had included one of Spingarn's essays in his *Modern Book of Criticism* (1919) and wildly praised Spingarn in the Introduction as one of the "shivering young Davids," who, like Lewisohn himself, were out to "face an army of Goliaths" (such as the Philistines Paul Elmer More or Irving Babbitt). In 1931, a year before the publication of *Expression in America*, Spingarn's most important book, *Creative Criticism* (first published in 1917) reappeared in a new and enlarged edition, so that Spingarn's vocabulary was very fresh in Lewisohn's mind.

45. Cf. van Deusen, *J. E. Spingarn*, 97–112.

46. Spingarn, *A Question of Academic Freedom*, 14.

47. Lea Ritter-Santini, "Maniera Grande: Über italienische Renaissance und deutsche Jahrhundertwende," in Roger Bauer, Eckhart Heftrich, Helmut Koopmann, Wolfdietrich Rasch et al., eds., *Fin de Siècle: Zur Literatur und Kunst der Jahrhundertwende* (Frankfurt am Main: Klostermann, 1977), 170–205.

48. Hugo von Hofmannsthal, *Sämtliche Werke 3: Dramen 1* (Frankfurt-am-Main: Fischer, 1982), 45.

49. But Spingarn made it clear that this was only "a vision of reality, not reality, imagination and not thought or morals." Quoted in van Deusen, *J. E. Spingarn*, 109.

50. Lewisohn, *Expression in America*, 421–422.

51. Quoted in van Deusen, *J. E. Spingarn*, 39.

52. Melville Crane, "The Woodberry Years," in Wesley First, ed., *University on the Heights* (Garden City: Doubleday, 1969), 96, 97. Alfred A. Knopf, who attended Spingarn's last seminar (1910–11), has high praise for the man whom Lewis Mumford called "'slim, erect, austere with dark brown eyes that would ignite under the first spark of thought,' 'proud as Dante,' and 'capable of advancing resolutely in the face of the enemy, without faltering because no one followed.' He was not well liked by many of his colleagues, and he was apparently a forbidding figure to some of his students" (*D* 49). Student Knopf, however, liked him. "Spingarn was a much more unconventional teacher [than John Erskine] but a really inspiring one. His enthusiasm for the classics, and indeed for any good writing, was contagious." Alfred A. Knopf, "The Columbia I Remember," in First, ed., *University on the Heights*, 183.

53. Jacob Zeitlin, "The Case of Mr. Lewisohn," *The Menorah Journal* 8 (June 1922): 189.

54. Even students who entered the academy as late as Meyer H. Abrams (born in 1912) or Leo Marx (born in 1919) were advised to reconsider their plans. M. H. Abrams, interview with the author, Cornell University, Ithaca, N.Y., 28 August 1988; Leo Marx, interview with the author, MIT, Cambridge, Mass., 13 May 1988.

55. Sidney Hook, "Anti-Semitism in the Academy: Some Pages of the Past," *Midstream* 25 (January 1979): 49–50.

56. Apart from Franz Boas and Felix Adler, there were Irwin Edman (philosophy); Edwin R. A. Seligman (economics), a member of the Columbia faculty since 1885; Gottheil (Semitic languages); Alexander Goldenweiser (anthropology); Isaac Leon Kandel (Teacher's College, education); Selig Hecht (biophysics); and Nathan Pfeffer (political science).

57. Hook, "Anti-Semitism," 50.

58. Wechsler, *The Qualified Student*, 151.

59. Zeitlin, "The Case of Mr. Lewisohn," 187.

60. Cf. M. Lincoln Schuster, "Four Historic Years," in First, ed., *University on the Heights*, 163.

61. Zeitlin, "The Case of Mr. Lewisohn," 189.

62. Customarily Mary Lewisohn, as she preferred to call herself, is referred to as Mary Arnold Crocker. Crocker was her maiden name; Childs was her first married name. She wrote poetry under the name Bosworth Crocker. Her death notices put her birthdate as 1866 or 1871, but the fact that her first marriage was in 1885 seems to exclude the later birthdate. For this information I am indebted to Dr. George M. Saiger; letter to the author, 25 December 1988.

63. Allen Guttmann, *The Jewish Writer in America: Assimilation and Crisis of Identity* (New York: Oxford University Press, 1971), 101.

64. Lainoff, *Lewisohn*, 28.

65. Lainoff suggests that the lost novel and Lewisohn's novel *Don Juan* are identical. In his monograph on Lewisohn, Lainoff analyzes *Don Juan* immediately after deailing with *The Broken Snare* (1908). Lainoff writes: "*Don Juan* (1923), written in twenty-nine days and published fifteeen years later, during which time Lewisohn had devoted himself to literary criticism and scholarship, stems from an autobiographical impulse" (28). But there is strong evidence against Lainoff's identification of the destroyed novel with *Don Juan*. In *Up Stream* (145) Lewisohn wrote that the destroyed novel, too, eventually got published. *Up Stream* came out in 1922, a year before *Don Juan*. In the second volume of his autobiography, *Mid-Channel* (1929), Lewisohn deals explicitly with the writing of *Don Juan*, dating it to "one of the last summers in America" [Lewisohn left for Europe in 1924] when he was told by his publisher, Horace Liveright, that "a book was needed for the fall. . . . I delayed to the last possible moment and then wrote the manuscript of *Don Juan* in exactly twenty-nine days." A little later, when he talks about the publication of *The Case of Mr. Crump* (1926), he states that "Very early in life I had a most harmless little book confiscated by Comstock's officers," without adding, as one might expect Lewisohn to do, that it was recently published. Ludwig Lewisohn, *Mid-Channel: An American Chronicle* (New York: Blue Ribbon Book, 1929), 66, 170. Further evidence for the late composition of *Don Juan* is that Helga Strong in *Don Juan* is clearly Thelma Spear, whom Lewisohn did not get to know until 1921 or 1922.

66. Stanley Chyet, "Ludwig Lewisohn: The Years of Becoming," *American Jewish Archives* 11 (October 1959): 141.

67. Ludwig Lewisohn, *The Spirit of Modern German Literature* (New York: B. W. Huebsch, 1916), 118.

68. See, for instance, the experience of the older Lord Chandos in Hugo von Hofmannsthal's "Ein Brief" (1902) in Hugo von Hofmannsthal, *Das erzählerische Werk* (Frankfurt-am-Main: Fischer, 1969), 102–113.

69. See, for instance, Robert Musil's concept of the "Augenblick" in *Die Verwirrungen des Zöglings Törless* (1903–06), or James Joyce's concept of epiphany in his *Portrait of the Artist as a Young Man* (1914–15).

70. Within that system nothing prevented the revaluation of a human being into a vermin (*Ungeziefer*) unworthy of life (*lebensunwert*) and the use of insecticide for "its" extermination.

71. Interesting in this context is Gotthart Wunberg's analysis of the obsession with unification in Austrian fin-de-siècle literature, which he calls *Monismus*. Cf. "Österreichische Literatur und allgemeiner zeitgenössischer Monismus um die Jahrhundertwende," in Peter Berner, Emil Brix, and Wolfgang Mantl, *Wien um 1900: Aufbruch in die Moderne* (Munich: R. Oldenbourg, 1986), 104–111.

72. Irving Howe, *Sherwood Anderson*, The American Men of Letters Series (New York: William Sloane, 1951), 100; see also 99.

73. Richard Hofstadter and Walter P. Metzger, *The Development of Academic Freedom in the United States* (New York: Columbia University Press, 1955), 495–496.

74. Chyet, "Ludwig Lewisohn," 144. The psychiatrist George M. Saiger, who has studied the Lewisohn family for many years, disagrees here with Chyet. Saiger points out that "there was insanity in the generation before Jacques Lewisohn" and that "Jacques himself was certifiably insane (or at least certified as insane)."

Looking at the generations following Jacques Lewisohn, Dr. Saiger observes that they "have escaped insanity only by other kinds of pathology." Minna Eloesser Lewisohn's death might have been a catalyst but was certainly not the reason for Jacques Lewisohn's insanity after 1912. (George M. Saiger, letter to the author, 25 December 1988).

75. Ludwig Lewisohn, *A Modern Book of Criticism* (New York: Boni & Liveright, 1919), 111.

76. Leslie Fiedler, "The Jew in the American Novel," in *The Collected Essays of Leslie Fiedler* (New York: Stein and Day, 1971), 81.

77. Lainoff, *Lewisohn*, 29.

78. "Eventually the book became for me a time machine through which to look backward and discover the origins of that deranged hypermorality to whose demands I had proved so hopelessly accessible in my early twenties. I was trying to come to some understanding of this destructive force, but separate from my own ordeal, to exorcise her power over me by taking it back to its local origins and tracing in detail the formative history of injury and disappointment right on down to its grisly consequences. . . ." Roth, *The Facts: A Novelist's Autobiography* (New York: Farrar, Straus & Giroux, 1988), 145.

79. "*My Life as a Man* would turn out to be far less my revenge on her than, given the unyielding problems it presented, hers on me. Writing it consisted of making one false start after another and, over the years it took to finish it, very nearly broke my will. The only experience worse than writing it, however, would have been for me to have endured that marriage without having been able to find ways of reimagining it into a fiction with a persuasive existence independent of myself." Roth, *The Facts*, 152.

80. Joseph Wood Krutch, "Significant Ugliness," *The Nation* 124 (9 February 1927): 150.

81. Krutch, "Significant Ugliness," 149.

82. Quoted in Robert M. Adams, "The Beast in the Jungle," review of Lyndall Gordon, *Eliot's New Life* and of Valerie Eliot, ed., *The Letters of T. S. Eliot: Vol. 1. 1898–1922*, in *The New York Review of Books* 35 (10 November 1988): 4.

83. Thomas Mann, in his 1926 preface to *The Case of Mr. Crump*, reprinted in the 1965 Farrar, Straus & Giroux edition of the novel (vii).

84. Robert Elias, ed., *Letters of Theodore Dreiser* (Philadelphia: University of Pennsylvania Press, 1959), 2:451–452.

85. Reinhold Niebuhr summarizes Lewisohn's volume, *The Permanent Horizon* (1934), as follows: "It embodies a series of essays on various subjects which achieve cohesion through their common polemic against all forms of modernism, liberal and radical." Reinhold Niebuhr, "'A Bourgeois Takes His Stand'," *The Nation* 139 (17 October 1934): 456.

86. Cf. the analyses in Robert Shafer, *Paul Elmer More and American Criticism* (New Haven: Yale University Press, 1935), 40–50; Louis Fraiberg, "Ludwig Lewisohn and the Puritan Inhibition of American Literature," chap. 7 of *Psychoanalysis and American Literary Criticism* (Detroit: Wayne State University Press, 1960), 145–160; and Jerrold Hirsch, "Ludwig Lewisohn: Can He Still Help Us? A Reconsideration of *Expression in America*," in Louis Filler, ed., *Seasoned Authors For a New Season: The Search For Standards in Popular Writing* (Bowling Green, Ohio: Bowling Green University Popular Press, 1980), 98–116.

87. Among the three alternatives, taking Freud seriously was in fact out of the question for Lewisohn, because probing the foundations of his "liberated" self might turn out to be a self-defeating activity. But Lewisohn would later use it as a

"bludgeon" (see Shafer, *Paul Elmer More*, 49) against those who deserved no better —the repressed Puritans in America's literary history.

88. Peter Gay, *A Godless Jew: Freud, Atheism, and the Making of Psychoanalysis* (New Haven: Yale University Press, in association with Hebrew Union College Press, Cincinnati, 1987), 131–132, 124.

89. Cf. Gershom Scholem, "Martin Bubers Deutung des Chassidismus," in *Judaica* (Frankfurt am Main: Suhrkamp, 1963), 166, 167.

90. These writings include such non-fiction as *Israel* (1925); the last part of *Mid-Channel* (1929); *The Permanent Horizon* (1934); two anthologies, *Rebirth: A Book of Modern Jewish Thought* (1935), and *Among the Nations* (1948); *The Answer — The Jew and the World: Past, Present and Future* (1939); *The American Jew: Character and Destiny* (1950); and his introduction to *The Great Jewish Book* (1952), ed. Samuel Caplan and Harold U. Ribalow; and such fiction as *Roman Summer* (1927); *The Island Within* (1928); *The Last Days of Shylock* (1931); *This People* (1933); *The Triumph of Jubilee* (1937); *The Renegade* (1942); and *Breathe Upon These* (1944). For analysis see Lainoff, *Lewisohn*, chaps. 3 and 6.

91. Norton Mezvinsky, "The Jewish Thought of Ludwig Lewisohn," *The Chicago Jewish Forum* 16 (Winter 1957–1958): 79.

92. Complaints about Lewisohn's carelessness concerning historical facts are a leitmotif in the writings of his critics. Edward Sapir, in his review of *Israel*, quite reasonably argues that "the reader whose attitudes are questioned in Mr. Lewisohn's pages will not lightly absolve him from the charges of unfairness, of an emotionally impelled misreading of facts, perhaps insincerity." Edward Sapir, "Lewisohn's View of the Jewish Problem," *Menorah Journal* 12 (April-May 1926): 124. Reinhold Niebuhr, in his review of *The Permanent Horizon*, points to such a deliberate misreading of the facts: "[Lewisohn] even allows himself a palpable falsification of history when he declares, speaking of German politics, that 'when in a given election the Nazis lost, the Communists gained and vice versa; the numerical strength of the parties of the middle remained fairly constant.' The real fact is that Communists gained at the expense of the Socialists as German desperation increased, while the fascists wiped out the parties of the middle." "A Bourgeois Takes His Stand," 456. And Oscar Cargill, in his analysis of *Expression in America*, is as exasperated at "the author's obvious unfamiliarity with the material," as at his "'abysmal ignorance of the authors cited"; he is even more irritated at his "unwillingness to examine the material." Lewisohn's chapter "The Polite Writers," in *Expression in America*, Cargill claims, "is nothing more than a wild harangue against a number of people in no sense related (Joaquin Miller is lumped with Longfellow, Sill and Lanier) whom Mr. Lewisohn suspects of perpetuating the 'Puritan' tradition, which he believes to have been stultifying. We do not know what the 'Puritan' tradition was since the author dismisses the colonial writers with a wave of his hand. If the force of Puritanism was as evil as he thinks it, it deserved a more adequate study than he has accorded it." Oscar Cargill, *Intellectual America: Ideas on the March* (New York: Macmillan, 1941), 734.

93. Lewisohn, *The American Jew: Character and Destiny* (New York: Farrar, Straus & Giroux, 1950) 47–48; 46; 114.

94. Lewisohn, *The American Jew*, 165.

95. Irwin Edman, "Odyssey," *The Menorah Journal* 14 (May 1928): 511.

96. For the following biographical information I am indebted to the psychiatrist George M. Saiger.

97. George M. Saiger, letter to the author, 25 December 1988. Dr. Saiger also compiled a bibliography of Lewisohn's writing for the *New Palestine*.

98. Lainoff, *Lewisohn*, 45.

99. George M. Saiger, letter to the author, 3 December 1988.

100. Lewisohn's accusation is confirmed by James Lewisohn's unpublished autobiography, to which Dr. George Saiger had access. Saiger, letter to the author, 25 December 1988.

101. Irving Howe, *A Margin of Hope: An Intellectual Autobiography* (New York: Harcourt, Brace, Jovanovich, 1982), 187.

102. Ibid., 184.

103. Ibid., 183–184.

104. Arthur Schnitzler, *Der Weg ins Freie*, in *Gesammelte Werke* (Berlin: Fischer, 1912), 3:175–176.

105. Howe, *A Margin of Hope*, 186.

106. Barbara Herrnstein Smith, interview with the author, Cambridge, Mass., 20 November 1988.

107. Harold Bloom, "A Speculation Upon American Jewish Culture," *Judaism* 31 (Summer 1982): 266.

108. Bloom, *Agon: Toward a Theory of Revisionism* (New York: Oxford University Press, 1982), 326. Gershon Shaked, "Alexandria: On Jews and Judaism in America," *The Jerusalem Quarterly* 49 (Winter 1989): 47–84.

109. Cf. Susan Handelman, *The Slayers of Moses*; Elias J. Bickerman, *The Jews in the Greek Age* (Cambridge: Harvard University Press, 1988).

110. Cf. Irving Howe, "Strangers," in Irving Howe, *Celebrations and Attacks: Thirty Years of Literary and Cultural Criticism* (New York: Horizon, 1979), 11–26.

111. Abraham Cahan, *The Rise of David Levinsky* (New York: Harper & Row, 1960), 110.

Chapter 5. A Professor of Literature

1. Morris Dickstein, "Lionel Trilling and *The Liberal Imagination*," *The Sewanee Review* 94 (Spring 1986): 334.

2. Eugene Goodheart, "Autobiographical," in Eugene Goodheart, *Pieces of Resistance* (Cambridge: Cambridge University Press, 1987), 2.

3. Eugene Goodheart, "William Chace's *Lionel Trilling: Criticism and Politics*," in Eugene Goodheart, *Pieces of Resistance*, 17.

4. Norman Podhoretz, *Making It* (New York: Harper Colophon, 1980), 3.

5. Phillip Lopate, "Remembering Lionel Trilling," *American Review* 25 (October 1976): 150.

6. Mark Krupnick, *Lionel Trilling and the Fate of Cultural Criticism* (Evanston: Northwestern University Press, 1986), 14.

7. Eugene Goodheart, interview with the author, Cambridge, Mass., 17 March 1989.

8. Morris Dickstein, *Gates of Eden: American Culture in the Sixties* (New York: Penguin, 1989), 21.

9. Krupnick, *Lionel Trilling*, 15.

10. For such attempts, see Mark Schechner, *After the Revolution: Studies in the Contemporary Jewish American Imagination* (Bloomington: Indiana University Press, 1987); Alexander Bloom, *Prodigal Sons: The New York Intellectuals and Their World* (New York: Oxford University Press, 1986).

11. In 1944 Trilling stated: "I do not think of myself as a 'Jewish writer.' I do not have it in mind to serve by my writing any Jewish purpose. I should resent it if a critic of my work were to discover in it faults or virtues which he called Jewish."

"Under Forty: A Symposium," *Contemporary Jewish Record* 7 (February 1944): 15.

12. Cynthia Ozick, interview with the author, New York, N.Y., 28 November 1989.

13. Geoffrey Hartman, "Lionel Trilling as Man in the Middle," in Geoffrey Hartman, *The Fate of Reading and Other Essays* (Chicago: University of Chicago Press, 1975), 299.

14. Richard Chase, *The American Novel and Its Tradition* (New York: Doubleday, 1957), 2.

15. This, at least, is how Mark Shechner reads Trilling: "Though we do not commonly think of Trilling as the historian of his own emotions, we can read the progression of moods he documented and the positions he championed as contributions to a Romantic autobiography of the sort that in the nineteenth century fairly defined the progress of the modern spirit: youthful precocity, mid-life emotional crisis, conversion, and revival." Schechner, *After the Revolution*, 72.

16. Dickstein, "Lionel Trilling," 330.

17. Daniel T. O'Hara, *Lionel Trilling: The Work of Liberation* (Madison: University of Wisconsin Press, 1988), 62.

18. Dickstein, "Lionel Trilling," 334.

19. Ibid.

20. Nathaniel Hawthorne, *The Scarlet Letter* (Columbus: Ohio State University Press, 1962), 240.

21. Dickstein, "Lionel Trilling," 334.

22. Gregory S. Jay, "Lionel Trilling," in *Dictionary of Literary Biography*, vol. 63, *Modern American Critics, 1920–1955*, ed. Gregory S. Jay (Detroit: Gale Research Company, 1988), 268.

23. Bialystok population in 1856: 13,787 (of which 9,547 were Jews); in 1895: 62,943 (of which 47,783 were Jews). Cf. *Encyclopaedia Judaica* (Jerusalem: Keter, 1972), "Bialystok."

24. Diana Trilling, "Lionel Trilling, A Jew at Columbia," *Commentary* 67 (March 1979): 42.

25. Mark Krupnick, "Lionel Trilling, 'Culture,' and Jewishness," *Denver Quarterly* 18 (Autumn 1983): 107; Diana Trilling, "Lionel Trilling," 41.

26. Cf. Lionel Trilling, "Some Notes for an Autobiographical Lecture," in Lionel Trilling, *The Last Decade: Essays and Reviews, 1965–1975*, ed. Diana Trilling (New York: Harcourt Brace Jovanovich, 1979). See also Lewis P. Simpson's analysis of Trilling's "Notebooks" in "Lionel Trilling and the Agency of Terror," *Partisan Review* 54 (Winter 1987): 18–35.

27. Diana Trilling, "Lionel Trilling," 42.

28. Ernest Samuels, *Bernard Berenson: The Making of a Connoisseur* (Cambridge: Harvard University Press, 1979), 21.

29. Diana Trilling, "Lionel Trilling," 42.

30. Ibid.

31. A notebook entry of 1945 reads: "The Victorians have lost all charm for me—they make my *parent* literature, the reading with which I was most cosily at home—I could feel their warmth and seemed always to know my way among them—now they bore me utterly . . . ." Trilling, "Notebooks 1," *Partisan Review* 51–52 (1984–1985): 505.

32. Cf. Tanner, *Lionel Trilling* (Boston: Twayne, 1988), 9.

33. The founding of Reconstructionism may be dated from the establishment of the Society for the Advancement of Judaism (SAJ) in January 1922. Kaplan's major work, *Judaism as a Civilization*, appeared in 1934. Concerning Trilling's

attitude toward Judaism, Kaplan's influence was stronger, in the long run, than Kadushin's. In his letter of endorsement to Elliot Cohen, the editor of the *Menorah Journal*, dated 2 December 1929, Trilling displays popularized Kaplanism: "The purpose of Jewish life is cultural, is it not?" Quoted in Elinor Grumet, "The Apprenticeship of Lionel Trilling," *Prooftexts* 4 (May 1984): 161.

34. A notebook entry of 1970 reads: "*Kim*—read first at age 12–13 . . . . Kadushin tells me it is *important*—with genuine seriousness—but when, after a service at S.A.J. I stop him to ask what its 'philosophy' is he snubs me, having to talk to some imp[ortan]t member of the congregation—as always, he disappoints . . . ." "From the Notebooks of Lionel Trilling, Part 2," *Partisan Review* 54 (Winter 1987): 15. Lionel Trilling, "Wordsworth and the Rabbis," in *The Opposing Self: Nine Essays in Criticism* (New York: Viking, 1955), 143.

35. Lionel Trilling, "Wordsworth," 123.

36. Grumet, "The Apprenticeship of Lionel Trilling," 164.

37. Richard Hofstadter and Walter P. Metzger, *The Development of Academic Freedom in the United States* (New York: Columbia University Press, 1955), 499.

38. President Butler's commencement address of 6 June 1917. Quoted in Hofstadter and Metzger, *Development*, 499.

39. Ibid.

40. Estelle Gilson, "Butler at Columbia," *Commentary* 81 (April 1986): 9, 10.

41. Ibid.

42. Wechsler, *The Qualified Student*, 159.

43. Ibid., 159–160.

44. Carleton Steven Coon, *The Races of Europe* (New York: Macmillan, 1939), pl. 2, fig. 4; pl. 3, fig. 1.

45. Wechsler, *The Qualified Student*, 159.

46. Herbert Hawkes letter to E. B. Wilbur, 16 June 1922. Quoted in Wechsler, *The Qualified Student*, 160–161.

47. Wechsler, *The Qualified Student*, 164. In the fall of 1929, the year Butler established a chair for Jewish studies, five hundred freshmen were admitted; ninety-two of them were Jews. Broun and Britt estimate that after the regulation of admissions the number of Jews admitted was kept between 19% and 26% (Broun and Britt, *Christians Only*, 74). This is an optimistic estimate. The figures for the thirties are much lower. In the fall of 1934, for instance, "572 freshmen were admitted of which 58% were Protestants, 25% were Catholics, and 17% were Jewish" (Wechsler, 168).

48. Diana Trilling, "Lionel Trilling," 40–41.

49. Helen Epstein, "Meyer Schapiro: 'A Passion to Know and Make Known,'" *Art News* (May 1983): 71; Tanner, *Lionel Trilling*, 20.

50. Francis Russel, speaking about his Jewish classmates at the elite Boston Latin School in the 1920s. Quoted in Steinberg, *The Ethnic Myth*, 232.

51. Steinberg, *The Ethnic Myth*, 230.

52. Diana Trilling, "Lionel Trilling," 43.

53. Epstein, "Schapiro," 71–72.

54. Mark Van Doren, "Jewish Students I Have Known," *Menorah Journal* 13 (June 1927): 266.

55. Ibid., 266, 267.

56. Ibid., 267–268. Jacques Barzun's portrait of the college student Trilling is quite similar: "To the superficial glance of another youth, fresh from Europe, the young Trilling appeared to be indulging himself in a borrowed bohemianism. He read much and wrote a few sketches of symbolist cast for campus publication. He

affected a languid, sauntering elegance (of manner, not of dress). And while I was dimly aware of a brooding strength, I failed to make out any particular direction it might take. Nor did I suspect the great shyness which was being masked by a manner and which persisted for a lifetime after the manner was gone." Jacques Barzun, "Remembering Lionel Trilling," *Encounter* 47 (September 1976): 83.

57. Jay, "Lionel Trilling," 271.

58. Cynthia Ozick, "The Question of Our Speech: The Return to Aural Culture," *Partisan Review* 51 (1984): 763. Reprinted in Cynthia Ozick, *Metaphor and Memory: Essays* (New York: Alfred Knopf, 1989): 146–172, at 161. Further references to this essay will be to *Metaphor and Memory*.

59. Ozick, "The Question of Our Speech," 160.

60. Ibid., 159, 160.

61. Henry James, *The American Scene* [1907] (Bloomington: Indiana University Press, 1960), 138, 139.

62. Cf. Trilling's exasperation with Paul Rosenfeld's novel, *The Boy in the Sun*. Trilling loses his patience when he arrives at the phrase "The doorbell burned." After a lengthy analysis he concludes: "Yet the idea, that to say a simple thing by a precious and fantastic use of words probably indicates the unclear perception of even a simple thing, is so elementary that it cannot far mislead. Curiously this practice, though not peculiar to Jewish writers, is frequent with them and when they exhibit it it is sometimes called 'Oriental ornateness.' The hypothesis is tempting that it is difficult for a Jew to accept English at its face value. Or, again, that he fails to get in modernity the completest sensory stimuli and seeks by language to key up a low sensory world." Lionel Trilling, "Burning Doorbells," *Menorah Journal* 15 (November 1928): 486.

63. Chace, *Trilling* 108, 111.

64. "The attack on my novel that it is gray, bloodless, intellectual, without passion, is always made with great personal feeling, with anger. — How dared I presume?" *N1* 509.

65. Chace, *Trilling*, 108.

66. Krupnick, *Trilling*, 104.

67. This legacy was pointed out by Stanley Cavell. The Enlightenment's appreciation of the ordinary (lost in the craze of Romanticism) is one of Cavell's fundamental assumptions in his book *In Quest of the Ordinary: Lines of Skepticism and Romanticism* (Chicago: University of Chicago Press, 1989).

68. Lionel Trilling, "Manners, Morals, and the Novel," in *The Liberal Imagination* (London: Secker and Warburg, 1951), 209.

69. Lionel Trilling, "Why We Read Jane Austen," in *The Last Decade*, 213–214.

70. Cynthia Ozick, "The Riddle of the Ordinary," *Moment* 1 (July-August 1975): 58, 59. Reprinted in Cynthia Ozick, *Art and Ardor* (New York: E. P. Dutton, 1984): 200–209. Further references to this essay will be to the printing in *Art and Ardor*.

71. Lionel Trilling, "Genuine Writing," review of Charles Reznikoff, *By the Waters of Manhattan*, in *Menorah Journal* 19 (October 1930): 89. This is the only thoroughly positive review of the eighteen that Trilling contributed to the *Menorah Journal* between 1927 and 1930.

72. Ozick, "The Riddle of the Ordinary," 206.

73. In Cynthia Ozick's essay, the sentence reads "we [Jews] swim in the sense of our dailiness. . . ." Ozick, "The Riddle of the Ordinary," 204.

74. Ibid., 206.

75. "Culture and the Present Moment: A Round-Table Discussion." Partici-

pants: Edward Grossman, Hilton Kramer, Michael Novak, Cynthia Ozick, Norman Podhoretz, Jack Richardson, Lionel Trilling. *Commentary* 58 (December 1974): 31–50, at 40.

76. Ozick, "The Riddle of the Ordinary," 203. "Cruelty and madness are likely to ensue when we start looking like gods to ourselves, when we start thinking that our new standpoint puts us above and beyond the ordinary, that we are able to look down on it. . . ." Richard Rorty, "Philosophy of the Oddball," *The New Republic* 200 (19 June 1989): 41.

77. Lionel Trilling, in "Culture and the Present Moment," 40.

78. "The Art of Fiction 95: Cynthia Ozick," *Paris Review* 29 (Spring 1987): 174. Interview by Tom Teicholz.

79. Cynthia Ozick, "What Literature Means," *Partisan Review* 49 (1982): 297, 296, 295. Reprinted in *Art and Ardor*, 244–248.

80. Dickstein, *Gates of Eden*, 250.

81. Trilling's view of the novel and novelistic fiction as an account of "circumstances and actuality" from which the observer detaches his or her own emotions and is thus enabled to pass judgment is already fully present in his first book reviews. Cf., for instance, "Despair Apotheosized," *Menorah Journal* 17 (October 1929): 91–94; "The Necessary Morals of Art," *Menorah Journal* 18 (February 1930): 182–186.

82. Harold Bloom, "The Free and Broken Tablets: The Cultural Prospects of American Jewry," in *Agon: Towards a Theory of Revisionism* (New York: Oxford University Press, 1982), 318–329.

83. Dickstein, "Lionel Trilling," 330.

84. The Latin *intellegere* or *intelligere* means "to perceive, to choose between."

85. Graff, *Professing Literature*, 81.

86. Thomas R. Nevin, *Irving Babbitt: An Intellectual Study* (Chapel Hill: University of North Carolina Press, 1984), 14. For much of the information on Babbitt I am indebted to Thomas Nevin's excellent study.

87. Nevin, *Irving Babbitt*, 16–17; 18.

88. Irving Babbitt, *Literature and the American College: Essays in Defense of the Humanities* [1908], intro. Russell Kirk (Washington, D.C.: National Humanities Institute, 1986), 75–76.

89. Nevin, *Irving Babbitt*, 31.

90. Ibid., 11.

91. Krupnick, *Lionel Trilling*, 49.

92. Nevin, *Irving Babbitt*, 28.

93. Lionel Trilling, "A Personal Memoir," in Dora B. Weiner and William R. Keylor, eds., *From Parnassus: Essays in Honor of Jacques Barzun* (New York: Harper and Row, 1976), xviii.

94. Diana Trilling, "Lionel Trilling," 46.

95. Lionel Trilling, "A Personal Memoir," xvii.

96. Ibid., xvi.

97. Ibid., xviii–xix.

98. Ibid.

99. Grumet, "Apprenticeship," 154. Grumet is probably mistaken about Solow's participation, because Trilling writes that he and Solow "had not known each other until after we had both graduated." Lionel Trilling, "A Novel of the Thirties," in *The Last Decade*, 7.

100. Jacques Barzun, "Remembering Lionel Trilling," *Encounter* 47 (September 1976): 83.

101. Lionel Trilling, "Impediments," in *Of This Time, of That Place, and Other Stories*. Selected by Diana Trilling (New York: Harcourt Brace Jovanovich, 1979), 3.

102. Harold Bloom, in his introduction to Browning in *The Oxford Anthology of English Literature*, vol. 2, *From Blake to Auden*, ed. Frank Kermode and John Hollander (New York: Oxford University Press, 1975), 969–970. The sections on Romantic poetry and prose and the Victorian poetry and prose were edited by Lionel Trilling and Harold Bloom.

103. Mary McCarthy's description for Meyer Schapiro; cf. Barrett, *The Truants: Adventures Among the Intellectuals* (Garden City: Anchor-Doubleday, 1982), 53. Unlike the generous Van Doren, Barrett gets annoyed with Schapiro. "I went once to the Museum of Modern Art with Meyer Schapiro, an erudite and brilliant scholar in the history of art, and the experience was exhilarating; but there came a moment when I could not help thinking: if only the man would stop talking for a bit, if only that spellbinding flow of words would cease, and some painting or other would stop him in his tracks and make him go silent. I had the feeling that the work of art was noticed only as the springboard to his discourse, a mere stimulus to set the verbal machinery going." Barrett, *The Truants*, 150.

104. Bloom, introduction to Browning, *Oxford Anthology of English Literature*, 970.

105. Alfred Kazin, *New York Jew* (New York: Vintage, 1978), 64.

106. See, for instance, Lionel Trilling's essays, "Competent, But—" *Menorah Journal* 13 (November 1927): 522–524; and "Burning Doorbells."

107. Mark Krupnick, "Lionel Trilling, 'Culture,' and Jewishness," *Denver Quarterly* 18 (Autumn 1983): 115.

108. Schechner, *After the Revolution*, 82–83.

109. Lionel Trilling, "A Recollection of Raymond Weaver," in First, ed., *University on the Heights*, 13.

110. Trilling, "Freud and Literature," in *The Liberal Imagination*, 40, 52. Trilling used exactly this formulation again in his address "Freud: Within and Beyond Culture," *Beyond Culture*, 79.

111. Chace, *Trilling*, 87.

112. Trilling, "Freud and Literature," 36.

113. The vilification of man's imagination (*yetser*; variant spelling: *yetzer*) in Jewish literature is as old as Gen. 8:21. When God is appeased by the pleasant odors of Noah's burnt offering he remarks somewhat strangely: *ki yetser lev ha-adam ra minurav*—"because the imagination of man's heart is evil from his youth." New Oxford Annotated Bible; or in Speiser's translation: "since the devisings of man's heart are evil from the start" (Anchor Bible). See also Geoffrey Hartman, "On the Jewish Imagination," *Prooftexts* 5 (1985): 201–220.

114. Schechner, *After the Revolution*, p. 84.

115. Lopate, "Remembering Lionel Trilling," 155–156.

116. An interesting consequence of this taboo is the failure of Hebrew to produce a language of interiority; this failure became a problem around the turn of the century when Hebrew writers began to produce modern prose fiction. Hebrew "could not provide persuasive access to the consciousness of characters to serve the purpose of a realism that was experiential rather than social or collective." Robert Alter, *The Invention of Hebrew Prose: Modern Fiction and the Language of Realism* (Seattle: University of Washington Press, 1988), 40.

117. Chace, *Trilling*, 20.

118. Van Doren, "Jewish Students," 264–265. "Rosenthal gave up his reli-

gious profession in the Thirties and took a degree in philosophy, which he now [1966] teaches" (*NT* 11).

119. Grumet, "The Apprenticeship of Lionel Trilling," 157.

120. Henry Rosenthal, "Inventions," *Menorah Journal* 14 (January 1928): 51; 49. Further references to this story will be indicated by *In*.

121. Lionel Trilling, "Chapter for a Fashionable Jewish Novel," *Menorah Journal* 12 (June–July 1926): 280.

122. Lionel Trilling, "Edmund Wilson: A Backward Glance," in *A Gathering of Fugitives* (New York: Harcourt Brace Jovanovich, 1978), 53.

123. Tanner, *Trilling*, 18.

124. Solow to the board of directors, quoted in Mark Krupnick, "The *Menorah Journal* Group and the Origins of Modern Jewish-American Radicalism," *Studies in American Jewish Literature* 5 (Winter 1979): 66.

125. Alan M. Wald, *The New York Intellectuals: The Rise and Decline of the Anti-Stalinist Left from the 1930s to the 1980s* (Chapel Hill: University of North Carolina Press, 1987), 42.

126. Krupnick, "The *Menorah Journal* Group," 65.

127. Wald, *The New York Intellectuals*, 42. For Magnus's program, see Arthur A. Goren, *Dissenter in Zion: From the Writings of Judah L. Magnus* (Cambridge: Harvard University Press, 1982), 34–37.

128. Krupnick, *Trilling*, 39.

129. On Trilling and Communism, see Krupnick, *Trilling*, 36–46.

130. For the political and economic reasons underlying the academicization of literary criticism, see Graff, *Professing Literature*. Trilling's regrets about the completion of this process are formulated in "On the Teaching of Modern Literature," in *Beyond Culture: Essays on Literature and Learning* (New York: Harcourt Brace Jovanovich, 1978) 3–27.

131. Krupnick, *Trilling*, 51.

132. Trilling, "Edmund Wilson," in *A Gathering of Fugitives*, 55.

133. Krupnick, *Trilling*, 51

134. Krupnick, "Lionel Trilling, 'Culture,' and Jewishness," 118. Krupnick bases his discussion of Trilling's appointment on a conversation he had with Sidney Hook. Hook published his account in "Anti-Semitism in the Academy: Some Pages of the Past," *Midstream* 25 (January 1979): 49–54. My account is based on Trilling's "Notebooks." It is unclear who headed the English department at that time. According to Christopher Zinn, who edited Trilling's "Notebooks," the chairman of the Columbia College English department was not Ernest Hunter Wright, but Harrison Ross Steeves. Cf. *N1* 498n6.

135. Chace, *Trilling*, 46, 58, 59, 53.

136. Lionel Trilling, *E. M. Forster* (New York: Harcourt Brace Jovanovich, 1980), 7, 8, 1.

137. Chace, *Trilling*, 74.

138. "What for me is so interesting in the intellectual middle class is the dramatic contradiction of its living with the greatest possibility (call it illusion) of conscious choice, its believing itself the inheritor of the great humanist and rationalist tradition, and the badness and stupidity of its action." Lionel Trilling, "The Situation in American Writing: A Symposium," *Partisan Review* 6 (Fall 1939): 111.

139. Lionel Trilling, "Of This Time, of That Place," in *Of This Time, of That Place*, 79.

140. Trilling also uses the emphasis on hands to signal a mind-body opposition in his essay on Raymond Weaver; cf. First, *University on the Heights*, 5–13.

141. That Matthew Arnold was not alone in his biased (if not revisionist) view of Greece is pointed out by Martin Bernal in *Black Athena: The Afroasiatic Roots of Classical Civilization*, Vol. 1: *The Fabrication of Ancient Greece, 1785–1985* (New Brunswick, N.J.: Rutgers University Press, 1987). Bernal writes about Matthew Arnold: "Where Dr. [Thomas] Arnold's love of Greece meshed with his Protestantism, Teutonism and anti-Semitism, his son's Hellenism was explicitly linked to the vision of the Indo-European or Aryan race in a perpetual struggle with the Semitic one, or to the conflict between 'cultivated' and bourgeois values. And in this, of course, he was following a well-beaten path. In theory—like Michelet, Renan and others—he accepted, as Bunsen put it, that 'If the Hebrew Semites are the priests of humanity, the Helleno-Roman Aryans are, and ever will be, its heroes.' All, however, clearly felt that in granting the Semites religion they were granting them too much" (348).

142. Trilling quotes from Hans Kohn's article, "The Teachings of Moses Hess," which had appeared in the *Menorah Journal* in May 1930: "The contrast between Judaism and Hellenism . . . came to concern all analytical and self-conscious Jews upon their entrance into European life at the close of the eighteenth century and their renewal of contact with the influence of Hellas. For Hess, the Greeks stand for multiplicity and variety, while the Hebrews represent unity. The former think of life as eternal *being*; the latter as eternal *becoming*. The Greeks seek to penetrate through the space dimension; they are the people of the eye, of nature and of plastic beauty. The Jews, on the contrary, are preoccupied with the *time* dimension. They are the people of the time sense, of the ear, of lyricism, of historical outlook and social ethics. The task of all cultural history is to effect a reconciliation between these opposing principles." Quoted in Lionel Trilling, *Matthew Arnold* (New York: Harcourt Brace Jovanovich, 1979), 256.

143. Ibid., 258.

144. Kallen, "Hebraism and Current Tendencies in Philosophy," 9.

145. This is the academic critic's indictment of Howe's poetry. It recalls the bottle of gin that the narrator of "Impediments" bought "to see if I couldn't get inspiration for the writing of a story" (*Im* 6). The rational Hettner "looked dubious" when offered a shot. "He probably never drank, but some idea of the 'validity' of Dionysian frenzy kept him from refusing the pungent, colorless stream I let trickle into his tea" (*Im* 7).

146. Lionel Trilling, "On the Teaching of Modern Literature," in *Beyond Culture: Essays on Literature and Learning* (New York: Harcourt Brace Jovanovich, 1978), 16.

147. Chace, *Trilling*, 27.

148. Lionel Trilling, *Sincerity and Authenticity* (Cambridge: Harvard University Press, 1972), 11.

149. Krupnick, "Lionel Trilling, 'Culture,' and Jewishness," 115.

150. Lionel Trilling, *Sincerity and Authenticity*, 12.

151. Cynthia Ozick, letter to the author, 20 March 1989.

152. Cynthia Ozick, letter to the author, 22 March 1989.

153. Cynthia Ozick, letter to the author, March 10, 1989. The allusion is to Conrad's "The Secret Sharer." Regarding Trilling's story "Of This Time, of That Place," Mark Krupnick points out that Trilling's "most important debt . . . is to 'The Secret Sharer.' " Krupnick, *Trilling*, 82.

154. Trilling, "On the Teaching of Modern Literature," 17.

155. "We know what happens when the impulse to make art resorts to the wrong instruments: those lampshades." Cynthia Ozick, letter to the author,

10 March 1989.

156. Cynthia Ozick, letter to the author, 6 May 1989.

157. Trilling, "On the Teaching of Modern Literature," 18.

158. Chace, *Trilling*, 29.

159. Trilling, "The Situation in American Writing," 109.

160. Shechner, *After the Revolution*, 76.

161. Such distinctions would be kosher/treyf; shabbat/workday; and, of course, Jew/Gentile. An entry for 12 December 1967 in Trilling's notebook reflects a clear awareness of separation: "Today a sudden recollection of the pleasure I had as a child in living in a world predominantly non-Jewish; it was not, in the main, thought of as a hostile world, although it was fairly resistant and it was this that made it attractive and *real*. I recall my non-Jewish teachers with more interest and affection than my Jewish ones, of whom there were few, and it seems to me that I thought of the Gentiles as having more reality than the Jews. This I am still likely to feel, that non-Jews are more 'real' than Jews, in whom I am likely to see a generic factitiousness. — I liked the non-Jewish holidays. Did I at any time feel 'ashamed' of being Jewish? Disadvantaged sometimes, but never ashamed" (N2, 13–14).

162. Krupnick, *Trilling*, 13.

163. Lionel Trilling, "Freud: Within and Beyond Culture," in *Beyond Culture*, 80.

164. It is part of Tertan's craziness to define his origins as "Of this time, of that place, of some parentage, what does it matter?" (78). And it is a sign of Howe's sanity to decide that "this" and "that" should point to specific circumstances.

165. Trilling, "Freud and Literature," 36.

166. Trilling, On the Teaching of Modern Literature," 24.

167. Ibid., 13ff.

168. Cynthia Ozick, letter to the author, 16 May 1989.

169. Trilling, "Freud: Within and Beyond Culture," 93.

170. Trilling, "Freud and Literature," 35.

171. Trilling, "Freud: Within and Beyond Culture," 93. Further references to this essay will be indicated by *FW*.

172. For individuals opposing culture on the basis of biology, Trilling chose a pagan, Socrates, and a Christian, Giordano Bruno, who died as intellectual martyrs.

173. Lionel Trilling, "Under Forty," in *Speaking of Literature and Society*, ed. Diana Trilling (New York: Harcourt Brace Jovanovich, 1980), 199.

174. Krupnick, *Trilling*, 172.

175. Lionel Trilling, "Isaac Babel," in *Beyond Culture*, 106.

176. Cynthia Ozick, letter to the author, 10 March 1989.

Chapter 6. Released into America

1. Lewis S. Feuer, "The Stages in the Social History of Jewish Professors in American Colleges and Universities," *American Jewish History* 71 (June 1982): 443–447. Regna Darnell, *Edward Sapir: Linguist, Anthropologist, Humanist* (Berkeley: University of California Press, 1990), 5–15.

2. Harry Levin, "A Personal Retrospect," *Grounds for Comparison* (Cambridge: Harvard University Press, 1972), 7.

3. Cf. Harry Levin's bibliography for the years 1936–1939 in Levin, *Grounds*

for Comparison, 399–400.

4. Henry Rosovsky, "From Periphery to Center," *The Jewish Experience at Harvard and Radcliffe*, 55.

5. Daniel Aaron, interview with the author, Cambridge, Mass., 30 June 1989. All quotations attributed to Prof. Aaron in the text are from this interview.

6. Meyer H. Abrams, interview with the author, Ithaca, N.Y., 28 August 1988. All quotations attributed to M. H. Abrams in the text are from this interview.

Index

Aaron, Daniel, 200, 201, 202–5
Abrams, Meyer, 200, 201, 205–6, 228n54
Academy for the Science of Judaism, 44
Acculturation, 162; education and, 221n134. *See also* Assimilation
Adler, Felix, 67–70, 101, 102; origins, xiii, 67; at Columbia, 66, 67, 68, 103; Ethical Culture, 66, 69, 70
Aleichem, Sholem, 57, 58, 59
Alter, Robert, 22, 42
America, 3, 34, 40, 47; perceptions of, xiii, 17, 34, 118–19
Americanization, xii, xiv, 36, 66, 152; Kallen on, 36, 39, 46, 47, 51
American Jewish culture, 135
Anderson, Sherwood, 119
Antebellum period: Jews in, 2, 3
Anti-Semitism, xi, 87, 92, 93, 145, 175, 201, 202; at universities, 1, 2, 4, 99–104, 112, 113; stereotypes, 2, 3–4, 110; restrictions, 4, 52, 101; Yiddish and 15–16; combating, 41, 79, 222n142; Lewisohn and, 92, 98, 127. *See also* Quotas
Arnold, Matthew, 94, 153, 160; *Culture and Anarchy,* 41, 43–44, 161, 181; Trilling and, 153, 161, 163, 175, 176, 178
Assimilation, xii, 16, 17, 42, 59, 110; views against, 22, 43, 47; Cohen on, 51–52, 53, 78, 80; national vs. personal, 85;

in Germany, 89; Lewisohn and, 127, 128
Augustine, 117, 141

Babbitt, Irving, 106, 111, 160–61, 162, 201, 203
Babel, Isaac, 195–98
Baron, Salo, 42, 79
Barzun, Jacques, 163, 166, 169, 177
Berenson, Bernard, 148
Berger, Arthur, 133
Bergson, Henri, 45, 52, 158
Bialystock, xiii, 8, 20, 142, 198
Bloom, Harold, 13, 127, 135, 158
Boas, Franz, 102, 146, 148, 200
Boorstin, Daniel, 204
Boston, 2, 14, 17, 20, 193
Bourne, Randolph, 43
Brandeis, Louis Dembitz, 49–50, 217n49
Brandeis University, 132–34, 226n34
Breadwinners' College, 66, 70
Brenner, Anita, 42
Buber, Martin, 82, 86, 126, 128, 129
Burgess, John, 103
Butler, Nicholas Murray, 102, 103, 114, 145, 146, 148, 178, 234n47; Spingarn and, 104, 106, 107
Cahan, Abraham, 53, 136
Cardozo, Benjamin, 101, 146
Chace, William, 154, 168, 178